LITERARY/CULTURAL THEORY

POSTCOLONIALISM
NOW

Literary/Cultural Theory provides concise and lucid introductions to a range of key concepts and theorists in contemporary literary and cultural theory. Original and contemporary in presentation, and eschewing jargon, each book in the series presents students of humanities and social sciences exhaustive overviews of theories and theorists, while also introducing them to the mechanics of reading literary/cultural texts using critical tools. Each book also carries glossaries of key terms and ideas, and pointers for further reading and research. Written by scholar-teachers who have taught critical theory for years, and vetted by some of the foremost experts in the field, the series Literary/Cultural Theory is indispensable to students and teachers.

Series Editors

Allen Hibbard
Middle Tennessee State University

Andrew Slade
University of Dayton

Herman Rapaport
Wake Forest University

Imre Szeman
University of Alberta

Krishna Sen
University of Calcutta

Scott Slovic
University of Idaho

Sumit Chakrabarti
Presidency University, Kolkata

Also in the series

Psychoanalytic Theory and Criticism
Feminisms
Jacques Lacan
Dalit Literature and Criticism
Ecocriticism
Postsecular Theory
Nations and Nationalisms
Periyar
Popular Culture
Life Writing
Queer Studies
Marxist Literary and Cultural Theory
Frantz Fanon
Mikhail Bakhtin
Deconstruction and Poststructuralism
Edward Said
Diaspora Theory and Transnationalism
Subaltern Studies

"This is an elegantly written book which deftly weaves together the most important thinking on anticolonialism, postcolonialism and decolonisation with sophisticated comparative readings of important literary texts from across the globe. With clarity and insight, Bhattacharya elaborates both the vital political and historical issues at stake in the world we now live in as well as the lasting importance of the literary in addressing them. This book is essential reading for those teaching and researching these issues."

Professor Priyamvada Gopal, Professor of Postcolonial Studies, University of Cambridge

"In narratives of emancipatory politics, 'postcolonialism' and 'decoloniality' have emerged as competing, if not contestatory, discourses on how legacies of empire have shaped our present and the desirable methods of engagement with it. *Postcolonialism Now* is an impressive book announcing the urgency to decolonise postcolonial studies. This insightful volume traces the evolving debates within postcolonial studies and using the insights gleaned from them, it undertakes a close analysis of texts ranging from novels, poetry and plays to films and graphic narratives from the perspective of their engagement with issues of caste, power, race, gender, utopia, sexuality, poverty, and globalization. Without disavowing the complexity of these categories, the book highlights how they are entangled with each other across the temporal and spatial axes of the postcolonial world. It underlines the significance of comparative and materialist reading strategies with a convincing case for 'reading for decolonising.'

The book is a reminder that despite differences, the decolonial and the postcolonial work towards the shared ambition of imagining futures beyond the colonial/imperial gaze. The uniqueness of the volume lies in its rich contribution both at empirical and theoretical levels."

Professor Nishat Zaidi, Department of English, Jamia Milia Islamia

"That the *postcolonial* is not a static marker and a theoretic category, but fully alive to current materialist shifts catalysing new hermeneutics of the present, is what is invoked in this new book by Sourit Bhattacharya. Building on the 'now' of historicist immediacy, Bhattacharya embeds the *postcolonial* within ongoing debates and signposts around minoritisation, migration, ethnic cleansing, and ecological traumas – familiar tropes but brilliantly retheorised through planetary and contemporary references. Animating the decolonial *epoche* within ongoing tides of discrimination, atrocities, extraction, malnutrition and pathologies, Bhattacharya justifies the 'why now' hinging current world-historical force-fields with new aesthetic *dissensus* across the globe. Growing political disquiet and literary furore over our 'damaged life' perhaps warrant a new 'melancholy science', or more engaged critical musings, something this book executes, within the interstices of the *decolonial* and the *public humanities*. The most fascinating hallmark of the book – its comprehensive engagement with foundational and existing theoretic icons in this field, amplified further through the inclusion of new critical voices from the Global South. The book, a must read for anyone looking for new directions and relevance for postcolonial studies in the current conjuncture."

Professor Anindya Purakayastha, Institute of Language Studies and Research, Kolkata and Kazi Nazrul University

"*Postcolonialism Now* persuasively argues that we should all be 'reading for decolonising': that is, reading so that we can link past struggles to our present moment and take part in those to come. Richly contextualized, lucidly argued, and historically and materially grounded, this is committed criticism of the best kind."

Dr Anna Bernard, Reader in Comparative Literature and English, King's College London

LITERARY/CULTURAL THEORY

POSTCOLONIALISM NOW

LITERATURE, READING, DECOLONISING

Sourit Bhattacharya
University of Edinburgh, Edinburgh

Series Editor
Sumit Chakrabarti
Presidency University, Kolkata

Orient BlackSwan

All rights reserved. No part of this book may be modified, reproduced or utilised in any form, or by any means, electronic or mechanical, including photocopying, recording or by any information storage and retrieval system, in any form of binding or cover other than in which it is published, without permission in writing from the publisher.

POSTCOLONIALISM NOW: LITERATURE, READING, DECOLONISING

ORIENT BLACKSWAN PRIVATE LIMITED

Registered Office
3-6-752 Himayatnagar, Hyderabad 500 029, Telangana, India
Email: centraloffice@orientblackswan.com

Other Offices
Bengaluru, Chennai, Guwahati, Hyderabad, Kolkata, Mumbai,
New Delhi, Noida, Patna

© Orient Blackswan Private Limited 2025
First published 2025

ISBN 978 93 5442 656 8

Typeset in Aldine 401 BT 10.5/13 *by*
K. Divya, Hyderabad 500 060

Printed at
B.B. Press, Tronica City, Ghaziabad 201 102

Published by
Orient Blackswan Private Limited
3-6-752, Himayatnagar,
Hyderabad 500 029, Telangana, India
Email: info@orientblackswan.com

The publisher has endeavoured to ensure that the URLs for external websites referred to in this book are correct and active at the time of going to press. However, the publisher has no responsibility for the websites and can make no guarantee that a site will remain live or that the content is or will remain appropriate.

For my father, Shri Sushil Kumar Bhattacharya (1943–2020)

Contents

Series Editor's Preface — xi

Acknowledgements — xv

1. The Decolonising Impulse in Postcolonial Studies, or, Why Now? — 1
2. Minorities: Nation, Caste, Race and Sexuality in Bama, Kay and Brand — 38
3. Migrations: Slavery, Diaspora and Refuge in McQueen, Hamid, Adichie and Bui — 77
4. Traumas: Genocide, Sexual Violence, Exile and Solidarity in Raihan, Nottage and Darwish — 121
5. Ecologies: Extraction, Hunger, Epidemics and Care in Devi, Mpe and Senior — 165
6. Futures: Utopia, Dystopia and Planetarity in Rokeya, Padmanabhan and Okorafor — 205

Conclusion: Postcolonial Studies in a Post-COVID World — 246

Series Editor's Preface

This volume, *Postcolonialism Now,* is the fourth book in the series that I have edited. In terms of chronology it could have been published earlier. Postcolonialism as a tool, a condition, a location, a politics, a problematic has been an academic engagement for a few decades now, spreading itself out to accommodate or assimilate various forms of postcolonial (with or without the hyphen) representations and habitations. Meanwhile, there have often been speculations and assertions that, as a theoretical tool postcolonialism had become unusable, obsolete or unnecessary. In a recent, almost livid essay, Mohamed Salah Eddine Madiou is vituperative about the inanities and falsities of postcolonialism:

> The inconsistencies and paradoxes this concept was born with and the *more* inconsistencies and paradoxes it came up with when it brushed past the postmodern advent have seduced critics who find those problems grist for the intellectual mill. The conceptual vulnerability of postcolonialism became a *distraction* and, for some reason, *more* important than the colonial problems it was supposed to study/criticize. Aside from conceptual problems, content problems such as hypocrisy make postcolonialism further dubious; *worse,* a dismal failure . . . Let us take stock. (Madiou 2)

As the readers take stock of the italicised accusations that emphasise the redundancy of postcolonialism as an analytical tool, it also reminds them, retrospectively, of the categories that postcolonialism has represented over several decades: race, caste, migration, gender, culture, nationalism, climate change and precarities of various other forms that have been pared and restored to their respective subjecthood by the minute sutures of postcolonial theoretical strategies. However, one must 'take stock' of the situation 'now' and the postcolonial critic has to rethink strategies. That the present volume appears now is perhaps to address the rethinkings.

This rethinking of strategies entails both a retrospective view of the playing field that was, and a looking ahead to understand whether it is indeed time for the postcolonialist to hang up their boots. This is not an easy task. Strategies of representation have evolved across both time and space. How does the postcolonial critic 'take stock' of terms such as 'anticolonial' and 'decolonial'? Is it through the internal heuristic of postcolonialism that these terms have gained currency? Or do they evolve from a separate set of discursive anxieties that are relationally at odds with the structural markers of postcolonialism? Is to rethink the postcolonial position therefore to reframe or reform one's problematic?

The idea of the historical has always been central to the evolution of postcolonial strategies. A large part of what we have, over the years, called postcolonial theory has grown around the critique of epistemic historiography and its Hegelian morphologies. One is reminded immediately of how Homi Bhabha foregrounded the idea of the performative contingency of representation that exposed the incommensurability of institutional historiography with the very contemporary moment of minority representation, or what one might call the 'now' of representation:

> Terms of cultural engagement whether antagonistic or affiliative, are produced performatively. The representation of difference must not be hastily read as the reflection of pre-given ethnic or cultural traits set in the fixed tablet of tradition. The social articulation of difference, from the minority perspective, is a complex, on-going negotiation that seeks to authorize cultural hybridities that emerge in moments of historical transformation. (Bhabha 2)

This is still in the final decade of the last century, and the postcolonial critic is trying to address the question of historical elision and the need to identify, acknowledge and celebrate hybridity and difference. But what began as a critique of the world-historical has now evolved into newer paradigms of the 'global' which has not only diversified and complicated the problems of representation but has also equipped the critic with insurgent tools of alterity that speak in different dialects of empowerment. Does postcolonialism now 'take stock' of these changed strategies? When the voice from the colonies speaks of entanglements or connections or networks or translations it speaks of a complex engagement with the very idea of representation within a post-capitalist, post-liberal, global space that cannot be immediately addressed by the tools of the past or the simple binaries of the Global North and the Global South. Likewise, the 'anticolonial' or the 'decolonial' are often not willing to share ideological space with different forms of their own meta-identities, let alone the space of the postcolonial. In representations of postcolonial spaces, the questions of contingency have left little scope for essentialisms, and thus the manifold plural is in urgent need of newer idioms defined differentially where the etymology of the word 'colonial' is incessantly refreshed.

We earnestly hope that this volume, *Postcolonialism Now* by Sourit Bhattacharya, will enrich the debates around both the ontology and the epistemology of postcolonialisms. Across the volume, Bhattacharya is indeed 'taking stock' of how the theoretical markers of postcolonialism are faring within a veritable battlefield of ideas of representation across histories and geographies, cultures and ecologies. He begins with the crucial question 'Why Now?' in the first chapter and intricately weaves his way through the chapters to arrive at a concluding chapter titled 'Postcolonial Studies in a Post-COVID World' marking an epistemological contemporaneity that tries to answer the question. Through the chapters Bhattacharya has attempted to unpack a 'method' of doing postcolonial studies now by consistently using the decolonial lens. On the one hand he revisits historiographical elisions and essentialisms in postcolonial methods of the past, their often assimilationist strategies that subsumed identities; on the other hand, he tries to develop narratives of articulation that elicit possibilities of connections, entanglements and networks of a global postcolonialism. Such discursively unstable narratives as 'Minorities', 'Migration', 'Traumas' or 'Ecologies' reiterate the contingencies and precarities inherent within manifest postcolonialisms across the globe and invest Bhattacharya's thesis in this volume with a nuance that will enrich scholarship on the subject. It is within these larger rubrics that Bhattacharya explores narratives of slavery, diaspora, exile, sexual violence, epidemics or solidarity. It will perhaps be fair to say that this volume 'takes stock' of where the theoretical problematic of postcolonialism stands now, and where does it lead to in the foreseeable future.

In the process of expanding his argument in this volume, Bhattacharya has referred to works of authors from diverse geographical, historical, and cultural contexts. His choice of literary texts is also a telling commentary on his vision of the literary canon and what talking about postcolonialism in seminars, conferences and literature classrooms of the future must account for. From Bama's *Karukku* to Thi Bui's *The Best We Could Do*, Zahir Raihan's *Stop Genocide* to Phaswane Mpe's *Welcome to Our Hillbrow*, Bhattacharya maps representations in their various precarities across multiple colonialisms. Bhattacharya's choice of texts is almost an exact ideological reflection of what Ato Quayson and Ankhi Mukherjee emphasise in their 'Introduction' to *Decolonizing The English Curriculum*: 'Substantive canon expansion . . . is nothing without an informed critique of the canonical method. Acknowledging a certain complexion of literary genealogy, we need to be mindful about not perpetuating its politics by perversely denying the diversity of literatures in English in the postcolonial, global world' (14–15).

This volume is an informed commentary on the 'method' that postcolonialism must acquire in order to assimilate the global in its manifest variety – the ideological, the phenomenal and the existential, not to mention the translational and the transnational. Bhattacharya's book is undoubtedly an important addition to the series.

Sumit Chakrabarti

REFERENCES

Bhabha, Homi K. *The Location of Culture*. Routledge, 1994.

Madiou, Mohamed Salah Eddine. "The Death of Postcolonialism: The Founder's Foreword". *Janus Unbound: Journal of Critical Studies*, vol. 1, no. 1, 2021, pp. 1–12.

Quayson, Ato, and Ankhi Mukherjee, editors. *Decolonizing The English Literary Curriculum*. Cambridge UP, 2024.

Acknowledgements

Despite the tremendous growth and popularity of the field of postcolonial studies in the last three decades, two key elements have been crucially missing for us, that is, its interested students and learners: how to read postcolonial literatures closely and comparatively, and how to do this through the lens of decolonisation and anticolonialism. The reasons for these absences are many, which I discuss in the first chapter of the book. As a postgraduate student in literary studies in India and interested in the field, I sought to be able to discuss the theories of decolonisation and postcolonialism through literary works, through the works' content, style, structure, form and comparability with other works, that is, through the strengths of the discipline. It occurred to me that our training in the field relied more on how a critical theory might define something as postcolonial and through this definition to interpret a literary text, rather than how a literary text might lead us to the theoretical complexity, conceptual depth and critical richness of what constitutes the predicament and the field of the postcolonial.

Thus, when the invitation to write this book came from Professor Sumit Chakrabarti in 2018, I saw the opportunity in fielding this idea. I sincerely thank Professor Chakrabarti for agreeing to see reason in my thoughts and allowing me to write the book, not as another primer for the series, but as a fresh contribution to the field. I also thank my teachers in Kolkata and Warwick who taught me how to closely read a literary text and critically appreciate literature through formal properties and political philosophy. Thanks are due to my colleagues in India and the UK from whose works and thoughts I have learnt so much about attentive reading, materialist criticism and committed politics.

Particular thanks to Professor Willy Maley, Dr Arka Chattopadhyay and Dr Arunima Bhattacharya for reading early drafts of the book and offering encouragement and helpful suggestions. Thanks are also due to the anonymous reviewers of the manuscript. Their suggestions and advice have been of immense help in revising the material for the book.

The practicable side of the book was tested in the modules I taught at IIT Roorkee and at the Universities of Glasgow and Edinburgh. In the Research Methodology course at Roorkee, I first trialled in workshops with students the method of closely reading a text in which we discussed how to understand if a poem was postcolonial. Similar thought and writing experiments were carried out in my Postcolonialism course at Glasgow and the Commodities of Empire course at Edinburgh, from which many of the texts in the current book are drawn. The ideas presented here are as much my own as they are insights garnered from students. In this way, the book has been written in the past six years through conversations with students to whom I offer my utmost gratitude and thankfulness.

The book is also a direct product of the past years that included the world-historical event of the COVID-19 pandemic, social and academic movements such as #BLM, and endless global wars. In 2019 I moved to the UK and faced the pandemic head on, whose most challenging episode was played out to me when I had to say goodbye to my father who passed away in 2020 during the flying suspension between the UK and India. Locked down in a flat and talking to my mother and family on the phone, it felt like an unending moment of irreconcilable grief. When it seemed the pandemic was finally over, colonial–imperialist wars in Russia and Ukraine and then in Israel and Palestine, and elsewhere, meant to us that there was no end to human suffering and grief, to our atrocities and indifference. We also noticed in these times significant moments of resistance, solidarity and fellow-feeling through social movements worldwide, which also affected me as a human being and as a scholar and shaped the way I wrote this book. I have no doubt that the local and global resonance through literary reading that I have aimed to establish in the book has a direct bearing upon this specific but comparable moment of grief, struggle and solidarity in our lives.

This is why my most sincere gratitude goes to my wife, Arunima, who like me was also far away from her 'home-land' and had to take care of a struggling me during the pandemic. It isn't an overstatement to say that this book exists today because of Arunima's support and the strength she gave to me during these periods.

Finally, I would like to thank Sreenath, Namrata Kartik and team at Orient BlackSwan for their patience and diligence in the copy-editing and production of the book. They have done an admirable job. Any errors and faults still in the book are solely my own and not theirs.

An earlier version of my work on Phaswane Mpe's *Welcome to Our Hillbrow* was published in R. Sreejith Verma and Ajanta Sircar's edited volume *Contagion Narratives: The Society, Culture and Ecology of the Global South* (Routledge, 2022). Shorter versions of my chapter-work on Mahasweta Devi's 'Mahadu: Ekti Rupkatha', and Zahir Raihan's 'Stop Genocide' are forthcoming in *The Cambridge Handbook of Literature and Plants*, edited by Bonnie Lander Johnson (Cambridge UP); and *The Routledge Companion to Literature and the Environment*, edited by Sharae Deckard, Treasa De Loughry, Kerstin Oloff and Claire Westall, respectively. I thank these publishers for giving me the opportunity to write and receive feedback on these topics. I have substantially worked on and revised the material for the current book.

Chapter One

The Decolonising Impulse in Postcolonial Studies, or, Why Now?

On 9 March 2015, Chumani Maxwele, a student at the University of Cape Town, travelled to campus by minibus with a bucketful of faeces. 'He took it to a bronze statue of the 19th-century British colonialist Cecil John Rhodes', Eva Fairbanks reports for *The Guardian*, 'that held pride of place on campus, just downhill from the convocation hall. "Where are *our* heroes and ancestors?" Maxwele shouted to a gathering, curious crowd. Then he opened the bucket and hurled its contents into Rhodes's face' ("The Birth of Rhodes Must Fall"). This incident inaugurated an influential academic campaign known as #RhodesMustFall or RMF (Chantiluke et al.) and sent ripples through South African academic and public spheres which were struggling to reckon with the immediate histories of race and racism in the post-apartheid context. But why defile a statue of a nineteenth-century industrialist? Cecil Rhodes, as Fairbanks mentions, was a colonialist and imperialist who held dehumanising views of black people and, as a hardcore white supremacist, was the first to implement policies of segregation and disenfranchisement along racial lines in South Africa. Writing a year after this incident for *The Guardian*, Amit Chaudhuri notes that in the draft 'Confession of Faith' (1877) attached to his financial bequests, including the prestigious Rhodes Scholarship, Rhodes had called for, '(T)he establishment, promotion and development of a Secret

Society, the true aim and object whereof shall be for the extension of British rule throughout the world, the perfecting of a system of emigration from the United Kingdom, and of colonisation by British subjects of all lands where the means of livelihood are attainable by energy, labour and enterprise' ("The Real Meaning of Rhodes Must Fall"). Chaudhuri clarifies that while vocal critics of RMF may euphemistically term Rhodes 'a man of his time', his vision and legacy continues to have a wide impact on Britain in giving it 'free passage to, and control of, the rest of the world, whether via business, expatriation, or military intervention – while those travelling to the west must be viewed as potential refugees or people posing as asylum seekers' ("The Real Meaning of Rhodes Must Fall").

As the struggles of RMF started to echo in Europe, another incident on 25 May 2020 in the United States of America infuriated the world. A forty-six-year-old black man named George Floyd was murdered by a white Minneapolis state police officer, Derek Chauvin, on the suspicion that he had used a counterfeit $20 bill to buy cigarettes from a shop. Chauvin pressed his knee to Floyd's neck for around ten minutes which asphyxiated and killed him, while Floyd gasped, 'I can't breathe' ("George Floyd"). Protests broke out in the US and globally against the murder and historical police brutality against black and ethnic minorities under the banner of #BlackLivesMatter which had begun as a social media movement in 2013 after the acquittal of George Zimmerman in the shooting death of an African-American teen, Trayvon Martin (Lebron). These protests, amidst a coronavirus pandemic, led to massive repercussions in Britain where a statue of the slave trader Edward Colston was toppled, defaced and pushed into Bristol Harbour (BBC). The incident reignited the RMF statue debate in Oxford, calling not only for the removal of the statue of Rhodes or statues of imperialists and slave traders in the country, but extending to questions of discrimination in teaching, learning, pedagogy, recruitment and the structure of institutions and organisations (Chigudu).

Postcolonialism Now takes its cue from these transformative social and academic movements in current times, which involve a radical gesture of 'uprooting' the colonising semiotics of statues and cultural establishments and pointing towards the racialised nature of police and state violence. This book reminds us that these movements are neither abrupt nor limited to 'western', formerly coloniser countries. The decolonising impulse and vigour of these movements derives from historical anti-abolitionist and global anticolonial struggles. That South Africa's racialised present or American slavery's white violence on black communities could resonate so widely in Britain and globally, serves to indicate that histories of colonialism and imperialism are deeply connected and ongoing. In this book, I argue that these histories and thoughts, their long-term anticolonial and ongoing decolonising agenda, have appeared in literary and cultural works of postcolonial nations through various socio-economic and cultural–geographical rubrics such as minority, migration, ecology, trauma, genre, and so forth. My chief aim in this chapter is to set up a hermeneutic of reading that identifies and explores the interconnectedness of these rubrics and, through them, the resonant decolonising impulse in postcolonial struggles and studies.

THEORISING THE POSTCOLONIAL: RETRIEVING THE ANTICOLONIAL

The word 'postcolonial' derives from the root word 'colony'. 'Colony', according to the *Oxford English Dictionary*, is 'a country or area under the control of another country and occupied by settlers from that country'. It draws from the Greek word *apoikia*, meaning settlement ('people far from home'; eighth century BCE), transitioning to Roman *colonus* in the fifth century CE, meaning farmer–tenant. From these agricultural and diasporic beginnings, postcolonial critic Robert J.C. Young informs us, two primary kinds of colonies grew in mid-sixteenth-century Europe, making their presence felt globally through travel, slavery, and commerce – 'exploitation colony' and 'settler colony'. The first stood for colonies such as India, Algeria or South Africa, which were used as hubs for resource extraction and cultural indoctrination and ruled from faraway 'metropolitan' centres such as London or Paris. Settler colonies in the Americas and Pacific Ocean territories too followed the route of force by exterminating or alienating Indigenous populations and settling on these lands (Young 28–33). Hence, this new European practice of occupying lands and building and controlling colonies was known as 'colonisation', while the ideology behind this practice geared towards economic and cultural profit was understood as 'colonialism'.

From the late-nineteenth century onwards, major European nations began to aggressively expand their overseas territories to extract resources and maintain national security, leading to the further disintegration of Africa and Asia thanks to a political–economic doctrine based on competitive occupation which came to be known as the doctrine of 'imperialism' (Howe 24–25). Of course, these settlements were not established without violence and resistance. Several peasant, Indigenous and workers' movements against forceful, imperialist seizures of land and commons broke out throughout the nineteenth and twentieth centuries, culminating in anticolonial nationalist movements that sought to retrieve and reclaim colonised land and cultures from European colonial rule in the wake of the Second World War; a phenomenon known as 'decolonisation'. The slow demise of the British Empire coincided with the ascent of the USA and the USSR. The rise of 'neocolonial' policies and proxy wars (such as the Cold War) in the 'Global South' until the dissolution of the USSR in the 1990s and the global neo-imperialist ascendancy of the USA, perpetuated neocolonialism and ongoing decolonising struggles in the postcolonial world.

The *Oxford English Dictionary* shows that the first use of the term 'post-colonial' dates back to 9 December 1955 and alludes to the threat of US hegemony supplanting British imperial influence in newly independent nation-states. Postcolonial critic Aijaz Ahmad writes that India's decolonisation; the Egyptian Revolution; the 1955 Bandung conference that advocated non-alignment in the Cold War; and other decolonisation movements in Africa, Asia and the Arab World had created a third force, sometimes sociologically known as the 'Third World' (USA–Europe and the USSR being First and Second Worlds respectively; *In Theory* 16–17). But the socialist agenda of these decolonisation movements was blunted in the wake of the 1973 global oil shock and the US-led neo-imperialist restructuring of the world through the forceful reintegration of Third World economies into a global capitalist system. This meant that the struggle-based, anticolonial and emancipatory philosophies of Amílcar Cabral, Mahatma Gandhi, Jawaharlal Nehru, Sukarno, Patrice Lumumba, Kwame Nkrumah or Gamal Abdel Nasser were denounced by economically and culturally richer countries through their influential media, public and academic platforms.

'Postcolonial' (at times meaning 'after colonisation', at others implying 'after independence') as an academic term, Marxist critic Neil Lazarus writes, began to appear in social science debates in the early 1970s to identify and analyse nations and societies at the historical conjunction of decolonisation and Non-Alignment movements in the post-Bandung era. But the political and cultural anti-emancipatory and anti-anticolonial atmosphere in Western academies in the 1980s meant that the term was co-opted into academic discourse analysis via theories of recovery and retrieval of the 'colonial' subject. This created narratives of despairing histories of neocolonial authoritarianism in most of the decolonised nations (Lazarus 9–11).

Edward W. Said's epochal work *Orientalism* set out the key 'postcolonial' task (note the absence of the hyphen) of retrieving the discursively colonised from 'a complex Orient suitable for study in the academy, for display in the museum, for reconstruction in the colonial office, for theoretical illustration in anthropological, biological, linguistic, racial, and historical theses about mankind and the universe' (8). Supported by the New Left's anti-humanist philosophical readings of Marxism; structuralism's linguistic, cultural and identity-driven projects; and poststructuralism's discursive and textualist emphasis, Said's Foucauldian theory of Orientalism was foundational to the rise of 'postcolonial theory' (*In Theory* 13). Said's writing coincided with Gayatri Chakravorty Spivak's and subaltern studies's radical historiographic and philosophical use of the Italian Marxist Antonio Gramsci's 1934 concept of the subaltern – originally 'of inferior rank' in the army, and coming to mean social groups that are subordinated and excluded from voice and representation to substantiate the cultural hegemony of dominant groups and are, thus, spoken for or represented by the masculine/elite (Gramsci). 'Subalternity', for Spivak, stood inversely for 'the space out of any serious touch with the logic of capitalism or socialism' ("Supplementing Marxism" 115). Merging revolutionary Marxism and humanism with continental philosophical methods of analysis such as psychoanalysis (Jacques Lacan), deconstruction (Jacques Derrida), intertextuality (Julia Kristeva), archaeology and genealogy (Michel Foucault) and micronarrative (Carlo Ginzburg), among others, these thinkers mobilised to retrieve the voice of the subaltern or the historically subordinated from colonial 'official' writing and cultural hegemony – a strategy that Bill Ashcroft, Gareth Griffiths and Helen Tiffin had famously defined as 'the empire writes back' or theoretically 'postcolonial' in 1989.

Retrieving voices and markers of material struggles apparently lost to colonisation/colonialism is an anticolonial task. But in the contemporary global–historical context of setbacks to and failures of the welfare state, and of decolonising nations now oppressed by neocolonial and neo-imperialist mechanisms, postcolonial critique in the western academy, as Aijaz Ahmad eloquently writes, was to a large extent mediated through the textual–philosophical agenda, at a remove from historical or ongoing anticolonial or postcolonial struggles. It focussed, rather, on questions of what constituted proper objects of enquiry – that is, meaning, method, language, text, historiography, discourse, representation, reality, subject, agency, and so forth (20–22). Dipesh Chakrabarty's nineteenth-century urban life-driven project on 'provincialising Europe' became an influential postcolonial method encouraged by Homi K. Bhabha's wide-ranging work on retrieving the colonised subject through theoretical methods of hybridity, mimicry, sly civility and ambivalence in *The Location of Culture*. In the context of capitalist globalisation and migrations of the middle-class Third World intellectual to the Western academy, most famously raised by Arif Dirlik, the 'postcolonial perspective' was read in Bhabha as a celebratory interrogation of the hybrid character of colonial and postcolonial lives (171–73).[1]

From the 1990s onwards, through several primers, anthologies, special issues of journals, new journals dedicated to the field, annual conferences and widespread university hiring in the Anglo-

American academy, postcolonialism was officially established as an academic discipline and a legitimate field of research and inquiry.[2] The institutionalisation of the term widened conversations on what constituted English literature or humanistic studies (Viswanathan), thereby opening up the canon to include writers and works from the Third World. However, the global primacy of the English language; the worldwide visibility of English-language Third World or immigrant writers in Euro-American countries; the importance given to theories of migrancy, post-nation, ambiguity, hybridity, radical indeterminacy and alterity as constituting the field of postcolonial studies; and the literary consecration of a handful of writers through prizes and critical work meant that writers such as Salman Rushdie, Toni Morrison, J. M. Coetzee, V. S. Naipaul or Gabriel García Márquez, among others, would be celebrated widely as literary and cultural bearers and markers of postcolonialism (Huggan, *The Postcolonial Exotic*; Parry; Brouillette; Ponzanesi).

In 'post-colonial' nations, the impact of postcolonial theory was visible, at least in the Indian literary context, in the inclusion of Indian English and translated Indian-language works in English literature university syllabi from the early 2000s onwards. But postcolonial theory was viewed in these nations with suspicion as another intellectual and methodological innovation constructed in the Western academy which was useful to analyse certain aspects of postcolonial life in the Third World, but was mostly at a remove from actual postcolonial realities of historic and everyday forms of oppression, struggle and resistance (Perusek; Ahmad, *The Politics of Postcoloniality*; San Juan Jr.; Krishnaswamy; Chibber; Bernard et al.). There was also the thorny issue that Arif Dirlik and Graham Huggan had notably raised – that, postcolonial authors and critics draw upon Third World issues to 'exoticise' these issues and cater to First World academic and cultural needs. Neil Lazarus acidly, and in my opinion correctly, suggests, 'in its prevailing and consolidated aspect at least', postcolonial studies as a discipline 'has been premised on a distinctive and conjuncturally determined set of assumptions, concepts, theories, and methods that have not only not been adequate to their putative object – the "postcolonial world" – but have served fairly systematically to mystify it' (16–17).

The USA's neo-imperialist invasion of West Asia for its War on Terror brought back the anticolonial vocabulary of imperialism, empire, colonialism, resistance and emancipatory struggle into mainstream postcolonial academic discussions (Young, *Postcolonialism*; Loomba et al.; Lazarus and Gopal). The Arab Spring, anti-racism, anti-patriarchy, anti-caste and climate-change movements in contemporary years have further emphasised conversations (this time encouraged by new media) on emancipatory struggles for justice, equality, and liberty – earlier discarded as 'grand narratives' – in post-colonial nations and post-imperial metropolises. The long-term, internationalist and interconnected nature of these struggles and narratives is provocatively captured in Priyamvada Gopal's reparative form of history-writing in *Insurgent Empire*, demonstrating how the nineteenth- or twentieth-century riots, insurgencies and uprisings in the colonies against the British Empire were crucial in developing the values of democracy, freedom and justice globally that the West had boasted of as having invented. Another postcolonial critic Yogita Goyal's *Runaway Genres*, which we will discuss in Chapter 3, shows how slave narratives were foundational to devising narrative strategies for anticolonial liberation struggles or the current refugee crisis, built as they were upon the universal concepts of humanity and justice (that is, abolitionists read the same constitutional narrative of the 'Declaration of the Rights of Man' to argue for their unjust subhuman treatment). As Susan Buck-Morss has argued, the narrative of liberty, equality and universal history propounded by thinkers such Georg Wilhelm Friedrich Hegel – to which list could be included Voltaire or Jean-Jacques Rousseau too – was not extended to the black slaves of Haiti, who rose against their French colonisers in favour of 'a new humanism'.

These contexts and questions have urged postcolonial scholars, in the last decades, to rethink the key concerns of the field; to balance 'the explosion of theory', to borrow from Ahmad; and to listen to and learn from the anticolonial/decolonising struggles of subjected populations worldwide, not necessarily only to study what precipitated such transformation – a slave rebellion or a colonial text – but also how a rebellion was popularly and historically read to effect this change.[3] What these academic initiatives have fundamentally asserted is that the anticolonial agenda is at the heart of decolonisation, or to put it differently: to decolonise is to reckon with the historical and ongoing colonial bases of contemporary knowledge systems and practices and to ceaselessly question them in imaginative works and grassroot struggles. Hence this book focuses on the decolonising agenda in postcolonial literatures and cultures which is different, in my reading, from decolonial studies. Decolonial studies and decoloniality, in the way that they have historically developed in Latin American academic contexts, are understood as an epistemological project of 'delinking' from 'western modernity', among other formulations. Decoloniality, as Walter Mignolo and other scholars have suggested, is less a political project of resistance and recovery than an epistemological one, that is, to begin to recognise how structures of colonial Western modernity are imposed on ex-colonised populations by postcolonial educated elites.[4] While this is a key condition for postcolonial life and living and a helpful feature for my analysis below, I use the transitive action verb 'decolonising' in the book as against the noun 'decolonisation'. As Anna Bernard notes, decolonising as an ongoing project 'requires us to consider how we know what we know, how we learned it, and how we might challenge or undo it' (7) – it is a process of pedagogic 'unlearning'. If neocolonial methods have meant that decolonisation is never fully achieved and is an ongoing process, postcolonial literary and cultural works, I argue, are best placed to demonstrate the decolonising impulse in the post-colonial world, that is, the active, self-reflexive, opposing process of not only 'considering' how colonial domination and anticolonial resistance have shaped much of the current socio-economic, political and cultural conditions in post-colonial nations but also acknowledging such consideration as key to continuous (anticolonial) initiatives and struggles for full decolonisation. As Gopal writes, 'it might be argued that no call to "decolonise" can really be fleshed out meaningfully without reference to the great movements of resistance, rebellion and opposition to empire which played a key role in initiating decolonisation (even if a substantial chunk of imperial history has been invested in minimising this or denying it to be the case)' ("On Decolonisation and the University" 887).

If discursively-oriented postcolonialism has taught us to retrieve the colonised from the coloniser's dematerialising textual strategies (a decolonising task, from my perspective), Marxist-oriented criticism has helped us see the historical conditions under which anticolonial and decolonising struggles, texts and utterances have found their ground. Reading material-struggles arising from contemporary colonialist ideologies and practices that go against the founding emancipatory principles of postcolonial constitutions and reading closely through or against the grain to retrieve and represent people's long-term anticolonial struggles, are both decolonising and reparative tasks. They cannot or should not be disengaged from each other. This is the meaning of 'postcolonial' (without the hyphen) in my reading – it is both a temporal condition in which neocolonial and decolonising power structures struggle for autonomy, and an interventionist method of reading literary–cultural works to mark this dialectical condition and to strive towards social transformation. Postcolonialism is the overall theoretical framework in which this reading practice happens, while postcolonial literature is a collection of literary and cultural works that helps us explore and implement this reading method and framework. *Postcolonialism Now*, then, sets out to read the presence of the originary anticolonial and decolonising agendas in contemporary postcolonial struggles and works. This warrants an appropriate method of active and engaged interpretation that I elucidate below as 'reading for decolonising'.

READING FOR DECOLONISING: LAND, CULTURE, METHOD

In an interview with *News24*, Chumani Maxwele – with whom we began the chapter – mentions anticolonial thinker Frantz Fanon as a chief inspiration behind his act of defiling the Rhodes statue. For Fanon, decolonisation is a violent process because colonialism was an utterly violent mechanism through which humans, animals, customs and values were systematically wiped out. As Fanon remarks in *The Wretched of the Earth*:

> Decolonization, which sets out to change the order of the world, is, obviously, a program of complete disorder. But it

cannot come as a result of magical practices, nor of a natural shock, nor of a friendly understanding. Decolonization, as we know, is a historical process: that is to say it cannot be understood, it cannot become intelligible nor clear to itself except in the exact measure that we can discern the movements which give it historical form and content. (36)

The ruling world order, for Fanon, is that of colonialism and capitalism in which history is written and validated by settlers and conquerors. Decolonisation sets out to vanquish this false history that had created a damaging and deceptive conception of the 'native' and, through colonial discourses of Enlightenment and 'modernity', forced upon the native inherent features of illiteracy, irrationality, laziness and promiscuity, among others. For Fanon, the history of colonisation is a 'history of pillage', while the history of decolonisation entails bringing into existence a 'history of nation' (51). National resistance and liberation unite people despite their irreducible heterogeneities because through decolonisation, colonised humans rendered into 'things' become human again (46). Therefore, decolonisation is not a sudden and shocking affair or a friendly understanding, but rather a slow but spectacular action that demands widespread re-cognition and acknowledgment. As Fanon observes, 'Decolonization never takes place unnoticed, for it influences individuals and modifies them fundamentally. It transforms spectators crushed with their inessentiality into privileged actors, with the grandiose glare of history's floodlights upon them' (36). These dramatic words about recognition and visibility, spectator and actor, strongly echo the passage cited above.

We may also notice in the above passage the use of words such as 'understood', 'intelligible', 'we' and 'discern' in the passage. But discernible or intelligible to whom? A population that is taking part in decolonisation movements as well as an audience that is witnessing and reading about them. Decolonisation, because of its historicity and spectacular visibility, is also a process of reading the conditions that make it opportune for populations and territories to attempt to gradually decolonise themselves. Fanon warns that until these conditions are ready, 'sly intellectuals' and the 'colonialist bourgeoisie' will attempt to collaborate with the ruling elite and neocolonial powers to teach the 'native' the higher values of tolerance, cooperation and 'peaceful' nation building (106; see also Ahmad, *In Theory* 28). But for the most enduring sufferers of colonisation – peasants, the working classes, oppressed castes, women and children – decolonisation means retrieving land, livelihoods, languages and cultures forcibly stolen from them and/or humiliatingly subordinated to colonising narratives. The question of land and culture is of primary importance for Fanon and my reading here. While peasant and tribal insurgencies in nineteenth-century colonial South Asia had already called for reclaiming land from zamindars – a British colonial land-lording settlement system (Guha) – probably the most cogent attack on land reclamation came from the Mexican Revolution in the early twentieth-century Americas which led to the establishment of land reform, worker rights, universal suffrage and women's rights in the country (Gonzalez). Indeed, Dalit scholar and activist Dr Bhimrao Ramji Ambedkar (a couple of decades after the revolution and probably unaware of it) wrote, in his undelivered speech *Annihilation of Caste* (1936), that the caste system was dehumanising for its classist gradation of human life: 'the caste system is not merely a division of labour. It is also a division of labourers. Civilised society undoubtedly needs division of labour. But in no civilised society is division of labour accompanied by this unnatural division of labourers into watertight compartments' (182). Awanish Kumar has shown that in numerous writings and speeches Ambedkar cogently attacked Indian society as being divided into touchable and untouchable castes and that the untouchables would never be able to purchase or own land until untouchability as an oppressive and inhuman social system was eradicated, land monopoly by caste Hindus was ended and agriculture was collectivised. Kumar writes, 'In Ambedkar's worldview, the land question for Dalits is a component part of the struggle to annihilate caste, which, in turn, is essential to establish democracy in India' (55).

It is not surprising that almost a hundred years from these events and thoughts, North American scholars and community workers Eve Tuck and K. Wayne Yang have written that decolonisation for Indigenous people is not a metaphor for reclaiming an imaginary or symbolic space lost to colonialism through transformational change in education and pedagogy, but that '[b]reaking the settler colonial triad, in direct terms, means repatriating land to sovereign Native tribes and nations, abolition of slavery in its contemporary forms, and the dismantling of the imperial metropole. Decolonization "here" is intimately connected to anti-imperialism elsewhere' (31). In conversations from Africa, South America, North America, Australia to South Asia in the last hundred years or so, activists, campaigners, anticolonialists and cultural critics have urged us to imagine the intellectual horizon of decolonisation as reclaiming land (and food) through which the colonised is able to reclaim dignity and humanity. Re-claiming land and decolonisation are not events that can be resolved overnight but, following Fanon, are historical processes which demand historical conditions to be prepared through an unceasing struggle between two antagonistic forces – the (neo)coloniser and the (neo)colonised – and to be able to 'read' these conditions and struggles appropriately for the 'utopian' socialist future of (global) egalitarian justice to come.

In these criticisms, decolonisation already appears as much about overthrowing oppressive material conditions as about being able to 'read' these conditions for a radical overhaul. This point on decolonising reading and culture has been compellingly raised by the Kenyan writer and intellectual, Ngũgĩ wa Thiong'o. In his influential book *Decolonising the Mind*, Ngũgĩ speaks about the need to overthrow the linguistic, cultural and educational forms of colonialism and imperialism with 'vernacular' languages and literatures, while in *Moving the Centre* he focuses on recognising the plurality of local cultures and languages in order to further anti-neocolonial struggles. Ngũgĩ mentions how English and dominant European languages, after contact with languages and societies in the so-called Third World, had systematically decimated the latter: 'If it was the gun which made possible the mining of this gold and which effected the political captivity of their owners, it was language which held captive their cultures, their values, and hence their minds. The latter was attempted in two ways, both of which are part of the same process' (*Moving the Centre* 49). The colonisation of resources and land could not happen without the colonisation of minds, languages and cultures – they were part of the same process.

The key finding for decolonisation, both for Fanon and Ngũgĩ, was that it had to be a people's revolution, coming from below, and that decolonising culture would need to take inspiration from the same people's cultures and languages. Fanon mentions community dance and popular storytelling techniques as anticolonial cultures in *The Wretched of the Earth*. Ngũgĩ proposes that a writer and cultural producer under the neocolonial state should align with people's struggles and cultures:

> In that situation, he will have to confront the languages spoken by the people in whose service he has put his pen. Such a writer will have to *rediscover* the real languages of struggle in the actions and speeches of his people, learn from their great heritage of orature, and above all, learn from their great optimism and faith in the capacity of human beings to remake their world and renew themselves. (*Moving the Centre* 92)

For Ngũgĩ, such an imaginative matrix that captured people's historical and cultural struggles in their everyday languages would become not only a crucial route for democracy and socialism but also usher in the possibility of decolonising education through indigenous means. Indeed, much of Ngũgĩ's corpus is aimed at recovering the local narrativising of events and creating a critical consciousness among the postcolonial educated elite about Western education's insidious connection with imperial power, as well as the dialogic means of pedagogy that 'African' learning methods have encouraged for centuries. This resonates with Paulo Freire's notion of implementing dialogue and science in local languages to resist colonial modernity's erasure of Indigenous methods and to recognise that (postcolonial) education is a two-way street based on liberating oppressed groups, and not oppressing them further (87–94). This could also be the method of 'righting wrongs' that Spivak refers to in *Other Asias* – that, postcolonial human rights activists and educational trainers must 'learn from below' in order to understand 'the structure of the role of alterity at work in subordinated cultures' (37). Acknowledging alterity, or the radical otherness between the educator and the educated, is to also take the responsibility to learn from them. For Spivak, humanities education and literary works allow for this kind of a critical pedagogic consciousness of

The Decolonising Impulse in Postcolonial Studies, or, Why Now?

listening – as Ngũgĩ or Freire urge us – to local and indigenous forms of thinking, learning to participate in them, and in so doing responsibly questioning one's class, caste, gender or race positionality in pedagogy (*Other Asias* 129).

To slightly stretch our intellectual horizon here, these positions on peoples' language, and pedagogy from below, as well as acknowledging the alterity of the oppressed, echo the American feminist scholar of Chicana cultural theory Gloria Evangelina Anzaldúa's notion of 'cross-over'. In *Borderlands*, a memoir of her social and cultural struggles, Anzaldúa documents the land and livelihoods lost due to US neocolonialism in Mexico and the birth of their migratory culture and border consciousness in a mixed narrative style: 'Barefooted, uneducated, Mexicans with hands like boot soles gather at night by the river where two worlds merge creating what Reagan calls a frontline, a war zone. The convergence has created a shock culture, a border culture, a third country, a closed country' (11). This country is 'closed' also because migrants have internalised racism and colonial violence built on a constant injection of suspicion and hostility towards their languages and cultures in order to live with the pressures of assimilation, particularly when seen in the context of an 'open' country like the US. This internalisation caused Anzaldúa to claim that the first important decolonising move in this context would be to restore women from the domestic and social forms of violence endemic to this world (18; 83–84). A decolonising culture and society for Anzaldúa would begin by uprooting, like Fanon, the rhetoric of us and them, settler and native, masculinity and femininity, and championing social justice and equity. This decolonising culture would also, like Ngũgĩ, acknowledge people's coeval social and linguistic heritage. As she writes, 'A massive uprooting of dualist thinking in the individual and collective consciousness is the beginning of a long struggle, but one that could, in our best hopes, bring us to the end of rape, of violence, of war' (80). Like Ngũgĩ's novel about a Kenyan insurgent peasant, *Matigari* (1986) – which he wrote in Kikuyu and then translated into English – Anzaldúa materialises this non-dualist collectivity in her memoir by adopting a sociocultural coevality: by writing the book in several languages

(English, Spanish, Indigenous, dialects and others); by raising an intersectional feminist resistance that is shaped by decolonisation struggles; and by deconstructing the genre of non-fiction through infusing essay writing with poetry, anecdotes, manifestos, stories and other cultural forms. This is what she considers the new borderland or 'mestiza' consciousness of contradictions, conjunctures and, above all, resistance (77).

Ngũgĩ and Anzaldúa, like Fanon and Ambedkar before them, are located in the margins of history from which they seek to restore dignity to their fellow humans through their anticolonial and decolonising agenda. They offer us, the generation of Tuck and Yang, a new mode of viewing and reading the world. This mode is based not only on retrieving stolen and suppressed histories but also on the ability to imagine and construct a future-world of dignified coexistence, or of 'affective communities' (to slightly inflect Leela Gandhi's phrasing of solidarity in *Affective Communities*). It is a world that fights for land and bread and aims to reclaim these from settlers. It is also a world that fights for values and cultures, to reclaim their humanity and collectivity. These two elements, material and epistemological, as I have been arguing in this chapter, are not mutually exclusive or even different fights for decolonisation. Therefore it is important to use 'decolonising' transitively – that is, reading prepares for decolonising material conditions while the latter calls for newer methods of reading for future material initiatives. In her inspiring book on social-science research *Decolonising Methodologies*, Indigenous scholar Linda Tuhiwai Smith writes that we need to decolonise our methodologies to be both self-reflexive about the manner and aim of the research undertaken on Indigenous communities and to be able to share our tools and knowledge with them, to feed back to the communities which have allowed researchers their valued knowledge and stories (52–53). Research in the postcolonial context by the historically subordinated, then, is reading to decolonising their colonial histories and knowledge systems in order to envision a future of giving back, of collectivity and community.

Following Tuhiwai Smith, representation is a crucial arena of struggle for postcolonial studies: that is, how to read material conditions and set up in literature, art, culture and criticism of these conditions imaginatively and critically for better, more opportune decolonising conditions to arrive. While representation in postcolonial theory, via Spivak's influential problematisation of the concept of the subaltern, is a much-debated topic about the authority and legitimacy of those who represent and speak of or for the subaltern, I am inclined to recall Said's prescient thought that, in this current global climate of authoritarianism and religious and economic fundamentalism, we cannot afford to not represent struggles:

> I don't think there is any way of getting away from them (representations) – they are as basic as language. What we must eliminate are systems of representation that carry with them the kind of authority which, to my mind, has been repressive because it doesn't permit or make room for interventions on the part of those represented . . . . The alternative would be a representational system that was participatory and collaborative, noncoercive, rather than imposed. ("In the Shadow of the West" 41–42)

Reflecting on the ethical and participatory urgency in these thoughts, Lazarus argues that representation is a matter of reading and strategic counter-reading. Authors and critics are aware of the vast and seemingly unbridgeable gap between elite and subaltern/subjected modes of life, thinking, and meaning-making. But their social and political responsibility is such that in these instances, at least, '"speaking the truth about" and "acquiring the authority to speak for" implicate one another' (Lazarus 126). For Lazarus, it is often through 'narratorial consciousness' – a self-reflexive strategy of acknowledging 'positionality' – that postcolonial authors have implemented this responsibility (156). This echoes Tuhiwai Smith's passionate and timely cry against the Eurocentric project of alienating and subordinating Indigenous struggles and knowledge systems in 'postcolonial theory' through the Indigenous researcher's (narratorial) alertness and vigilance. Smith writes,

> To acquiesce is to lose ourselves entirely and implicitly agree with all that has been said about us. To resist is to retrench in the margins, retrieve "what we were and remake ourselves".

The past, our stories local and global, the present, our communities, cultures, languages and social practices – all may be spaces of marginalization, but they have also become spaces of resistance and hope. (35)

Reading in postcolonial (literary) studies is thus an interventionist, participatory and decolonising task. However, Ahmad warns us that during the ascendancy of 'postcolonial theory', reading replaces activism and struggle as 'the appropriate form of politics' (*In Theory* 4). The point here is to not replace activism and struggle with reading but to find, complicate and enrich struggle-based politics with reading in such a manner that reading and practice are co-constitutive. In contemporary global anti(neo)colonial struggles, it is important we implement a form of reading that remains committed to retrieving the historical, ongoing and comparable contexts of decolonisation through literary content, form, style and aesthetics. One such reading method is imagined by Elleke Boehmer as being an interactive, interpretation-based theory that goes beyond symptomatic or sociological methods and exposes, through semantic processes, how meaning unfurls (*Postcolonial Poetics* 8). Boehmer's interpretive study follows Ato Quayson's useful concept of 'calibration' in reading literary texts for 'the social': to understand how literary texts have used aesthetic properties or thresholds to interrogate 'structures of transformation, process, and contradiction that inform both literature and society' (*Calibrations* xvi–xviii). While, like them, I use close and comparative readings of literary works to understand how these works have constructed decolonising 'arguments', my reading is not solely aimed at reception or the effect that literary works have created among readers. It interrogates history through style; politics through aesthetics; context through form; and, above all, the postcolonial through the anticolonial for which a historical materialist method is warranted. Walter Benjamin addresses this point in 'On the Concept of History', that in the course of history, thoughts are arrested and crystallised into monads, inspiring a historical materialist to uncover sedimentations of suppressed and subordinated histories in the monad. A historical materialist is analytical, self-reflexive and cautious about received histories and traditions, taking cognisance of the monad 'in order to blast a specific era out of the homogenous course of history—blasting a specific life out of the era or a specific work out of the lifework' (Benjamin 396).

A close analytical framework for such a historical materialist enquiry in comparative literary studies is offered by the Warwick Research Collective's (WReC) reading of 'world-literature' as 'literature of the modern capitalist world-system' (8). WReC urges critics to explore how literary writings from 'peripheral' or 'semi-peripheral zones' have registered the uneven and combined matrix of capitalist and non-capitalist social relationships in the works' aesthetics, which they read as 'peripheral realism' (71). While WReC considers world capitalism as the 'political horizon' for combined and uneven development, I argue that colonialism and imperialism substantiate world capitalism's peculiar means of governance (extractive, racist and segregationist); geography (local and specific); and culture (inferiority and resistance) – through which economic and cultural accumulation can continue at a global scale and which can also invite historical means of resistance. This book's methodological agenda, thus, comes close to Benita Parry's materialist reading of British colonial literature (2004) and, more specifically, to Robert Spencer and Anastasia Valassopoulos' work *Postcolonial Locations*, in which they define reading as 'a directly political activity' in postcolonial studies which has (however) not always paid attention to the specificities of the works' locations and articulations, however systemic and global their dispositions and struggles are (2–3).[5] It further draws inspiration from Anna Bernard's work on *Decolonizing Literature* in which Bernard offers multiple ways of decolonising literary studies including teaching diverse Anglophone and translated work in the curriculum to reading collective anticolonial struggles through women's autobiographies to implementing a 'contrapuntal' method of reading colonial and anticolonial works together that can 'expose the falsehoods and omissions of imperial cultural production' and become 'an effective way of conceiving world literature' (80).[6]

Like these critics, I also show through close materialist readings that literary and cultural works and their key thematic registers – class, caste, race, gender, nation, religion, land, water and so on – are never abstract but rather historical and concrete and connected; that reading different registers and rubrics together (as we will see below) can expose imperialist falsehoods but also critical comparability. As Fanon, Ambedkar, or Tuck and Yang have noted, concerns of dignity and humanity are associated with those of land and food. Concerns and movements of caste, class and gender are widely connected with those of liberation and justice, as the latter are with those of land, ecology and food. Thus, reading for decolonising entails an acknowledgement of what Darren Lenard Hutchinson calls the 'multidimensionality' of neo-imperialist oppressions and historical liberations (309). As decolonial feminist scholar, Françoise Vergès, reading Hutchinson, argues, 'A multidimensional approach makes it possible to avoid a hierarchy of struggles based on a scale of urgency whose framework often remains dictated by prejudice. The challenge is to hold several threads at once, to override ideologically induced segmentation, and "to grasp how production and social reproduction are historically articulated"' for a social relation of totality (20–21). In my decolonising reading of literary and cultural works I apply a multidimensional approach, arguing for the intersectionality of broad analytical categories or rubrics and close thematic registers and, through them, seek a totality of social relationships. Reading in this historical materialist framework thus becomes an interrogative method and ethical imperative through which one can recover the continuity and resonance of global decolonising struggles for land and culture.

The Decolonising Impulse in Postcolonial Literature: An Example

Let me offer a brief reading of the final episode of the Sudanese–Scottish writer Leila Aboulela's short story 'The Museum', winner of the 2000 Caine Prize for African Writing, to elucidate the method of reading for decolonising of postcolonial literatures in the book. The short story is about a young, middle-class, international Sudanese woman, Shadia, in a Scottish university who finds herself alienated by majoritarian 'white' people and culture. She longs to go home but is against her imminent marriage with a well-off but narrow-minded Sudanese businessman. She strikes upon a support network with African international students and finds in Islam, for the first time, peace and solace from her anxiety and depression. Later in the story, she begins to develop a romantic affection for her white, working-class, Scottish classmate Bryan. The final episode is set in a visit to the museum with Bryan. In the museum, Shadia discovers that African culture is projected in a pejorative, dehumanising light as against the heroism of Scottish travellers and soldiers. She reads a poster on a display cabinet which proclaims *'During the 18th and 19th centuries, north-east Scotland made a disproportionate impact on the world at large by contributing so many skilled and committed individuals . . . In serving an empire they gave and received, changed others and were themselves changed and often returned home with tangible reminders of their experiences'* (Aboulela 15; italics in the original). These tangible reminders are little statues of iron and copper which not only give a skewed and outmoded portrayal of colonial Africa but also a reductive and objective one for current viewers: frozen in time, 'cold and old' (15). In the colonial–imperialist message of serving an empire that changed others, the display narrative becomes a one-way street where Africa is a dark continent, a vast land of savages that need to be civilised; a project most violently carried out by King Leopold in his Congo Free State and aptly summed up by Joseph Conrad's narrator Marlow in *Heart of Darkness*:

> The conquest of the earth, which mostly means taking it away from those who have a different complexion or slightly flatter noses than ourselves, is not a pretty thing when you look into it too much. What redeems it is the idea only. An idea at the back of it; not a sentimental pretence but an idea; and an unselfish belief in the idea. (10)

It is this ideology of imperialism that Shadia encounters in the museum and in her mind:

> Biographies of explorers who were educated in Edinburgh; they knew what to take to Africa: doctors, courage, Christianity, commerce, civilisation. They knew what they wanted to bring back: cotton, watered by the blue Nile, the Zambezi river . . . She touched the glass of a cabinet showing papyrus rolls, copper pots. She pressed her forehead and nose against the cool glass. If she could enter the cabinet, she would not make a good exhibit. She wasn't right, she was too modern, too full of mathematics. (16)

This is an advanced decolonising reading in the story for critical museum or literary studies. While museums in the wake of postcolonial studies in the Western academy and institutions had begun to address questions of empire and objects (as Tim Barringer and Tom Flynn's edited volume *Colonialism and the Object* shows), museum-related activisms or initiatives for decolonising the colonial institution was at an early stage when the story was first published in 1997 (Arora 122). Sumaya Kassim has written about the emotionally draining task of putting together a curatorial event at Birmingham Museum and Art Gallery (2017–18) about its colonial extraction of objects and its colonising narratives because of, among others, the affective labour involved:

> Too often people of colour are rolled in to provide natural resources – our bodies and our "decolonial" thoughts – which are exploited, and then discarded. The human cost, the emotional labour, are seen as worthy sacrifices in the name of an exhibition which can be celebrated as a successful attempt by the museum at "inclusion" and "decolonising", as a marker that it – and, indeed, Britain – is dealing with its past.

What Shadia experiences is the emotional pain of being reduced to an object that has no agency in the dimly lit walls of the museum. She sits on a chair, her chest tight with pain and her mind seething with anger about the dehumanising portrayal of her country and continent – a disorientating experience for the ex-colonised. From this emotional pain to undergoing the emotional labour of working to develop a project (by Kassim et al.) about the colossal nature of this pain, we have walked a few important miles. The museum episode, or the story itself, thus, can be read as Aboulela's Benjaminian 'monad' of history. It is the postcolonial literary critic's task to read, through the narrative, the decolonising intellectual moment of reckoning with an imperialist museum for ex-colonised people in a globalised world captured in soulless and irresponsible display units, hence setting up the imaginative horizon for what an anticolonial museum might look like through Kassim and her colleagues' (historical materialist) work.

The clues for implementing the method of 'reading for decolonising' are more apparent here. Note that Shadia's anti-imperialist thoughts arise from reading the posters and displays. Reading, here, is as much about the literal act of viewing texts as about sensing and experiencing the colonialist atmosphere and the colonising 'narrative' that is thrust into the minds of Scottish people through the museum. Indeed, Shadia notices that Bryan reads everything with 'an intent expression on his face' (Aboulela 15) or Bryan 'was preoccupied with reading the caption' (16). Bryan then tells her that like these soldiers and travellers who wanted to get away from Scotland in order to benefit (from empire) and contribute to society, he would like to travel to Mecca one day (because 'we did Islam in school' so he learned a little about Mecca from a book). While Shadia likes his interest in travel, we know through the diegetic narrator that Bryan was not ready to absorb the 'throbbing' nature of life and customs in 'ex-colonised' countries. He has been misled – interpellated as it were – through colonising narratives and discourses in public institutions in Britain which have, for centuries, misrepresented and distorted Africa, Asia and the postcolonial world. The quotes from the story are an apt reminder that travel, adventure and colonialism went hand in hand, enabled and corroborated by 'findings' hatched and validated in the chief academic bastions of the Scottish Enlightenment – Edinburgh, Glasgow and Aberdeen – or in their English counterparts – Oxford, Cambridge and London. For all of these, Shadia is too modern an African subject, too unfitting for the current project.

The quote about Shadia's thoughts on encountering the exhibits could also be read as an example of the self-reflexive narratorial consciousness that Neil Lazarus mentions. Through Shadia's disorientating encounter with the colonial museum and her deconstructive reading of what lies beneath the biased and superficial display of that institution, Aboulela manages to set up the interconnectedness of masculine imperialism, travel narrative, colonised space and the Enlightenment – in our critical reading, the multidimensional totality of social relationships. This interconnectedness, on the other hand, enables a racialised, gendered and spatialised feeling of disorientation in Shadia from which the only response that she can offer to Bryan was that he 'did not understand'. There are no appropriate material or intellectual conditions ready for Shadia to show Bryan the shameful and disorientating experience she feels. Thus, Bryan's generous though abstract response appears naïve in its optimism: 'Museums change, I can change' (19).

Bryan's honest intention for him and the museum to change is a huge leap for which Shadia does not have the time and energy to encourage. But twenty-five years from Shadia's (or Aboulela's) material and symbolic experience, enabled by social movements in the postcolonial world as well as the impact of RMF and BLM movements on social media, museums have found more robust grounds on which to address these disorientating issues (as the work of Kassim et al. might suggest). Museums, archives, statues and syllabi are not abstract domains of teaching, learning and enterprise in a historical vacuum. They shape the way we conduct and react to things around their colonial agenda. In Shadia's responses of frustration, anger and despair, there is an anticolonial reading, questioning the imperialist one-sidedness of narratives and their historical and ongoing – tacit and dominant – validations by citizens, cultural ambassadors and politicians. It also questions their relevance in an increasingly globalised world of student and worker traffic from ex-colonised countries to post-imperial metropolises who encounter reductive renderings of and stolen objects from their countries and feel ashamed, outraged, and ask questions. These questions from postcolonial populations inside (ethnic minorities based here for historical reasons of colonialism and slavery) and outside (tourists, students, workers and a global population accessing materials online) will set up the contexts for more strategic anticolonial counter-readings to come, the opportune conditions upon which further decolonising initiatives and readings will rest.

Here it is also important to note that Shadia, a middle-class woman who judges Bryan's working-class character through the same shirt he wears every day and through his rough accent against her 'BBC World' English, are keen suggestions from Aboulela, with respect to Ngũgĩ, about the colonial impact on the learning cultures of the postcolonial educated elite. Here, 'class' is introduced against colonial privilege in an intersectional move that complicates a one-sided reading of the story (Aboulela's characters are self-questioning, not self-righteous). Much of the postcolonial/ decolonial activism from international student populations in the UK, in the Indian context at least, comes from those belonging to a middle-class, upper-caste background, encountering, often for the first time, the dehumanising experiences of social marginalisation. Aboulela's story is also about this self-reflexivity of the middle-class postcolonial intellectual who will need to decolonise intellectual and material conditions in their own knowledge systems and their own countries by standing in solidarity with the 'minorities' there (as working-class, anti-patriarchy, Dalit, peasant and student activism in these countries have done) and mark the internationalism of these struggles – which, in my opinion, is intently underway encouraged by the globalism of social and news media. To quote from Priyamvada Gopal's essay on decolonisation and the university, 'This horizon of decolonisation requires the hard work of examining both the moment and the afterlife of empire, unflinchingly, both in former colony and metropole' (896–97).

Such a critical self-awareness, or what I have referred to above as a critic's 'positionality', can often be at its most telling when the postcolonial student/intellectual is uprooted, either by force or choice, from their comfortable locations and arrives in the contentious domain of the post-imperial metropolis. Indeed, Aboulela says in an interview that she would have never written the story if she had not come first to London and then to Scotland ("Moving Away" 204– 05). Therefore, the responsibility to analyse colonialist–imperialist or anticolonial/decolonising conditions underpinning a literary work (sometimes from a distance) has to include positionality – that is, a critic's or researcher's political–ethical position (commitment) and their socio-economic and geographic location (peripheral or metropolitan as they may relationally stand for) (England; Vanner). Although Aboulela's story ends with an exhausted, distraught Shadia, its self-reflexive anticolonial vigour and contemporaneous decolonising initiatives and solidarity struggles worldwide may indicate that its 'decolonising impulse' is well served. This goes back to the point raised before through the #RhodesMustFall campaign in the introductory paragraphs – defacing the Rhodes statue at the

University of Cape Town or asking to remove it from Oriel College, Oxford is not a sudden or isolated outburst. It is a consequence of the conditions built through a historical process of encountering, both literally and pedagogically, the violent nature of colonialism as a system that needs to be self-reflexively negotiated and 'uprooted' for a properly decolonising culture and society, or for Gopal the anticolonial university (888–90), to arrive.

Framing the Book: Why Now

Drawing from this example, I read in the book 'current' postcolonial literary expressions of violence, oppression, dislocation and dispossession, and their immediate, slow or complex forms of resistance. The works chosen were mostly published in the last two decades of the twenty-first century, hence the 'now-ness' of the project. But there are also works from the early 1990s, late 1980s, early 1970s, and even from the first decade of the twentieth century. By choosing these works away from an immediate now-ness, the book also suggests that many of the struggles in colonial and postcolonial periods are fought on similar grounds: to ensure access and claims to land, water, food and to imagine conditions for equitable, just, socialist transformations. Writing or commenting on the present while imagining a historical past or an egalitarian future is a form of counter-reading which writers and cultural producers have long pursued. In the current neoliberal climate, it is our training and urgent task, as literary and cultural studies scholars, to read through the radical and transformative agenda in such works, that is, their anticolonial spirit and decolonising impulse. The now-ness thus, is both strategic and ideological. *Postcolonialism Now* stands for the retrospective vantage point of how the field has developed – the field's key issues and what could be done (its reading strategy) to see through and strive towards its transformative agenda. In this light, 'postcolonialism', as suggested above, is the theoretical framework of organising and reading literary works and concepts in order to recognise the continuous and co-constitutive process of social transformation.

For this, I have chosen literary–cultural examples from different parts of the postcolonial world: India, Bangladesh, Pakistan,

Vietnam, Israel/Palestine, Nigeria, South Africa, the Democratic Republic of the Congo, USA, Scotland/UK, Antigua, Granada/Canada, and so on. These works are either originally composed in or translated into English, which means that they are available to a wider readership. Yet, most of these works may not have received wide scholarly attention. In this way, such works can extend our intellectual horizon on the global nature of postcolonial conditions and the comparative (mis)fortunes of minorities and oppressed populations who continue to face threats that are similar in nature. It is important to mention that the writers/filmmakers discussed here are not always those who have been oppressed themselves; neither does the book make an argument about what an authentic portrayal of postcolonial communities and resistance should look or feel like. As I have suggested above, representation is a form of anticolonial counter-reading to fight oppression and build communities of trust, inclusion and solidarity. What I have offered to do in the book, rather, is to build a method of reading that would not necessarily depend on the question of one's compatibility with a 'native' language, on translation or the market.

To give a sense of the materialist framework and method of reading, I have brought at least three works from three different nations/writers together under a broad conceptual rubric. These works have key thematic registers or topics in postcolonial studies – race, gender, language, hunger, et cetera – as their putative literary object. Together, these topics/themes are placed under five conceptual rubrics to suggest, apropos the question of multidimensionality, that these topics and their rubrics are not isolated but connected with each other. So, the conceptual rubric of Chapter 2 is 'minorities' which includes three texts addressing topics of caste, race and sexuality to understand the multidimensional struggle of minorities and margins in postcolonial nations. I first interrogate, through minority struggles, the decolonising meaning and use of the term 'nation' in postcolonial contexts and then show how these struggles are complexly captured in their literary and cultural representations. I illustrate through Dalit writer Bama's autobiography that the struggles of the caste minority in India are not disengaged from those of class, gender or land minority ('minority' here standing for structural dispossession). Similarly, gender minority in Scotland represented by a black writer, Jackie Kay, cannot be understood without its racial, class, territorial, linguistic or biological contexts. I further read Dionne Brand's queer poetry through the minority lens of sexuality, empire and solidarity.

In Chapter 3, I read 'migrations' through the valences of forced migration in Steve McQueen's film based on a slave narrative and Thi Bui's graphic conjuration of the Vietnamese-American refugee crisis, and of professional migration to richer/ex-imperial nations for opportunity through Chimamanda Ngozi Adichie's and Mohsin Hamid's novels on post-racial and religious issues in the postcolonial context. Chapter 4 introduces 'traumas' and their postcolonial dimensions through war, genocide and memory as well as their recovery through solidarity-based struggles by reading Zahir Raihan's documentary cinema on the Bangladesh War of Liberation; Lynn Nottage's play on rape and female bonds in the Democratic Republic of the Congo; and Mahmoud Darwish's poetry on the Israel–Palestine conflict. Chapter 5 engages with postcolonial 'ecologies' through Mahasweta Devi's short story on extraction, hunger and tribal life in India; Phaswane Mpe's novella on the AIDS epidemic in South Africa; and Olive Senior's poetry on plant consciousness and postcolonial resilience in the Caribbean. In the final chapter on 'futures', I demonstrate how postcolonial writers have envisioned different futures – utopia in Rokeya Sakhawat Hossain's short fiction; AI and dystopia in Manjula Padmanabhan's theatre; and planetarity in Nnedi Okorafor's speculative fiction.

This broad comparative framework helps us see the interconnectedness of these thematic and analytical registers and their conceptual rubrics (hence the usage of the plural 'rubrics'). In suggesting the individual works' resistant spirit and their composite, complex, and multidimensional representational contexts, *Postcolonialism Now* offers an understanding of the totality of anticolonial struggles. For this reason, the book does not follow the more established path of discursive readings of postcolonial theories in the last decades in themselves or through a handful of literary works – of which many excellent critical surveys, primers and anthologies remain, some of which I have referred to above. What

I argue has been broadly missing from the field, is a sustained basis of materialist and comparative reading of literary and cultural works through key postcolonial topics/rubrics. In this context, the book can be seen as an offering of committed readings, or an interpretive register to establish postcolonial literature's thematic and stylistic resonances – and hence, there will be in specific chapters reminders of a text's resonance in other texts and other chapters of the book. This may mean there are several texts and comparative critical readings in the book (as opposed to fewer texts and 'in depth' readings – a pattern humanistic scholars are trained with). As suggested above, I have attempted to smoothen out this issue by historicising and complicating a rubric in the beginning; contextualising a topic in it; introducing a text to explain the topic; picking up on a particular aspect in a text (imagery, genre or narrative structure) for concision; reading it using extensive secondary literature; and setting up comparative discussions in texts between a chapter and across the book as a way of suggesting how to read postcolonial texts closely, critically and comparatively. This approach, I believe, will offer undergraduates and postgraduates, as well as specialists – this book's primary target audience – a reading method and toolkit to attend to the cultural and literary specificities of a literary work and to bring together works and cultures from global postcolonial contexts and genres to understand their comparative aesthetic properties and resonant decolonising agenda.

Finally, a few words on genres and works. I have studied in this book novels, short stories, poems, plays, graphic novels, films and nonfiction works, among others, under five rubrics (chapters) while placing these genres in the title of the book under the broad heading of 'literature'. This is because I implement a close historical materialist reading of content, style and form of these 'works' and do not offer a specialised reading of non-literary genres such as cinema, for which I do not have the expertise. By bringing together several different literary and cultural genres I am more inclined to argue for a holistic postcolonial reading of literatures and cultures in this book – a training in comparative critical reading that students of literature should not be unfamiliar with. However, as a historical materialist, I have repeated in each chapter that every genre and form is unique in their own light and in the context they are implemented. Close attention to their generic and historical specificities is key to informed postcolonial readings (I have raised the issue on 'genre' more explicitly in the chapter on 'futures'). These genres can hold on to their stylistic peculiarities, and when placed alongside other genres and contexts, accentuate their interconnectedness, long-term continuity and holistic nature. Studying them in the manner of critically surveying postcolonial topics and texts to retrieve their anticolonial agenda and placing them under rubrics, can also demonstrate the extraordinary spectrum of works in the postcolonial literary world which may otherwise be routinely rendered invisible by scholarly over-reliance on the novel genre and a list of 'canonised' authors thanks to global marketing politics (Brouillette; Dwivedi and Lau; Bernard).

What this interconnected reading is finally able to do, in my judgement, is demonstrate that these five conceptual rubrics are also categorically connected and hermeneutically resonant – that a fight for reclaiming caste dignity can also be a fight for land reclamation and ecological reparation; or that a moment of confronting a reductive representation of Africa in a Scottish museum is also a moment of reckoning with the 'ongoing' pasts of slavery and empire (migrations), resource extraction (ecologies), racist and masculine narratives (minorities), deep-seated anxiety (traumas), and the call for social and material transformation (futures). While it is thus possible to read across these rubrics through one literary work, I have chosen to read several works which at their heart have a comparable and cogent anticolonial demand: standing up to the oppression of historical and ongoing global colonialisms. These rubrics and their literary works are not used in an instructive or exhaustive manner (there are many colonial empires, postcolonial geographies, topics or works that could not be read here for space). Rather, the chief reason behind the selection of works and topics, as I have suggested above, is pedagogic and methodological; that this critical reading is a way to identify and analyse the specific, irreducible, resonant, and decolonising contexts of postcolonial histories and texts. So, while the book is about introducing students and scholars to the discursive complexities in the field (hence rubrics and key topics), what it has primarily aimed to do for the 'now' is activate a committed reading of literary and cultural works for postcolonial studies scholars. By doing so, and by acknowledging scholarly positionalities, the book looks forward to constituting a community of readers and citizens which would remain vigilant to neoliberal and neocolonial attacks on critique, dissent and, more broadly, humanistic studies. We may end this chapter with Edward Said's prophetic reminders that the postcolonial critic or intellectual is

> (S)omeone whose place it is publicly to raise embarrassing questions, to confront orthodoxy and dogma (rather than to produce them), to be someone who cannot easily be co-opted by governments or corporations, and whose raison d'être is to represent all those people and issues that are routinely forgotten or swept under the rug. . . . individuals with a vocation for the art of representing, whether that is talking, writing, teaching, appearing on television. And that vocation is important to the extent that it is publicly recognizable and involves both commitment and risk, boldness and vulnerability. (*Representations of the Intellectual* 11, 13)

NOTES

1. For opposing notions, see Appiah; McClintock; Dirlik; and Parry, among others.

2. See, for instance, Ashcroft, et al.; Boehmer; Childs and Williams; Gandhi; and Loomba's *Colonialism/Postcolonialism*, among others.

3. For works aimed at historicising the field and reading critically about neocolonial capitalism, popular struggle and resistance see Quayson's *Cambridge History*; Huggan; Malreddy, et al.; Kennedy; and Spencer and Valassopoulos.

4. It is important to note longer forms of colonial settlement and socio-ecological relations, since at least the early-fifteenth century, in Latin America. See, in this context, Walsh and Mignolo; and Bhambra.

5. See also Jenni Ramone's use of 'located reading' in the contexts of the local literary marketplace (23–24).

6. Also see in this context, the 'Introduction' by Ato Quayson and Ankhi Mukherjee in their edited volume *Decolonising the English Literary Curriculum*.

REFERENCES

Aboulela, Leila. "The Museum". *An African Quilt: 24 Modern African Stories*, edited by Barbara H. Solomon and W. Reginald Rampone, Jr., Signet, 2012, pp. 1–17.

---. "Moving Away from Accuracy". *Alif: Journal of Comparative Politics*, vol. 22, 2002, pp. 198–207.

Ahmad, Aijaz. *In Theory: Classes, Nations, Literatures*. Verso, 1992.

---. "The Politics of Literary Postcoloniality". *Race & Class*, vol. 36, no. 3, 1995, pp. 1–20.

Ambedkar, B.R. *Annihilation of Caste*. 1936. Verso, 2014.

Anzaldúa, Gloria E. *Borderlands/La Frontera: The New Mestiza*. Aunt Lute Book Company, 1987.

Appiah, Kwame Anthony. "Is the Post- in Postmodernism the Post- in Postcolonial?" *Critical Inquiry*, vol. 17, no. 2, 1991, pp. 336–57.

Arora, Anupama. "Decolonizing the Museum: Leila Aboulela's 'The Museum'". *Journal of Postcolonial Writing*, vol. 57, no. 1, 2021, pp. 121–34.

Ashcroft, Bill, Gareth Griffiths, and Helen Tiffin, editors. *The Empire Writes Back: Theory and Practice in Post-colonial Literature*. Routledge, 1989.

Barringer, Tim, and Tom Flynn, editors. *Colonialism and the Object: Empire, Material Culture, and the Museum*. Routledge, 1998.

BBC. "Edward Colston Statue: Protesters Tear Down Slave Trader Monument". *BBC*, 8 June 2020, https://www.bbc.com/news/uk-52954305. Accessed 27 April 2022.

Benjamin, Walter. "On the Concept of History". *Walter Benjamin: Selected Writings, Vol. 4: 1938-1940*, edited by Howard Eiland and Michael E. Jennings, Harvard UP, 2003, pp. 389–400.

Bernard, Anna, Ziad Elmarsafy, and Stuart Murray, editors. *What Postcolonial Theory Doesn't Say*. Routledge, 2018.

Bernard, Anna. *Decolonizing Literature: An Introduction*. Polity Press, 2023.

Bhabha, Homi K. *The Location of Culture*. Routledge, 1994.

Bhambra, Gurminder K. "Postcolonial and Decolonial Dialogues". *Postcolonial Studies*, vol. 17, no. 2, 2014, pp. 115–21.

Boehmer, Elleke. *Colonial and Post-Colonial Literature*. Oxford UP, 1995.

---. *Postcolonial Poetics: 21st Century Critical Readings*. Palgrave Macmillan, 2018.

Brouillette, Sarah. *Postcolonial Writers in the Global Literary Marketplace*. Palgrave Macmillan, 2007.

Buck-Morss, Susan. *Hegel, Haiti, and Universal History*. U of Pittsburgh P, 2009.

Chakrabarty, Dipesh. *Provincialising Europe: Postcolonial Thought and Historical Difference*. Princeton UP, 2000.

Chantiluke, Roseanne, Brian Kwoba, and Athinangamso Nkopo, editors. *Rhodes Must Fall: The Struggle to Decolonise the Racist Heart of the Empire*. Zed Books, 2018.

Chaudhuri, Amit. "The Real Meaning of Rhodes Must Fall". *The Guardian*, 16 March 2016, https://www.theguardian.com/uk-news/2016/mar/16/the-real-meaning-of-rhodes-must-fall. Accessed 27 April 2022.

Chibber, Vivek. *Postcolonial Theory and the Spectre of Capital*. Verso, 2013.

Chigudu, Simukai. "Rhodes Must Fall in Oxford: A Critical Testimony". *Critical African Studies*, vol. 12, no. 3, 2020, pp. 302–12.

Childs, Peter, and Patrick Williams, editors. *An Introduction to Postcolonial Theory*. Routledge, 1997.

'Colony'. *Oxford English Dictionary*, https://www.oed.com/search/dictionary/?scope=Entries&q=colony. Accessed May 26, 2022.

Conrad, Joseph. *Heart of Darkness*. 1899. Penguin Books, 1991.

Dirlik, Arif. "The Postcolonial Aura: Third World Criticisms in the Age of Global Capitalism". *Critical Inquiry*, vol. 20, no. 2, 1994, pp. 328–56.

Dwivedi, Omi P., and Lisa Lau, editors. *Indian Writing in English and the Global Literary Market*. Palgrave Macmillan, 2014.

England, Kim V.L. "Getting Personal: Reflexivity, Positionality, and Feminist Research". *The Professional Geographer*, vol. 46, no. 1, 1994, pp. 80–89.

Fairbanks, Eve. "The Birth of Rhodes Must Fall". *The Guardian*, 18 November 2015, https://www.theguardian.com/news/2015/nov/18/why-south-african-students-have-turned-on-their-parents-generation. Accessed 26 May 2022.

Fanon, Frantz. *The Wretched of the Earth*. Translated by Constance Farrington, Grove Press, 1963.

Freire, Paulo. *Pedagogies of the Oppressed*. 1970. Continuum, 2000.

Gandhi, Leela. *Affective Communities: Anticolonial Thought, Fin-de-Siècle Radicalism, and the Politics of Friendship*. Duke UP, 2006.

---. *Postcolonial Theory: A Critical Introduction*. Allen and Unwin, 1997.

"George Floyd: What happened in the final moments of his life". *BBC*, 16 July 2020, https://www.bbc.com/news/world-us-canada-52861726. Accessed 5 September 2023.

Gonzalez, Michael J. *The Mexican Revolution, 1910-1940*. U of New Mexico P, 2002.

Gopal, Priyamvada. *Insurgent Empire. Anticolonial Resistance and British Dissent*. Verso, 2019.

---. "On Decolonisation and the University". *Textual Practice*, vol. 35, no. 6, 2021, pp. 873–99.

Gramsci, Antonio. *Subaltern Social Groups: A Critical Edition of Prison Notebook 25*. 1934. Translated and edited by Joseph Buttigieg and Marcus E Green, Columbia UP, 2021.

Guha, Ranajit. *Elementary Aspects of Peasant Insurgency in India*. Oxford UP, 1983.

---, and Gayatri Chakravorty Spivak, editors. *Selected Subaltern Studies*. Oxford UP, 1988.

Howe, Stephen. *Empire: A Very Short Introduction*. Oxford UP, 2002.

Hutchinson, Darren Lenard. "Identity Crisis: "Intersectionality," "Multidimensionality," and the Development of an Adequate Theory of Subordination". *Michigan Journal of Race and Law*, vol. 6, 2001, pp. 285–317.

Huggan, Graham. *The Postcolonial Exotic: Marketing the Margins*. Routledge, 2001.

---, editor. *The Oxford Handbook of Postcolonial Studies*. Oxford UP, 2013.

Kassim, Sumaya. "The Museum will not be Decolonised". *Media Diversified*. 15 November 2017, https://mediadiversified.org/2017/

11/15/the-museum-will-not-be-decolonised/. Accessed 21 April 2022.

Kennedy, Melissa. *Narratives of Inequality: Postcolonial Literary Economics*. Palgrave Macmillan, 2017.

Krishnaswamy, Revathi. "Globalization and its Postcolonial (Dis)contents: Reading Dalit Writing". *Journal of Postcolonial Writing*, vol. 41, no. 1, 2005, pp. 69–82.

Kumar, Awanish. "BR Ambedkar on Caste and Land Relations in India". *Review of Agrarian Studies*, vol. 10, no. 1, 2020, pp. 37–56.

Lazarus, Neil. *The Postcolonial Unconscious*. Cambridge UP, 2011.

---, and Priyamvada Gopal, editors. "After Iraq: Reframing Postcolonial Studies". New Formations (Special Issue), vol. 59, 2006, pp. 7–171. *The Postcolonial Unconscious*. Cambridge UP, 2011.

Lebron, Christopher J. *The Making of Black Lives Matter: A Short History of an Idea*. Oxford UP, 2017.

Loomba, Ania. *Colonialism/Postcolonialism*. Routledge, 1998.

---, et al, editors. *Postcolonial Studies and Beyond*. Duke UP, 2005.

Malreddy, Pavan, et al, editors. *Reworking Postcolonialism: Globalization, Labour and Rights*. Palgrave Macmillan, 2015.

Maxwele, Chumani. "Newsmaker: Chumani Maxwele: No Regrets for Throwing Faeces at Rhodes Statue". *News24*, https://www.news24.com/news24/newsmaker-chumani-maxwele-no-regrets-for-throwing-faeces-at-rhodes-statue-20150429, 29 March 2015. Accessed 20 May 2022.

McClintock, Anne. "The Angel of Progress: Pitfalls of the Term Post-Colonialism". *Social Text*, vol. 31, no. 2, 1992, pp. 84–98.

Parry, Benita. *Postcolonial Studies: A Materialist Critique*. Routledge, 2004.

Perusek, Darshan. "Post-Colonial Realities, Post-Structuralist Diversions: An Unamused Exchange". *Economic and Political Weekly*, vol. 29, no. 5, 1994, pp. 243–49.

Ponzanesi, Sandra. "Publishing, Prizes, and Postcolonial Literary Production". *The Cambridge History of Postcolonial Literature*, edited by Ato Quayson, vol. 2, Cambridge UP, 2012, pp. 1127–54.

'Post-colonial'. *Oxford English Dictionary*, https://www.oed.com/dictionary/postcolonialism_n?tab=meaning_and_use#10377158. Accessed 26 May 2022.

Quayson, Ato. *Calibrations: Reading for the Social*. Minneapolis: U of Minnesota P, 2003.

---. *The Cambridge History of Postcolonial Literature*. Cambridge UP, 2012. 2 vols.

Quayson, Ato, and Ankhi Mukherjee. Introduction. *Decolonising the English Curriculum*, Cambridge UP, 2023, pp. 1–20.

Ramone, Jenni. *Postcolonial Literatures in the Local Literary Marketplace: Located Readings*. Palgrave Macmillan, 2020.

Rose, Gillian. "Situated Knowledges: Positionality, Reflexivities and Other Tactics". *Progress in Human Geography*, vol. 21, no. 3, 1997, pp. 305–20.

San Juan Jr, E. *Beyond Postcolonial Theory*. Macmillan, 1998.

Said, Edward W. "In the Shadow of the West". 1985. *Power, Politics and Culture: Interviews with Edward W. Said*, edited by Gauri Vishwanathan, Bloomsbury, 2004, pp. 39–52.

---. *Orientalism*. 1978. Penguin Books, 2005.

---. *Power, Politics and Culture: Interviews with Edward W. Said*, edited by Gauri Viswanathan. Bloomsbury, 2004, pp. 39–52.

---. *Representations of the Intellectual: The 1993 Reith Lectures*. Vintage, 1994.

Spencer, Robert, and Anastasia Valassopoulos. *Postcolonial Locations: New Issues and Directions in Postcolonial Studies*. Routledge, 2021.

Spivak, Gayatri Chakravorty. "Can the Subaltern Speak?". *Marxism and the Interpretation of Culture*, edited by Carl Nelson and Lawrence Grossberg, Macmillan, 1988, pp. 271–313.

---. *Other Asias*. Blackwell, 2008.

---. "Supplementing Marxism". *Whither Marxism?: Global Crises in International Perspective*, edited by Bernd Magnus and Stephen Cullenberg, Routledge, 1995, pp. 109–20.

Tuck, Eve, and K. Wayne Yang. "Decolonization is not a Metaphor". *Decolonization: Indigeneity, Education & Society*, vol. 1, no. 1, 2012, pp. 1–40.

Tuhiwai Smith, Linda. *Decolonising Methodologies: Research and Indigenous People*. Zed Books, 2012.

Vanner, Catherine. "Positionality at the Center: Constructing an Epistemological and Methodological Approach for a Western Feminist Doctoral Candidate Conducting Research in the

Postcolonial". *International Journal of Qualitative Methods*, 2015, pp. 1–12.

Vergès, Françoise. *Taking Sides: A Decolonial Feminism*. Translated by Ashley J. Bohrer with Françoise Vergès, Pluto Press, 2021.

Viswanathan, Gauri. *Masks of Conquest: Literary Studies and British Rule in India*. Columbia UP, 1989.

Wa Thiong'o Ngũgĩ. *Decolonising the Mind: The Politics of Language in African Literature*. 1986. Zimbabwe House Publishing, 1994.

----. *Matigari ma Njiruungi*. Heinemann, 1986.

___. *Moving the Centre. The Struggle for Cultural Freedoms*. James Currey, 1993.

Walsh, Catherine E., and Walter D. Mignolo. *On Decoloniality: Concepts, Analytics, Praxis*. Duke UP, 2018.

Warwick Research Collective. *Uneven and Combined Development: Towards a New Theory of World-Literature*. Liverpool UP, 2015.

Young, Robert J.C. *Empire, Colony, Postcolony*. Wiley-Blackwell, 2016.

---. *Postcolonialism: An Historical Introduction*. Wiley-Blackwell, 2003.

Chapter Two

Minorities

NATION, CASTE, RACE AND SEXUALITY IN BAMA, KAY AND BRAND

The nation and its fragments (margins and minorities) are at the heart of postcolonial studies. Nation states, marked by territorial, linguistic, cultural and social borders, demand a life-long allegiance to their ethos from their citizen subjects, celebrated by participating in 'national' festivals such as Independence Day or global sporting and cultural events. By doing so, postcolonial nations have often warranted the creation of an imagined 'homogeneous' community of citizen subjects (Anderson). In a socially, religiously and culturally diverse postcolonial nation, such as India or Nigeria, this may also lead to a willing or coerced submission from citizens to a majoritarian politics which may result in social unrest. For instance, the Citizenship Amendment Act in India (CAA, 2019) – which is marked by an assertive, religion-based juridical imagination as to who could and could not belong to the nation – was widely questioned by people and critics for its majoritarian Hindu agenda in a constitutionally secular country (Anupama Roy 4). Postcolonial scholars of nations and nationalisms have urged us to confront critical questions of how to imagine a nation which is essentially composed of what Partha Chatterjee calls 'fragments', or heterogeneous groups, cultures and interests. They have called on us to read the nation and its works – when produced by majoritarian and ruling groups in which subalterns are essentially voiceless – against their grain to retrieve marginalised and suppressed voices, and encouraged us to seek out works written from the margins. Calling this phenomenon of resistance as 'writing back', Bill Ashcroft, Gareth Griffiths and Helen Tiffin noted in their influential book, *The Empire Writes Back* (1989), 'the alienating process which initially served to relegate the post-colonial world to the "margin" turned upon itself and acted to push that world through a kind of mental barrier into a position from which all experience could be viewed as uncentred, pluralistic, and multifarious. Marginality thus became an unprecedented source of creative energy' (12).

In this chapter, I will discuss the complex and urgent presence of a heterogeneous, anticolonial and creative margin in the nation through the analytical rubric of 'Minorities'. I will engage with this rubric via the critical lenses of caste, race and sexuality – social categories or analytical topics in my reading which were either engineered or accelerated by colonialism and imperialism, and which have witnessed fierce politics of resistance, particularly in post-colonial times, leading to various rights-based and decolonising movements in metropolitan and ex-colonial nations. I will also point out that these topics need to be understood through their multidimensional intersections and ontological discontinuities which literary works are able to finely distinguish between and explore.

Minorities, Nations and Intersectional Struggles: Displacing the Centre

Although 'margin' is understood as a creative and radical term, philosophical complexities between margin and centre arise when we note that the margin is often defined by its binary, the centre. But if postcolonial studies attempts to displace the centre, does the process lead to establishing multiple margins or centres, or does it exhort to abolishing these concepts altogether? European colonialism, as postcolonial critics have pointed out, did not work through economic relationships alone but also through the systematic appropriation of social, cultural, political and ontological possibilities in the colonies and by establishing the hierarchical racist superiority of white Europe (Fanon; Said 6–7; Viswanathan 40–41). As Ngũgĩ wa Thiong'o famously argued, decolonising the mind must begin with decolonising our learning traditions, and in this context, by abolishing English departments in the post-colony (16–18). While abolishing English departments was not going to be an easy task because of the global primacy of English, English literature as a discipline or subject area has expanded upon its teaching canon since the 1990s by including literatures written in English by writers variously affected by colonialism and imperialism, thanks to continuous questioning of its racist and imperialist biases. An English literature undergraduate or postgraduate degree in most parts of the world today includes national, regional or global postcolonial texts (Anglophone or translated). These texts attempt not only to displace the canonicity of English literature but also help imagine how non-English peoples' (English) literatures may envision language, place, environment and human interaction with the nonhuman (in short, the world) differently. In this context, 'decentring' – a key term since the poststructuralist influence on postcolonial critical scholarship (as argued in the previous chapter) – includes not only displacing the centre imaginatively and philosophically, but also being suspicious of the concept of the centre itself as something different, superior, pure or homogeneous. This goes back to the discussion of centre and margin from Ashcroft, et al. in their work on postcolonial *Key Concepts*: '(T)he dismantling of centre/margin (periphery) models of culture calls into question the claims of any culture to possess a fixed, pure and homogenous body of values, and exposes them all as historically constructed, and thus corrigible formations' (33).

While these discussions may give us an appropriate context to understand the plurality of margins in postcolonial studies, it would be naïve to think that centres and margins do not continue to exist in the post-colonial world. That a London or Paris continues to hold cultural supremacy over the globe's mind-map or that a decolonising movement in an Oxford or a Sorbonne attracts more (social) media and public attention, is testament to the power and allure of colonial centres and their global educational and cultural heritage. Conversely, because of this heritage which has forced or encouraged people from colonised territories or ex-colonised nations to come to these cities and universities as tourists, students and workers, and experience historical and structural prejudice (as we noticed through Aboulela's story in the previous chapter), postcolonial residents and citizens in these centres have been vocal about discrimination against them, their rights and struggles. This does not mean that postcolonial struggles begin at metropolitan centres – they cannot, as suggested before – but, for reasons of historical discrimination and global power dynamics, postcolonial struggles are recognised and become more widely visible when they arrive at these centres. These struggles, then, both learn from and lend their intellectual and practical tools to relevant struggles elsewhere.

Here, Gayatri Chakravorty Spivak's understanding of margin and centre may shed light on the topic. Spivak writes that the culture of explanation presupposes there is a self and a world that is knowable and explainable, that can be controlled and managed with knowledge. If it is through explanation that we constitute our sovereign subjectivity or our politics, then an alternative politics must arise allowing for the possibility of the 'radically heterogeneous', which for Spivak, must arrive through a deconstruction or displacing of the centre (Spivak 104). As an example of the centre at work, Spivak writes about how women are forced to adopt a 'masculinist centralism' to be recognised at work. The point of displacing this framework of recognition, not a reversal of it, is to acknowledge that the centre itself is a margin constituted by a handful of people controlling an institution and shaping the outside of it, the majority, as *its* margin. Reminding us of Anzaldúa's observations on 'cross-over' in the previous chapter, a properly deconstructive praxis from the margins, Spivak posits, begins not when one remains outside of the centre and accuses it of control, but rather when one 'can shuttle between the centre (inside) and the margin (outside) and narrate a displacement' (107).

This structural element of narrating a displacement is particularly relevant for the (anticolonial) rise of minority studies in the Anglo-American academy, which has been the 'centre' of academic postcolonial studies. In their two-volume special issue on 'Minority Discourses', Abdul JanMohamed and David Lloyd observe that minority studies began to appear through the 'special programs' of ethnic studies, women's and gender studies, and gay and lesbian studies offered in major American universities in the aftermath of the radical social movements of the 1960s and 70s. Though meagrely funded, these programmes pointed out that culture (following Stuart Hall) was an arena of struggle which the minority or oppressed, having lost their socio-economic power in the coloniser/majority world, could envision working on at centres of power to compel these centres to confront their multiple margins. The study of minorities, thus, is dedicated to understanding 'the particularities of the cultural struggles waged by minorities in the effort to "represent themselves" . . . and on the epistemological, political, and cultural consequences which the struggle with the hegemonic culture entails' (JanMohamed and Lloyd, "Introduction" 6).

If retrieving the archive from a hegemonic system and critiquing the apparatus for its uncritical universal humanism is a properly decolonising/postcolonial task (as discussed in the previous chapter) and remains key to such studies, the other important element is to explore 'a critical-discursive articulation of alternative practices and values which are embedded in the often damaged, fragmentary, hampered, occluded works of the minorities' (10). JanMohamed and Lloyd state that the realm of the minor or of the margins is one of continuous violence and damage, both physical and spiritual. Thus, transforming a historically negative position of coercion and violence (from the perspective of Western humanism) to a positive one requires support and coalition between damaged communities, despite their irreducible heterogeneities. They assert, 'Out of the damage inflicted upon minority cultures . . . emerges the possibility of collective subjectivity formed in practice rather than contemplation . . . (T)he function of cultural forms is not therefore, as in the west, ethical leading to the formation of a universal subject but on the contrary political, collectively produced and provisional' (JanMohamed and Lloyd 10–11). These arguments echo the philosophical dwelling on minor and minority literatures in Gilles Deleuze and Félix Guattari, who consider 'minor' a political term manifested through a collective belonging to subordinated and repressed groups and their constant displacement of subjectivities. Deleuze and Guattari point towards a constant 'becoming' of minor literatures which is de-territorialising but at the same time rhizomatic – by which they suggest embodying a network of multiple identities and concerns (601–05).

These critical contexts offer a solid gateway to engage with the minorities of caste, race and sexuality which, as we will see, are damaged, displacing, collective, provisional, and at their heart, anticolonial identities. These categories were invented or used to mark the hierarchical structure and homogeneous character of the ruling 'majority' (variously, Hindu; white; male; or, heterosexual) which are not always numerical majorities. When used in minority contexts however, these categories betray their epistemologically decolonising agenda of displacing the concept of the 'majority' through political and narrative emphasis: their communities were often collectively damaged by the intersection of these categories and thus could only be reclaimed by demonstrating the multidimensional and intersectional function of their resisting identity. It will be useful, thus, to read them through Kimberlé Crenshaw's concept of 'intersectionality', by which she meant the intersectional identity of gender and colour for black women in North America which leads to their being doubly oppressed by racism and sexism (1244). As Sara Salem has shown, this concept had arisen through postcolonial and black feminist interventions in the 1970s Anglo-American academy which posed 'a double critique: on the one hand, a critique of a feminism that saw gender as the main source of oppression for women universally; and on the other hand, a critique of a Marxism that saw imperialism and colonialism – and by extension race and nation – as peripheral to the capitalist system and its expansion and development' (411). I will argue in this chapter that minority writers and literatures from postcolonial nations and periods have narrated nation and nationalism through the autonomous yet intersecting and critical categories of caste, class, race, gender and sexuality. That is, a text written by a Dalit woman on her life experience often includes how the overlapping, collective forces of caste, class, religion and gender have worked together (to take from JanMohamed and Lloyd) to inflict historical damage on Dalit communities and cultures. These writers have variously shown how 'national' or 'transnational' categories of race or sexuality have controlled and configured postcolonial lives, and how their art forms have critiqued, protested, and subverted these categories through offering anticolonial imaginings of the nation by displacing the centre. To read these imaginings to explore their intersectional struggles is also to frame a multidimensional and decolonising reading of their totality, as argued in the first chapter.

I will offer here close stylistic readings of Bama's autobiographical work, *Karukku*; Jackie Kay's poems in *The Adoption Papers*; and Dionne Brand's poetry collection, *No Language is Neutral* – for postcolonial literature warrants a 'decolonising impulse' which it is our task as readers and critics to retrieve and explore, as I have argued in the first chapter. I will show that all of these literary works implement autobiographical lenses such as confession, testimonio or life writing, but powerfully displace and dismantle the bourgeois, colonialist, standardised and Eurocentric usage of these lenses to retrieve their decolonising agenda. Also, while these works were written in the early 1990s when postcolonial studies as an academic field was emerging, their selection should be able to suggest the two chief aims of the chapter: that the 'now' of caste, class, race, gender and sexuality struggles in the postcolonial world – marked by Dalit, Black, and Indigenous 'Lives Matter' movements – often rose through socio-political contexts in the latter half of the twentieth century. These struggles are compellingly captured by these not very visible postcolonial voices who command wide critical scrutiny. Second, while these writers do not always imagine and invent new literary forms and genres to represent historical or everyday forms of colonialist oppression and minority discourses of resistance, they certainly expand, twist and modify existing genres and styles, thus enforcing an anticolonial reclamation and reinvention of their coeval postcolonial cultures and traditions.

BAMA'S *KARUKKU* AND DALIT FEMINIST LITERATURE

Karukku is a confessional narrative that interweaves the categories of caste, class, gender, religion and colonialism to bring attention to the socio-economic, physical and philosophical damage inflicted on Dalit women. 'Dalit', as Raj Kumar writes in *Dalit Literature and Criticism*, is a 'political' term. It refers to

> (T)he existential condition of a group of people who were earlier known as "untouchables". These marginalised peoples are a product of the Hindu caste system. Following caste rules, the untouchables were subject to all forms of oppression – be it social, political, economic, cultural or religious. The term "Dalit", therefore, is an act of rebellion used by the former "untouchables" to acquire a new identity, which stands for pride and self-respect. (13)

The key word for us here is untouchable. In the Hindu caste system, the lowest of the castes, which constituted more than one third of the population and was involved in manual and menial forms of labour, were considered polluted or untouchable. The consolidation of brahminical rule through Hindu classical scriptures and literatures proved fatal for the dignity, respect and uplift of Dalits (a sociopolitical term like 'black' below). British colonialism, by modernising the territory through bureaucracy, technology and social reformation, and by implementing philanthropic initiatives (or rather, conversion propaganda) through missionary programmes, enabled Hindu upper and middle classes, religious groups and upper castes to hold onto socio-economic and religious power over other classes, castes and groups (Omvedt viii; 3–7). Contact with Western educational and philosophical systems also meant that from the mid-nineteenth century onward, social reformers such as Jyotirao Phule in Maharashtra (standing on the back of religious literature written by Sufi and Bhakti communities) could speak about the social ills of the Hindu caste system and the need for its eradication (O'Hanlon 105–121). These movements led to the Self-Respect Movement by Tamil social activist and philosopher, 'Periyar' E. V. Ramasamy in the early-twentieth century which argued for Dalit self-respect, and that political liberation without individual self-respect was meaningless. Periyar, like Savitribai Phule (Jyotirao's wife), also spoke about gender discrimination and the social and political mobilisation of women (Geetha 180–203).

In the late-colonial period, Dr B. R. Ambedkar offered passionate speeches and wrote widely on the abolition of untouchability and the politico-economic uplift of oppressed groups (most notably in *Annihilation of Caste*). While Ambedkar encouraged anti-caste movements in India, the term 'Dalit' in literature and culture began to be widely used in Dalit literary and political movements (such as the Dalit Panthers) in Maharashtra in the post-independence period (Paswan and Jaideva 321–26). This helped consolidate the term Dalit literature for future use as 'writing by Dalits with a Dalit consciousness' but not necessarily limited to Dalit castes (Sharankumar Limbale qtd. in Joshil and Mishrahi-Barak 17–20). It is in this complex context of multidimensional and intersecting forces of caste; class; gender; Christianity; colonialism; self-consciousness practices among untouchable groups; and coalition-based, revolutionary anti-caste movements in Dalit communities that Bama's autobiographical narrative becomes particularly relevant for a decolonising reading of nation and minorities.

Bama's debut work *Karukku* (1992; translated into English by Lakshmi Holmström in 2000), meaning double-edged sword or a serrated palmyra leaf in Tamil, begins with the childhood of the unnamed protagonist (probably Bama herself) and her early realisation of social segregation in her village. Her community, the Parayas, live on the outskirts of the village as polluted untouchables, while the Naickars (the upper castes), and the Nadars and Thevars (the agricultural communities) live mostly around the centre of commerce and public activity. This autobiography however, clarifies from the beginning that it will not follow the traditional linear narrative of a *bildungsroman*. It mixes the individual experience of the protagonist with different phases in Dalit life, such as festivities, daily work and the community's suffering at the hands of repressive forces of the upper castes, the Church, and police. The protagonist does well in school and joins a nunnery believing it to be the best way to tackle social and caste harassment as well as to uphold her community's Christian belief in social equality. However, she soon realises that the order is controlled by upper-caste, upper-class women and that there is a deep-rooted casteism in the academic decisions and sociocultural practices of the nunnery. The protagonist has a moment of self-realisation before she leaves the order to become a schoolteacher and an atheist:

I felt in my heart that I could go and speak directly to God without their intervention. I could no longer believe that God could only be reached, as they taught us, through prayer learned by rote, through pious practices, through the novena and rosary. I came to realize that you could see God through the mind's eye, in nature, and in the ordinary events of every day. So all the rituals that I had followed and believed in so far suddenly began to seem meaningless and just a sham. (Bama 102)

As Christians, the protagonist's Dalit community is taught to believe all humans are equal. In the nunnery, however, this is not practised. Here is a strict hierarchy as to what could be taught and done and what is considered casteist 'sacrilege'. She notices that the churches, schools, convent, and priests' bungalows are located in areas where the upper castes live – pointing to the socio-geographical apartheid that the caste system is.[1] It is from the upper castes, who donate much of the Church's wealth and endowments, that many of the administrative positions in the nunnery are filled (88). If Dalits become priests and nuns, 'they are pushed aside and marginalized . . . before the rest go about their business' (80). They cannot preach or minister to the congregation but must continue to toil and do hard labour for the upper castes. This is a gradation of labour that Ambedkar analyses in *Annihilation of Caste*, and we mentioned in Chapter 1: 'the caste system is not merely a division of labour. It is also a division of labourers' (Ambedkar 182). Bama's protagonist, despite being educated and socially sophisticated, falls short of caste-driven gradations of voice and speech. The protagonist decides to leave the order and chooses not to marry. The autobiography ends with an observation that it is tremendously difficult for women like her to survive in a hierarchical, Hindu moralistic society that cannot tolerate the independence of a single, educated woman – especially one who is Dalit and yet holds all means of production and commerce in her hands. It also points out the Hindu caste values regarding unmarried women that Dalit males have absorbed and are unjustly implemented in their societies (recall Anzaldúa's prescient words on border cultures and gender violence in the previous chapter). I read Bama's narrative as a Dalit feminist reminder that Dalit subjectivity, as Gopal Guru argues, is as much about rising up against the Hindu caste system as against Dalit patriarchy (Arya and Rathore 151). In the rest of the section, I will discuss the question of the colonialist nature of brahminical and patriarchal caste oppression and how autobiography or, in this context, testimonio attempts to represent a countering perspective of critical Dalit collectivity.

The Dalit Christian identity is a colonial and intersectional identity. European colonialism, broadly speaking, began with Catholic Christian missionaries. Colonialism coopted Catholic and Protestant missions and religious institutions into a covert agenda for cultural and ideological conversion propounded through missionary literature (Viswanathan 213–14; Thorne 48). As Orientalists substantially translated Hindu scriptures and created a canon of 'classical' scriptures in which the lives of peasants and Dalits were marginalised, colonisation and Christianity continued to consolidate the caste system (Webster 11). Conversely, in many instances Protestant missionaries encouraged Dalits and the lower castes toward social reformation via colonial bureaucracy (Oddie; Taneti; Viswanath). While I do not suggest that Catholic missionaries contributed little to the uplift of Dalits, the conservative elements of the caste system resonated with similar elements found in Catholic values. Uma Chakravarti has further argued that Dalits have historically suffered what Ambedkar called 'Brahminical patriarchy'– by 'brahminical' he meant not only the brahmins, but 'virtually all castes and peoples who thought humans and their identities can be categorised based on the hierarchical structures set up by Brahminical discourses' – which was absorbed by Dalit males as well (Chakravarti 581–82). Thus, by standing against the caste system and the Catholic nunnery, Bama's protagonist takes a historical anticolonial stand which is also an anti-conservative, anti-patriarchal, Dalit feminist position. Current conversations regarding decolonising the education and curriculum in India have only recently begun to address anti-casteism (Manoharan). What Bama's protagonist suggests is that self-purification or self-respect cannot be established without revolting against the intersectionality of class, caste, religion, colonialism and gender – as raised by Dalit feminists Mary E. John and Meena Gopal. Dalits suffer every day from multiple forms of colonialist power structures, emancipation from which will require an anticolonial, intersectional solidarity (Arya and Rathore 195).

These theoretical discussions help set up how Dalit women are oppressed by intersecting collective forces which Bama eloquently presents in *Karukku*, not only through the question of oppression but also through the anticolonial solidarity between Dalit women against casteist–colonialist violence. For instance, In the third chapter on police torture, the women stand up to the injustice and devise strategies to save their men from police hounding and torture. In an episode when a beaten, fugitive father comes to the village in disguise, amidst heavy police presence, to bid farewell to his dead son, the women find means to lead him to his son and protect him from the police. Bama writes,

> They kept a vigil all night, and even before cock-crow the women set out the dead body and buried him themselves, in the cemetery. Before dawn broke properly, the boy's father set off in this sari with the two women accompanying him some distance; then, he disappeared into the same mandavam fields. . . . they said how clever the women had been and how smartly they had managed everything themselves. (43)

Women must find means to survive, but their survival and resilience have also made them resourceful in saving their men. What this passage further suggests is the bond between men and women over affective causes. Not being able to say goodbye to one's deceased son is harrowing. The women work together and find ways to help meet the father with his dead son, digging out and burying him again in the middle of the night as well as accompanying the father back to safety. This is an extraordinary achievement in a curfewed village. What this act also hints at is the question of solidarity through intersectionality, as John and Gopal raise above.

Bama's protagonist is disgusted by the wealth and wastage of resources in the nunnery, and the core hatred of the nuns for the poor and the oppressed. She rejects the institution and calls for, like Periyar, the 'earning of consciousness' for Dalits. Dalits cannot be marginalised when they begin to practise self-respect and organise to fight casteism. Bama writes,

> They realized that they have been maintained as the stone steps that others have trodden on as they raised themselves up. They have become aware that they have been made slaves in the name of God, the Pusai (Jesus), the Church . . . But Dalits . . . have become aware that they too were created in the likeness of God. There is a new strength within them, urging them to reclaim the likeness which has been so far repressed, ruined, obliterated; and to begin to live again with honour, self-respect, and with a love towards all humankind. To my mind, this alone is true devotion. (109)

Recalling Fanon's call for reclaiming dignity and humanity through decolonisation, these statements demonstrate both self-conviction and pride in one's community and living together in peace, which casteism and patriarchy, along with colonialism, will not allow. What brahminical patriarchy has done is create an illusion of freedom through religiosity, an instance of which is Gandhi's term 'Harijan' for Dalits that anti-caste activists such as Ambedkar heavily criticised (Bayly 255–63). In the convictions expressed above on rising against oppression and practising self-respect, we find the thoughts of Ambedkar, Phule and Periyar rekindled. In the question of rising up itself, there is also a suggestion of the rise of the Dalit Panthers and Dalitbahujan movements in India, which this work is probably a consequence of. But there is also a clear Dalit feminist stand – that Dalits cannot reproduce brahminical patriarchy. Self-respect is a call for equality among the sexes and the end of caste-based discrimination. It is a call for forming a coalition between oppressed communities and groups and recognising the differences and heterogeneities among them. Like Periyar who wrote widely about women empowerment, Bama's work calls for an anticolonial Dalit feminist standpoint of radical heterogeneity and collectivity which means 'rethinking notions of patriarchy, feminism, and "difference" in a caste-sensitive manner . . . further(ing) the feminist ideals of freedom, equality, and solidarity, where they can acquire a more collective tone' (Arya and Rathore 2).

This discursive stand against brahminical and Dalit patriarchy is decolonising in that it breaks open the colonialist preponderance of the forces that underlie patriarchy, and suggests the fight has to be slow, collective and on multiple fronts. Such a stand, thus, needs a narrative form that can articulate the robustness and nuance of the challenges that need to be faced. Critics have commented on the use of the autobiographical mode for Dalit cultural expression and compared it with the testimonio genre of American and Australian Indigenous people, such as the works by Rigoberto Manchu. Pramod Nayar tells us that testimonio is,

> (A) narrative that exists at the margins of literature, representing those subjects excluded from authorized representation. In most cases *testimonio* narratives are documents of atrocities and suffering, bringing one into contact with the victimized. The *testimonio* is the voice of one who witnesses for the sake of another, who remains voiceless: That is, the speaking subaltern subject of the narrative gives voice to the lived experiences of herself and of those who are victims of social and linguistic-literary marginalization. (84; emphasis in the original)

Not only does testimonio as a genre fully respond to the questions of margins and marginality, it also talks about the notion of a communal and collective life that is abused and silenced but not erased. Sharmila Rege argues that Dalit testimonios offer the solid purpose of destabilising the Western bourgeois 'I' in the autobiography with a communal 'we' (13–15); what Laura Brueck reads as the 'witnessing' of Dalit plight and suffering (34). While Bama's narrative is about the protagonist, it never loses sight of the village, the people and the collective – witnessing the life of collective living and marginalisation around herself – which she reclaims in an anticolonial spirit and which, for JanMohamed and Lloyd, critical minority discourses are born with. The work offers acute insights into the protagonist's community in the very first chapters. In a short space, the text succeeds in developing the protagonist's character from her childhood, her inquisitiveness, precocity and empathetic character, as well as offering descriptions of everyday Dalit rural life, reminding one of Chinua Achebe's monumental *Things Fall Apart*. This balance destabilises the bourgeois individual subjectivity, as

Rege suggests, and proposes a dual, collective self formed by society and caste-based spatial segregation. Bama's 'autobiography' also questions linearity. Discussions on the protagonist's current feelings in the nunnery are set against her experience in school without much clarification.[2] The observations waver around various aspects of Dalit life such as caste, society, food, poverty and renunciation, among others, offering a horizontal perspective of her collective subjectivity rather than a vertical lens of an individualistic (Western) subject. As she leaves school and its damaging caste practices and waits, jobless, at a bus-stand about to meet a friend, she realises, 'It is now, for the very first time that I must learn to be truly alone. It may be difficult at first, but in due time I would get used to it' (Bama 116). While these lines may suggest the enduring strength of the protagonist – her resilience in deciding to live alone despite the challenging path ahead – we also anticipate that this is not going to be a romantic journey of adventure and thrill but one of exhaustion and angst because of routine discrimination at every stage of her life. Nonetheless, it also reminds us, via Spivak, that a historical minority such as Dalit women cannot simply refuse to engage with or leave the centre of casteist, classist and patriarchal power dynamics controlled by the ruling majority. Despite uncertainty and insecurity, as in the case of the protagonist here, one must continue to engage with the centre and form radical alliances to displace it altogether, which, according to Holmström, Bama does through belonging to and writing about her Dalit female community in *Sangati* (Holmström xviii). Recent testimonios of Dalits, notably Yashica Dutt's *Coming Out as Dalit* and Suraj Yengde's *Caste Matters*, continue to use destabilising and decolonising narrative means to emphasise and interrogate the multidimensional, intersecting forces of oppression that casteism is.

JACKIE KAY'S *THE ADOPTION PAPERS* AND BLACK BRITISH POETRY

Like for caste struggles in 1970s India, the contexts of centre–margin and intersectionality received new currency in the race and gender debates encouraged by civil rights and other post-war movements in the USA and Britain (Lorde; hooks). In Britain, the arrival of Caribbean and Asian people from the colonies in the wake of the Second World War and rapid decolonisation resulted in a media-induced social and economic crisis. Gurminder Bhambra notes that this was not a question of mobility: whiter subjects from the Commonwealth had been migrating to and settling in Britain for a long time, as well as those from Eastern European countries during the labour shortages in the 1960s. But it is only when darker subjects had arrived, media and public concerns were raised over who belonged in this country: 'The construction of darker citizens as aliens over the 1960s was based on a visceral understanding of difference predicated on race rather than in relation to any legal basis' (Bhambra 402–03). The question of race was not given due attention by white working-class movements in their struggle against oppressive classes. A. Sivanandan, pointing to the colonialist deracination of black communities, advocated for a Periyar-like consciousness-based approach where '[t]he blacks must through the consciousness of their colour, through the consciousness, that is, of that in which they perceive their oppression, arrive at a consciousness of class; and the white working class must in recovering its class instinct, its sense of oppression, both from technological alienation and a white-oriented culture, arrive at a consciousness of racial oppression' (82). Hazel Carby and Catherine Hall, among others, called out the Eurocentrism in feminist work in Britain (Carby 90) and anticipated the memory-based legacy work of the British Empire and slavery that Hall and others started at University College London (C. Hall, et al.). The everyday material struggles of black, Asian and ethnic minority communities, the new 'imperial nostalgia' and 'postcolonial melancholia' in the Thatcher-era Britain resulted in 'race riots' (Gilroy). Consequently, heated cultural and academic discussions on race led to the intellectual establishment of what Stuart Hall called 'black' as a political category, pointing out black artists' and activists' struggle for access to representation and the contestation of their marginality. Hall further observed that Thatcherism and the neoliberal discourses of the 1980s, however, developed a new 'politics of representation meaning that representation had a constitutive rather than expressive role in the formation of social and political life' (S. Hall 442–43). These conversations interrogating nation and citizenship, class and race, writing, access and representation emerged from, what Alison Donnell calls, 'two periods of critical history that have emphasised transnational, international, and cosmopolitan affiliations both in terms of cultural aesthetics and politics' – decolonisation, and postcolonial and Black Atlantic studies – and would be crucial to the emergence of Black British writing (14–15).

The tense climate of contemporary citizenship debates, social and political struggles and cultural representation was not very different in Scotland either. While the notion of Scottish exceptionalism, that there was racial harmony north of the border, had prevailed in public and academic discourses (narratives encouraged by newspapers in the seventies), these works, however, conveniently excluded ethnic minorities in imagining national consciousnesses and publics. Neil Davidson and Satnam Virdee have tracked these exclusionary practices and the 'entrenched narrative of an absent racism' in Scotland in *No Problem Here* (9). As scholars have already noted, it was in the 1970s and 80s that various black and Asian organisations began to be established, many of them by and for women, addressing structures of marginalisation and discrimination as well as calling for collective unity, action and enterprise in Scotland (Henderson and Mackay 118–22). Further, Scotland benefitted from the British Empire and developed values and cultures that were manifestly Eurocentric, as we noted in the discussion of Leila Aboulela's story in the previous chapter. But Scotland also had a complicated history with England/Great Britain. The Act of Union was seen as an act of conspiracy and betrayal by the elite Scottish and English ruling classes for a substantial portion of the Scottish population. It is no surprise that some of the most exciting conversations on nation and nationality in the last decades came from Scotland in the context of 'devolution' (Tom Nairn; Neil Davidson, *The Origins of Scottish Nationhood*). But these conversations did not always acknowledge the existence of a sizeable and diverse ethnic minority population in the country, which was a direct result of slavery, empire and decolonisation – paradoxically, key drivers behind the discussions of nation and nationalism. As Joseph Jackson comments in

Writing Black Scotland, decolonisation allowed the use of a suite of postcolonial tools which were useful in talking about national and nationality in Scotland, but also made effective the discussion of race and racialisation here, leading people to interrogate a unitary understanding of nation or blackness in Britain. These views also offered for Jackson a crucial understanding of 'the discursive production of blackness within a Scottish national-cultural frame, rather than a canon of "black writing" determined by author' (17).

This is where Jackie Kay's poetry becomes particularly significant for our discussion of nation and minority. Kay, a Scottish poet of Nigerian descent, brings her marginalising, autobiographical experience of growing up in a 'white' Scotland to the fore, hence becoming part of a comparable framework for Bama's female Dalit experience. She also interrogates questions of empire, minority, nation, Britishness and exceptionalism – or the discursive production of blackness – in Scotland through the tropes of transracial adoption and 'lineage', urging one to consider her anticolonial retrieval of an intersecting, heterogeneous 'Scottishness'. Further, as a lesbian, many of Kay's poems and literary work draw from a radical notion of love – a point that I will make more expressly in the next section on Dionne Brand's queer poetry. My reading of poetry in the two sections below will follow Jahan Ramazani's provocative remarks that 'Postcolonial poetry is responsive to, and emerges out of, social and political realities such as global inequities, racial oppression, and imperial violence, and yet it is also responsive to internal histories of form and language, lifting off from current realities even as it answers them, playing in the gap between its linguistic surfaces and the world it engages' (6). A historical materialist study of postcolonial poetry will acknowledge both historical specificities and formal peculiarities as it will look for global resonance through these peculiarities.

Kay's *The Adoption Papers* (1991), first broadcast on BBC 3, is composed of two sections: 'The Adoption Papers' and 'Severe Gale 8'. My discussions will focus on the first section. 'The Adoption Papers' is divided into three parts charting the protagonist's life story from 1961–62, 1967–71, to 1980–90 – a black child's adoption by white, Marxist working-class parents and her growing up in the north of Glasgow in a white majority area (understandably Kay's own life-stories as reflected in her memoir, *Red Dust Road*). Sara Dorow has asked how we might imagine transracial adoption – inevitably linked to the world of colonialism, imperialism and conflict – to be 'the joyful intimacy of making family next to the unjust history that it might recall' (3). Kay seems to respond to the complexity by adopting a triadic voice narrative of the baby's black birth mother, her white adopted mother and the baby-teen herself, fracturing, like Bama does above, the colonialist concept of a unitary self and subjectivity. The first poems in 1961–62 are about the birth mother's pain of delivering a child as her Nigerian partner withdraws from the relationship. Yet she still loves him; his 'high laugh'; his 'eyes intense as the whirlwind' (*The Adoption Papers* 12). In the poem, 'The Waiting List,' Kay introduces the protagonist's adopted mother and her frustrations at not finding an appropriate adoption agency. But as soon as she declares that the child's colour is not a problem, she gets numerous options easily:

> Just as we were going out the door
>
> I said oh you know we don't mind the colour
>
> Just like that the waiting was over (14)

This emotional realisation is able to point at two things, among others: that Scottish parents hardly wanted a black child, at least in the sixties, and that there were many children of colour available to adopt from.

The bureaucratic aspects of adoption appear more insidiously in questions of surrogacy and mothering in the next poem, 'Baby Lazarus'. While the agency clears the adopted family, the child suffers ill health at birth. This is a powerful poem that swings from the birth mother's intense emotions for her baby, about having to give the baby away, and the adopted mother's pain and rage at being made to wait longer for the baby. These lines capture these two sides well:

> Land moves like driven cattle
>
> My eyes snatch pieces of news

Headline strung out on a line
MOTHER DROWNS BABY IN THE CLYDE

....

The adoption papers
Can't be signed. I put the phone down
I felt all hot. Don't get overwrought.
What does she expect? I'm not a mother
Until I've signed the piece of paper. (16)

The first perspective is of the birth mother who is traveling in a train from Aberdeen to Edinburgh for her delivery. Throughout, her perspective and language are poetic and emotional, allowing her motherly anxiety to take up a correlating language. On the other hand, the language of the adoptive mother is one of reason and rage. Note also the prosaic composition of the adoptive mother's narrative. Hers is a bureaucratic anxiety about having to clear papers and being frustrated at being denied on different grounds. The final lines in both the stanzas have similar emotions of anxiety and pain and yet very different expressions. While the birth mother feels she is betraying her body and child by remembering newspapers stories about mothers drowning children in the Clyde river, the adoptive mother is outraged at being told that she will not be a mother until the adoption papers are signed, represented through the linguistic use of 'all hot' and 'overwrought'.

By intermeshing the bureaucratic world with the affective, and by foregrounding oral forms and storytelling methods in the triad of voices, Kay seems to hint at what Valerie Popp calls an 'improper communication'. For Popp, Kay uses the oral forms because, as we noted through Bhambra above, Britain's passport history is full of racialised implementation. At the same time, Scotland's fraught relations with Britain forces Kay to record 'the rift between legal nationality and informal national identity in postcolonial Britain' (293). Thus, Kay's biblical imagery of Lazarus rising from the dead alludes to the regeneration of a child with ill health and from a different mother coming back to life again in a new abode, the prospect of child rearing signifying growth and animation. This is something which she hardly allows for her birth mother who is given a non-direct, lyrical and intensely emotional voice throughout. The intensely affective and paradoxical use of language and imagery for the birth mother further suggests what John McLeod calls the biocentricism of family and kinship networks in transcultural adoption, in which 'normative consanguineous families' are favoured, resulting in 'vexed and anxious lives for those inward of the adoption triad'. McLeod perceptively adds, 'The pathologization of birth-mothers as "unnatural" rather than as oppressed by unkind social circumstances has sentenced many to deeply traumatizing experience of pernicious stigmatization' (15–16).

The traumatic experience of stigmatisation is most compellingly captured in the poems' thematic and stylistic uses of 'paperwork', as suggested above, and of blood and transnational solidarity. A black child (like Kay) in a white family and neighbourhood is an anomaly. Thus, the teenager protagonist continuously searches for her birth mother. Indeed, the second poem in the first year-group is about her search for her original birth certificate. What she finally manages to discover upsets her, 'I was a midnight baby after all' (12). The paperwork is not always about material documentation but can also be racialised body marks, forceps-induced scars, 'stitches', 'swollen' belly and 'leaking' (13) as well as a realisation of her different skin complexion which points at her slavery and diasporic heritage – what Pamela Fox calls 'staking out Scotland as a "multiracial" territory of Black British hybridity' (Fox 282).

Probably the most powerful poem in the collection, 'Black Bottom' begins with the teenager protagonist's adopted mother who angrily reacts to racist discrimination in society but can only implore her daughter to be strong. The perspective then shifts to the teenager who regularly fights her peers in school for their racist taunts and remarks. As she punches a boy in the gut and is jeered at as 'Dirty Darkie', the schoolteacher punishes her for being truant and aggressive and calls her a 'juvenile delinquent' in the classroom:

>Do you know what that is? Look it up in the dictionary
>She spells each word with slow pleasure
>Read it out to the class

Thug. Vandal. Hooligan. Speak up. Have you lost your tongue? (*The Adoption Papers* 24)

This paints a vivid picture of racism in contemporary Scottish schools. Associating a black child with delinquency brings back the rhetoric of aggression and stigma around black teenagers, especially in contemporary Britain and the USA. Another instance of pedagogical racism in 'Black Bottom' is when in a dance competition the protagonist does 'a Cha Cha' and fails to do the feet movements, the teacher shouts at her

> Come on, show
>
> us what you can do I thought
>
> you people had it in your blood (25)

The metaphor of blood occurs in the poem repeatedly as she keeps thinking 'What is in my blood' although her mother sincerely asks to 'ignore' it. In the previous poem, 'The Telling', the child protagonist keeps asking her mother 'Mammy why aren't you and me the same colour,' to which her painstaking reply is that she is not her real 'mammy'. Countering Katy Massey's insistence that the repetition of blood tropes in the poems is mainly familial, Fox finds a racial angle in recent transracial adoption debates which have 'revived interest in racial matching to protect not only individual black children's psychic health but also the literal survival of black communities in the wake of race-unconscious philosophies still often espoused by the mainstream adoption industry and white prospective adoptive parents' (Fox 284).

In 'Black Bottom', the child having found no black people she can identify with in her school and neighbourhood (apart from a nurse) finds an identifying figure in Angela Davis while watching news about her on TV; an act of transnational solidarity. Davis, as we know, is a very influential black activist for the civil rights and sexual and reproductive rights movements who was charged with murder. This is what Fox, in her psychoanalytic reading of the text, calls 'an erotic moment of blurred self/group recognition' for the child (285). The child prays for Davis as the news of her being wanted is broadcasted on TV. She even kisses goodbye to Davis's photo and wears a badge advocating for Davis's freedom to school, whom no one recognises. As I have been arguing, the formation of her (anticolonial) racialised identity is made as much from racist stereotypes in the ideological state apparatus that forms the school and dance society, as with finding an 'affective community' in powerful black artists and political leaders such as Davis. Throughout the collection, love and blood relationships are questioned and consolidated. The intertextual references and the posters are important here as she continues to search for the meaning of her blood. As she calls family, makes appointments with adoption agencies, explores her blood history and is confused that 'I know my blood. It's dark ruby red and comes / regular and I use Lillets' (*The Adoption Papers* 29), she realises that there is no point in establishing a bloodline when she will always look different. There is also no point searching for her birth mother who she has never seen and who remains elusive throughout, turning her longing into a fictive autobiography. Thus, in the final poem 'The Meeting Dream', the poet speaks her anguish at her trace narrative:

> She is too many imaginings to be flesh and blood
>
> there is nothing left to say
>
> Neither of us mentions meeting again (33)

Despite all the demands made on her blood, she comes to the surety that her birth mother will not matter to her growing self. She will have to continue to fight for her own existence and skin colour. This offers an ironic rejoinder to the adoption papers which will not be relevant to her anymore. Her paper is not her skin and body.

This is also a reminder of the cultural meaning of the poem, 'Black Bottom' – a popular black song and performance piece in 1920s Harlem which was a key seat for black arts movements and civil rights activities – offering for her what Cynthia Young has termed 'a certain geographic and ideological fluidity that cohered into a revolutionary internationalism' (206; 186). Like the teenager embracing the identity and force of Davis at the end of 'Black Bottom', 'The Adoption Papers' concludes that skin colour will not take over the universality and sameness of blood amongst humankind, and that she will fight for her rights and existence: a 'civic nationalism' that questions the mythology of Scottish exceptionalism and national homogeneity (McFarlane 2). Although she will have the solidarity of her white parents and peers, in a white majority Scotland – like for Bama in a majoritarian Hindu India – often the fight will be lonely and exhausting, fraught with love for her people and birthplace and her bordered identities.

Kay has spoken about these issues in many of her interviews including in her introduction to *Bessie Smith* – about the irreconcilable opposites in transracial adopted families and about her marginal, bordered and political identities (*Bessie Smith* 9–10) that shuttle between the centre and the margin, to reference Spivak's suggestion of displaced centres. The use of multiple perspectives in the poem, the generous mix of Glaswegian and English and use of affective imagery and free verse suggests the impossibility of the colonialist concept of a unitary self or the fixed notion of an individual speaking 'I', especially for an adopted child. Nancy K. Gish calls this 'multiple presence' in Kay. For Gish, Kay uses 'the multiple "different" forms of identity she attributes to adoption to challenge dominant culture through the fusion of Black and Scottish and Blue' (Gish 184). Gish's reading of fluidity and multiplicity in the speaking 'I' also resonates with Bama's testimonial 'we' – that minority poets and prose writers continuously twist existing genres to carve out anticolonial differences in aesthetics and politics to stand up to heteronormative, casteist and racist societies. In order to combat the intersectional oppressive forces of race, nation, belonging, blood and language, Kay's poetry and her affective community will have to build up an anticolonial and multidimensional meaning of *bildungsroman* that is able to further fracture the illusion of a unitary self, which these oppressive forces essentially hide under.

ANTICOLONIAL, CREOLE, QUEER: DIONNE BRAND'S *NO LANGUAGE IS NEUTRAL*

In an interview with Charles Henry Rowell, Jackie Kay stated that the complexity of her emotion for her birthplace and people might have derived from her fluid and bordered identity of being black, Scottish and lesbian, which encourages a politically radical notion of love in her poems (Rowell 268; 273). Nowhere is this radical notion more forcefully presented than in postcolonial queer poetry. While academic and public discussions of 'queer' sexuality consolidated in the turbulent sociopolitical climate of civil war and the Lesbian, Gay, Bisexual and Transgender (LGBT) rights movements in the 1960s and 70s (both in North America and globally; Belmonte), postcolonial studies of queer – not just literary works based on the topic – arrived much later. In *Postcolonial, Queer* – the first major collection of queer theories from postcolonial perspectives – John C. Hawley, following Annamarie Jagose, observed that the term defied an easy fix or a fixity of identity. For Hawley, 'queer' was often associated with lesbian and gay identities which stressed an essentialist notion of a sexual rather than a social constructionist nature being embodied in queer theory, while 'this queering of gay and lesbian studies is both a protest against the foreclosure of possible inclusion and a demand that liberal (white, yuppified, western) gay and lesbian establishment recognize the "subalterns" in its midst' (Hawley 6). This is where Hawley draws upon the postcolonial angle of queering sexuality. Postcolonial queer theory not only aims to understand the liberal, elitist dimensions of LGBT movements in the West, but the intersections of race, gender norms, caste, religion and othering on which it rests. Gayatri Gopinath and Jasbir Puar, among others, have argued that not only are queer identities routinely read through anterior, pre-modern terms needing Western theoretical/socio-economic engagement (recall Carby's perspective discussed in the section on Kay), but they are read through the liberal imperialist and 'homonationalist' agendas that force the valuing of sexual freedoms which are also often, conversely, never extended to minority or 'alien' communities and non-conforming bodies (Gopinath; Puar). What these scholars have stressed is that postcolonial queering ultimately calls for an (anticolonial) solidarity within and between differences; a solidarity where one's fluid gender and sexual identities, and their complicated colonial and postcolonial heritage are retrieved and recognised. As Donna McCormack writes, in postcoloniality there is a desire to be fluid, to transgress boundaries and a non-adherence to exclusionary nationalist ideologies which is reflected in queerness. Queer postcolonial texts, thus, 'both resist mimicking the prominent trope of the coming out story (even while characters may discover their queer sexualities and genders) and portray the violence of implementing a supposed plan of modernization through a white, heteronormative colonial regime' (McCormack 8).

These insightful and decolonising propositions may help us think through the question of postcolonial queer sexuality and solidarity in Dionne Brand's poetry collection, *No Language is Neutral*. Together with Austin Clarke and Marlene NourbeSe Philip, Brand represents one of the most complex and uncompromising voices that have emerged from the Caribbean literary community in Canada. Originally from Trinidad and Tobago, Brand (as Simona Bertacco notes) has been active within black and feminist communities which 'represented a crucial experience both in terms of political commitment and disillusionment, and in terms of how it affected her writing' (Bertacco 10). As the title makes clear, these poems are interventions in sociolinguistic and psychosomatic landscapes that argue that language is a deeply political act. The collection focuses on everyday, long-forgotten or noted 'creole' female figures who have either been victims of slavery and colonialism or led anticolonial and anti-neoliberal struggles. 'Phyllis' is dedicated to Phyllis Coard, Minister of Women's Affairs for the People's Revolutionary Government of Grenada, 1979–83, who is now imprisoned at Richmond Hill Prison in Grenada, the poet informs us. As the first Minister of Women's Affairs, she worked to raise women's living standards, literacy levels and job prospects by establishing the National Women's Organisation, and had Grenada admitted into the Women's International Democratic Federation which campaigned for women's political and sexual rights. She was subsequently imprisoned for life by the invading US force in Grenada for alleged involvement in the assassination of Grenada's Prime Minister, Maurice Bishop (Mandle and Mandle 295–96). Brand thus begins her poem on this extraordinary woman,

> Phyllis, quite here, I hear from you
>
> not even from your own hand in a note
>
> but from stranger who dragged it
>
> from a prison wall (*No Language is Neutral* 8)

Written in 1990 when Coard was already in prison, Brand reminisces about their meeting where Phyllis talks about her ideas and 'the revolution, it did sound sweet and it did sound possible' (8). Reminiscent of Davis's impact on the young protagonist in Kay's poems, this poem repeats two images: Coard's laugh and womanhood. Brand compares her laugh with a 'bronze bauble / hanging' in the evening when she taught Brand about the revolution that was possible. Comparing the laugh with bronze baubles, Brand suggests the laugh's celebratory and tactile power – it is infectious and touches hearts. In a transferred epithet, the evening is configured as revolutionary – meaning that the air is filled with the thrilling discussion of overthrowing a colonial and capitalist hierarchy and setting up egalitarianism and female solidarity in Grenada. This laugh is then remembered as 'luminous and bubbling' (9). Here the tactile elements receive a visual image of swelling luminosity. In the third and final image, Brand stretches the laugh to an aural dimension (10). This laughter is not bubbling and joyous anymore but is a clanging that can break through the stone walls of prison.

Through the sensorium of her laugh, Brand then arrives at the vulnerable yet unorthodox nature of her womanhood:

> I know they treat you bad
>
> like a woman
>
> called you *hyena*, a name enjoining
>
> you alone to biology and not science (*No Language is Neutral* 10)

These lines betray the dominant colonialist, patriarchal metaphor of sexual violence. Treating Coard 'like a woman' is a clear indication of sexual subjugation in society or prison. She campaigned for women's sexual rights and was understood by the colonialist invading armies as a danger to the status quo. She would, thus, be reminded of what it meant to be a woman: that is, by forcing themselves on her and sexually abusing her. This is consolidated by the use of the cryptic image of 'the skill of your womb' a few lines later. Brand insinuates that Coard knew when she joined the revolution that once caught, she would have to pay a double punishment for being a revolutionary and a woman. The imagery of jumping on the 'skill of your womb' is historical here. Warring groups have historically been the most violent on women, raping and forcing them to give birth to war babies as a thumping sign of victory over a country or community. As we will see in Chapter 3, in Lynn Nottage's Congo based play, *Ruined*, raping women by military and militant forces means sending a message that an adjacent land (one's 'motherland') is vulnerable and has been triumphed over. The 'skill of her womb', thus, is about women's reproductive abilities, and in this context, the scarred lives of war babies.

What is redemptive in these imagining is the comparison of Coard with a hyena (*No Language is Neutral* 10). Hyenas have been understood in popular culture as tricksters or cheats. Because of their physiognomy and scavenging practices, hyenas have been called ugly, filthy and schematic. It is also difficult to distinguish male and female hyenas as female hyenas have pseudo-penises, which made Ovid call them hermaphrodites in *Metamorphosis* (Mwangi 173–74). Coard has been compared to hyenas (biologically) because she has short hair and is resourceful and strong – traits associated with a male. She is also a political campaigner for women, to make women recognised as strong and important contributors to the anticolonial life of the country. For these reasons, she is understood as treacherous and untrustworthy by (a masculine) polity, and seen as feeding on the dead body of the prime minister. But what is compelling about this imagery is that hyenas always work in packs and have tremendous verbal and communication techniques. Their laugh is famous for its giggling and throbbing nature. Hyenas, thus, also point to the work of collectivity and solidarity in developing methods to successfully quell an enemy. Like the double-edged nature of *karukku* for Bama or the resistant spirit of 'Black Bottom' for Kay, Coard is a hyena for the prison guards and for the many admirers and sympathisers of her cause like Brand. Her laughter is like the laughter of the hyena, a warning call for the enemy that hyenas will gather and devise decolonising strategies for food and survival (psychoanalytically, for 'male castration'), and in this case for sociopolitical liberation. Stretching an image to reveal its underlying historical and aesthetically comparable basis recalls Ramazani's thoughtful remarks on the idea of radical resonance we are arguing for in the book: 'We should read such poetry because we can learn from it, perhaps more vividly than we can from a textbook recounting of politics, history, and society, how the world and the self and society feel, look, and sound to people both like and unlike ourselves, emerging from colonial histories, whether or not we ourselves are' (Ramazani 11).

Omise'eke Natasha Tinsley argues that Brand uses 'a pedagogy of crossing' in this collection, by which she means both her own temporary Middle Passage in revolutionary Grenada and her 'tracing of a conceptual map' which continually connects personal history with the complex 'fragmented, often violent past' of oceanic history 'to imagine yet unrealized, potential junctures between Caribbean erotic and political landscapes and desires' (Tinsley 211, 228). Here, Brand's key medium is to build a creole language that lies at the intersections between the slave, oceanic and coloniser's tongues. Brand offers a glimpse of this complex linguistic matrix in the long prose poem 'No Language is Neutral', where the memory of a place is tinged with memories of its violent historical pasts, like in the remarkable poem 'Blues Spiritual for Mammy Prater' about a 115-year-old ex-slave whose photography captures her historical patience against the *longue durée* of colonial and imperialist violence on her body and community. 'No Language is Neutral' takes an aural route to capture the past,

> people does here things in this heliconia peace
> the morphology of rolling chain and copper gong
> now shape this twang, falsettos of whip and air
> rudiment this grammar. (23)

Sensory and acoustic elements are predominant in Brand's poetic rendering of slavery: from gong and rolling chain, to falsettos. This poem was written in the 1990s, when postcolonial studies was emerging in Canada and the Canadian Multiculturalism Act was proposed. It appears to hark back to a notion of language that is asymmetrical and dialectical; in which standard English and sensory elements in creolised languages, or what Kamau Braithwaite called the dialectical relation between dialect and nation language (311), germinate into an ambiguous and ambivalent poetic prose. As Jason Wiens thoughtfully writes, through conjurations of Liney (an old woman) and her non-standard English dialect, Brand offers not only another compelling portrayal of a strong black woman in the post-slavery Caribbean, but also the possibility of acknowledging the varieties of creolised language in a post-settlement, postcolonial society like Canada (Wiens 91–93).

Love and intimacy, the antidotes to historicist, colonialist and masculine pasts, are most explicit in the section of short poems titled 'Hard against the Soul'. Brand, here, establishes her lesbian love in language that is as sensuous as it is revolutionary:

> You can hardly hear my voice but I heard you
>
> in my sleep big as waves reciting their prayers
>
> so hourly the heart rocks to its real meaning,
>
> saying, we must make a sense here to living,
>
> this allegiance is as flesh to bone but older
>
> (*No Language is Neutral* 39)

This poem, whose first line is repeated in three short poems in this section, continues the oceanic imagery that sees their relationship as a 'shell murmuring and / yawning' in a previous poem (38). The lover hears her beloved like waves reciting prayers. In using the word 'rocks', the poem makes a pathetic fallacy of lovemaking, as if waves were making love to rocks. Her love for her beloved is as strong and consummative as the waves; it is an 'allegiance of flesh and bone' which, as she says later, has no poems dedicated to it. As Brand suggests throughout, the love for women by women is historically everywhere and yet this intimacy has been denied; a history which she attempts to erect through her anticolonial poetry. Here, queerness, following Hawley's words above, is not only the radical homosexual love between lesbians or gay people, but the ability to remind one through the collection that this love includes respect for women who have struggled throughout the last five hundred years to survive, bonded in chains and forced to work by their white masters. This love is also about how they have stood the test of time, often sitting patiently like Mama Prater or revolutionising social practices like Phyllis Coard. 'Hard against the Soul' has a reference to Marta Beatriz, economist and staunch critic of Fidel Castro's political attempts at gagging women and minorities in Cuba: 'because she said she loved women and you wanted to believe her' (45). In these conjurations, lesbianism receives a hallmark of anticolonial transnational solidarity between women, a love that is as sexual as it is political – reminiscent of James Baldwin's literary and activist work on gay rights as a civil and anticolonial right.

Brand wrote about the negative reaction to her black feminist revolutionary work by Marxist and conservatives alike:

> To dream about a Black woman, even an old Black woman, is dangerous even in a Black dream, an old dream, a Black woman's dream, even in a dream where you are the dreamer. Even in a Black dream, where I, too, am a dreamer, a lesbian is suspect; a woman is suspect even to other women, especially if she dreams of women. (*Bread out of Stone* 14)

She never gave up on the dream though. Her response is to offer a larger notion of love that enables her reader to see the transforming effect of solidarity, sexuality and faith against a colonising patriarchy. As she writes in one of the poems in the section 'Hard against the Soul', 'But perhaps I always had it in my mind to be an old woman / darkening, with another old woman' (*No Language is Neutral* 46). Lesbianism is the bond of solidarity that allows the beloved to acknowledge the beauty of intimacy and fellow feeling. The poems here end with a historical reminder:

> . . . They say this place
>
> does not exist, then, my tongue is mythic. I was here
>
> before (51)

Note the monosyllabic strength of the public imposition that these female and lesbian places of love and solidarity never existed; that what she said was only found in a poet's imagination. This changes with the disyllabic word 'mythic' which is contrastingly set with 'before'. The change of tense from present to past also sends a response back to the imposing present indefinite. She has been here before and thus knows that this has happened, never acknowledged in authoritative histories but also profoundly present in poetic readings. Her poetry, thus, is an anticolonial retrieval of ordinary women's extraordinary feat of standing up to sexual, social and political authoritarianism as well as their 'authoritative' writings of history.

Thirty years after Brand's collection, Natalie Diaz – a Mojave American poet – published her critically acclaimed collection, *Postcolonial Love Poem*. Awarded the Pulitzer Prize in Poetry in 2021, this collection alludes to an expansive notion of love, intimacy and female solidarity through including non-binary and transgender topics that Brand anticipated. In poems like 'Grief Work' or 'From the Desire Field', Diaz also tackled the issues of intersectional and border identities (such as seen in Kay or Anzaldúa) and the watery oceanic crossing of Brand, pointing to the affective success of, at least, three decades of writing on socio-historically marginalised issues by socio-historically marginalised people. As theories of queer attend to heated debates on non-binary and transgender issues today, literary and cultural representations of queer – such as that of Diaz or Arundhati Roy (*The Ministry of Utmost Happiness*) – will only point to a further cultural and social decolonising of the field.

In this chapter I have argued that the postcolonial minority is a coeval and intersectional concept that forms against the overlapping oppressive forces that constitute nationhood, to identify and interrogate which we will need a multidimensional and decolonising lens of totality. Drawing from relevant theoretical conversations, I have showed that minority lives are conflicted and radically uncertain from within, which continue to question majoritarian and fixed notions of identity established through the key social categories or academic rubrics of nation, race, caste, class, gender, religion and sexuality. For writers who inhabit the borders of this fluid and 'deterritorialising' path, the genre and form of writing is an important gateway to address the complex ontological retrievals of self and culture and its challenging identifications with solidarity. In topic-based case studies, I have explained that Bama takes up the testimonio genre to counter the colonialist–bourgeois novelistic narrative of individual and collective progress, pointing to the layered and endless sufferings of Dalits. Jackie Kay and Dionne Brand adopt poetry to voice intersectional racial and sexual identities. While Kay blunts the lyric 'I' through a triadic formation of voices and suggests a collective, homoerotic identity formation with political agents such as Davis, Brand uses historical figures and an expansive notion of love and revolutionary struggle mixed with creole voices and oceanic imagery to dismantle the colonising ethos of patriarchy and bondage. Echoing the broad theoretical framework of rubrics, topics and close, comparative materialist readings found in this book, I have established that the works discussed in this chapter, in their peculiar and resonant means, stand up to the heteronormativity of majoritarian ethno-nationalist practices and remind us, through their marginalised yet strident voices, of a dawning consciousness for the marginalised that is displacing the centre by shuttling between majoritarian cultures and fluid identities. Following Anzaldúa in the first chapter, this may be called the 'new mestizo consciousness' which is 'a source of intense pain, (but) its energy comes from continual creative motion that keeps breaking down the unitary aspect of each new paradigm' (Anzaldúa 80). Through another set of topics and texts, we will see in the next chapter how this disruptive and creative motion works through a complex interplay of history, choice and coercion in the rubric of postcolonial migration.

NOTES

1. Here, Fanon's observations on colonialism as a racialised and spatialised apartheid comes to mind (*The Wretched of the Earth* 37–38). It is no wonder that European colonialism quickly found a worthy ally in Hindu casteism for perpetuating its rule.
2. See chapters 6 and 7 in *Karukku* for further explication.

REFERENCES

Abraham, Joshil K., and Judith Misrahi-Barak, editors. *Dalit Literatures in India*. Routledge, 2015.

Ambedkar, B.R. *Annihilation of Caste*. 1936. Verso, 2014.

Anderson, Benedict. *Imagined Communities: The Origin and Spread of Nationalism*. Verso, 1983.

Anzaldúa, Gloria. *Borderlands/La Frontera: The New Mestiza*. Aunt Lute Book Company, 1987.

Arya, Sunaina, and Aakash Singh Rathore, editors. *Dalit Feminist Theory: A Reader*. Routledge, 2020.

Ashcroft, Bill, Gareth Griffiths, and Helen Tiffin, editors. *The Empire Writes Back: Theory and Practice in Post-colonial Literature*. Routledge, 1989.

---. *Post-Colonial Studies: The Key Concepts*. 2000. Routledge, 2007.

Bama. *Karukku*. Translated by Laxmi Holström, Oxford UP, 2001.

Baldwin, James. *No Name in the Street*. Joseph, 1972.

Bayly, Susan. *Caste, Society and Politics in India from the Eighteenth Century to the Modern Age*. Cambridge UP, 1999.

Belmonte, Laura A. *The International LGBT Rights Movement: A History*. Bloomsbury, 2020.

Bertacco, Simona. "Imagining Bodies in the Work of Dionne Brand". *Altre Modernitá*, vol. 1, no. 3, 2009, pp. 9–17.

Bhambra, Gurminder. "The Current Crisis of Europe: Refugees, Colonialism, and the Limits of Cosmopolitanism". *European Law Journal*, vol. 23, 2017, pp. 395–405.

Braithwaite, Kamau. "Nation Language". *The History of the Voice: The Development of Nation Language in Anglophone Caribbean Poetry*. New Beacon, 1984, pp. 309–13.

Brand, Dionne. *Bread out of Stone: Recollections, Sex, Recognitions, Race, Dreaming, Politics*. Coach House Press, 1994.

---. *No Language is Neutral*. Coach House Press, 1990.

Brueck, Laura R. "Narrating Dalit Womanhood and the Aesthetics of Autobiography".*Journal of Commonwealth Literature*, vol. 54, no. 1, 2019, pp. 25–37.

Carby, Hazel V. "'White Woman Listen!': Black Feminism and the Boundaries of Sisterhood". *Black British Culture and Society: A Text Reader*, edited by Kwesi Owusu, Routledge, 2005, pp. 86–93.

Chakravarti, Uma. "Conceptualising Brahminical Patriarchy in Early India: Gender, Caste, Class and State". *Economic and Political Weekly*, vol. 28, no. 14, 1993, pp. 579–85.

Chatterjee, Partha. *The Nation and Its Fragments: Colonial and Postcolonial Histories*. Princeton UP, 1993.

Crenshaw, Kimberlé. "Mapping the Margins: Intersectionality, Identity Politics and Violence against Women of Color". *Stanford Law Review*, vol. 43, no. 6, 1991, pp. 1241–99.

Davidson, Neil. *The Origins of Scottish Nationhood*. Pluto Press, 2000.

---, and Satnam Virdee. "Understanding Racism in Scotland". *No Problem Here: Understanding Racism in Scotland*, edited by Neil Davidson, et al., Luath Press, 2018, pp. 9–12.

Deleuze, Giles and Félix Guattari. "Kafka: Toward a Minor Literature: The Components of Expression". *New Literary History*, vol. 16, no. 3, 1985, pp. 591–608.

Diaz, Natalie. *Postcolonial Love Poem*. Faber & Faber, 2020.

Donnell, Alison. "Nation and Contestation: Black British Writing". *Wasafiri*, vol. 17, no. 36, 2002, pp. 11–17.

Dorow, Sara K. *Transnational Adoption: A Cultural Economy of Race, Gender, and Kinship*. New York UP, 2006.

Dutt, Yashica. *Coming Out as Dalit*. Aleph Book Co., 2019.

Fanon, Frantz. *The Wretched of the Earth*. Translated by Constance Farrington, Grove Press, 1963.

Fox, Pamela. "The "Telling Part": Reimagining Racial Recognition in Jackie Kay's Adoptee Search Narratives". *Contemporary Women's Writing*, vol. 9, no. 2, 2015, pp. 277–96, https://doi.org/10.1093/cww/vpu041. Accessed 9 March 2022.

Geetha, V. "Periyar, Women, and Ethic of Citizenship". *Gender and Caste*, edited by Anupama Rao, Zed Books, 2005, pp. 180–203

Gilroy, Paul. *Postcolonial Melancholia*. Columbia UP, 2004.

Gish, Nancy K. "Adoption, Identity, Voice: Jackie Kay's Invention of Self". *Imagining Adoption: Essays on Literature and Culture*, edited by Marianne Novy, U of Michigan P, 2001, pp. 171–91.

Gopinath, Gayatri. *Impossible Desires. Queer Diasporas and South Asian Public Cultures*. Duke UP, 2005.

Guru, Gopal. "Dalit Women Talk Differently". *Dalit Feminist Theory: A Reader*, edited by Sunaina Arya and Aakash Singh Rathore, Routledge, 2020, pp. 150–53.

Hall, Catherine, et al. *Legacies of British Slave-Ownership: Colonial Slavery and the Formation of Victorian Britain*. Cambridge UP, 2014.

Hall, Stuart. "New Ethnicities". *Stuart Hall: Critical Dialogues in Cultural Studies*, edited by David Morley and Kuan-Hsing Chen, Routledge, 1996, pp. 442–51.

Hawley, John C., editor. *Postcolonial, Queer: Theoretical Intersections*. Albany, State U of New York P, 2001.

Henderson, Shirley, and Allison Mackay, editors. *Grit and Diamonds: Women in Scotland Making History 1980-1990*. Stramullion/ Cauldron Collective, 1990.

Holström, Laxmi. Introduction. *Karukku*, by Bama, Oxford UP, 2012, pp. xv–xxii.

hooks, bell. *Ain't I A Woman: Black Women and Feminism*. 1982. Pluto Press, 1990.

Jackson, Joseph. *Writing Black Scotland: Race, Nation, and Devolution of Black Britain*. Edinburgh UP, 2020.

JanMohamed, Abdul, and David Lloyd. "Introduction: Toward a Theory of Minority Discourse". *Cultural Critique*, vol. 6, 1987, pp. 5–12.

John, Mary E., and Meena Gopal. "Responses to Indian Feminists' Objections". *Dalit Feminist Theory: A Reader*, edited by Sunaina Arya and Aakash Singh Rathore, Routledge, 2020, pp. 188–98.

Kay, Jackie. *Bessie Smith*. Absolute, 1997.

---. *The Adoption Papers*. Bloodaxe Books, 1991.

Kumar, Raj. *Dalit Literature and Criticism*. Orient BlackSwan, 2019.

Lorde, Audre. "The Master's Tools will Never Dismantle the Master's House". *Sister Outsider: Essays and Speeches*, U of California P, 1984, pp. 110–113.

Mandle, Jay R., and Joan D. Mandle. "The Coards and the Grenada Revolution". *New West Indian Guide*, vol. 94, no. 3-4, 2020, pp. 293–99, https://www.jstor.org/stable/27130306. Accessed 3 Sept. 2021.

Manoharan, Karthick Ram. "Debrahminizing Decolonization: Imagining a New Curriculum". *All About Ambedkar: A Journal of Theory and Praxis*, vol. 1, no. 1, 2020, https://www.allaboutambedkaronline.com/post/debrahminizing-decolonization-imagining-a-new-curriculum-:~:text=Debrahminization%20as%20an%20academic%20 exercise,to%20the%20study%20of%20disciplines. Accessed 12 May 2022

McCormack, Donna. *Queer Postcolonial Narratives and the Ethics of Witnessing*. Bloomsbury, 2014.

McFarlane, Anna. "The Poetry of Civic Nationalism: Jackie Kay's 'Bronze Head from Ife'". *C21 Literature: Journal of 21st-century Writings*, vol. 5, no. 2, 2017, pp.1–18, https://c21.openlibhums.org/article/id/530/-:~:text=This%20is%20particularly%20apparent%20in,to%20synthesise%20identity%20from%20difference. Accessed 8 March 2022.

McLeod, John. *Life Lines: Writing Transcultural Adoption*. Bloomsbury, 2015.

Mohanty, Chandra Talpade, "Under Western Eyes: Feminist Scholarship and Colonial Discourses". *boundary 2*, vol. 12, no. 3, 1984, pp. 333–58.

Mwangi, Evan. *The Postcolonial Animal: African Literature and Posthuman Ethics*. U of Michigan P, 2019.

Nairn, Tom. *The Break-Up of Britain: Crisis and Neo-nationalism*. NLB, 1977.

Nayar, Pramod K. "Bama's *Karukku*: Dalit Autobiography as Testimonio". *Journal of Commonwealth Literature*, vol. 41, no. 2, 2006, pp. 83–100.

Oddie, Geoffrey. *Social Protest in India: British Protestant Missionaries and Social Reforms, 1850–1900*. Manohar, 1979.

O'Hanlon, Rosalind. *Caste, Conflict, and Ideology: Mahatma Jotirao Phule and Low Caste Protest in Nineteenth Century Western India*. Cambridge UP, 1985.

Omvedt, Gail. *Understanding Caste. From Buddha to Ambedkar and Beyond*. Orient BlackSwan, 2011.

Paswan, Sanjay, and Paramanshi Jaideva, editors. *Encyclopaedia of Dalits in India, Vol. 3: Movements*. Gyan Publishing House, 2004.

Popp, Valerie L. "Improper Identification Required: Passports, Papers, and Identity Formation in Jackie Kay's "The Adoption Papers"". *Contemporary Literature*, vol. 53, no. 2, 2012, pp. 292–318.

Puar, Jasbir. *Terrorist Assemblages: Homonationalism in Queer Times*. Duke UP, 2007.

Ramazani, Jahan. "Introduction". *The Cambridge Companion to Postcolonial Poetry*, edited by Jahan Ramazani, Cambridge UP, 2017, pp. 1–18.

Rege, Sharmila. *Writing Caste/Writing Gender: Reading Dalit Women's Testimonios*. Zubaan, 2006.

Rowell, Charles Henry. "An Interview with Jackie Kay". *Callaloo*, vol. 37, no. 2, 2014, pp. 268–80.

Roy, Anupama. *Citizenship Regimes, Law, and Belonging. The CAA and the NRC*. Oxford UP, 2022.

Roy, Arundhati. *The Ministry of Utmost Happiness*. Hamish Hamilton, 2017.

Said, Edward. *Orientalism*. 1978. Penguin, 2003.

Salem, Sara. "Intersectionality and Its Discontents: Intersectionality as Traveling Theory". *European Journal of Women's Studies*, vol. 25, no. 4, 2018, pp. 403–18.

Sivanandan, A. "The Liberation of the Black Intellectual". *Black British Culture and Society: A Text Reader*, edited by Kwesi Owusu, Routledge, 2005, pp. 73–85.

Spivak, Gayatri Chakravorty. *In Other Worlds: Essays in Cultural Politics*. Methuen, 1987.

Taneti, James Elisha. *Caste, Gender, and Christianity in Colonial India: Telugu Women in Mission*. Palgrave Macmillan, 2013.

Thorne, Susan. "Missionary-Imperial Feminism". *Gendered Missions: Women and Men in Missionary Discourse and Practice*, edited by Mary T. Huber and Nancy C. Lutkehoaus, U of Michigan P, 1999, pp. 39–66.

Tinsley, Omise'eke Natasha. *Thiefing Sugar: Eroticism between Women in Caribbean Literature*. Duke UP, 2010.

Viswanath, Rupa. *The Pariah Problem. Caste, Religion, and the Social in Modern India*. Columbia UP, 2014.

Viswanathan, Gauri. *Masks of Conquest: Literary Study and British Rule in India*. Oxford UP, 1989.

---. *Outside the Fold: Conversion, Modernity and Belief*. Princeton UP, 1998.

wa Thiong'o, Ngũgĩ. *Decolonising the Mind: The Politics of Language in African Literature*. Zimbabwe Publishing House, 1981.

Webster, John. *The Dalit Christians: A History*. Indian Society for Promoting Christian Knowledge, 1994.

Wiens, Jason. ""Language Seemed to Split in Two": National Ambivalence(s) and Dionne Brand's "No Language Is Neutral"". *Essays on Canadian Writing*, vol. 70, 2000, pp. 81–102.

Yengde, Suraj. *Caste Matters*. Penguin, 2019.

Young, Cynthia. *A Soul Power: Culture, Radicalism, and the Making of a U.S. Third World Left*. Duke UP, 2006.

Chapter Three

Migrations

SLAVERY, DIASPORA AND REFUGE IN MCQUEEN, HAMID, ADICHIE AND BUI

'Colony', as we noted in the first chapter, means travel to and settlement in faraway lands. Migration, that is contact with new cultures in adopted lands and imagining and reconstituting home and nation there, is key to colonial and postcolonial studies. From the fifteenth century onward, with the invention of the printing press in Germany and its mass use in Europe – especially through the production of the Bible and other religious, educational, political and cultural works – words and ideas travelled across 'the globe' (referring mainly to Western power centres) in an unprecedented fashion. The print revolution (as it came to be known) also coincided with 'New World discoveries' by Iberian (Spanish and Portuguese) empires (Young, *Empire, Colony, Postcolony* 16–17). People in the 'West' wrote about coming into contact with Indigenous and native communities in the Americas as well as with the spectacular civilisations of the Chinese, Ottoman and Indian empires. The Iberian empires, armed with superior weaponry and naval technology and riddled with new diseases, had wiped out Indigenous communities from the Americas while in search of commodities and raw material, thus establishing a blueprint for European settlement and plantation systems (Pratt; Bailyn). In the sixteenth and seventeenth centuries, the Dutch, French and English followed the successful pattern of establishing plantation economies, then colonial settlement and the religious and political discourses of European supremacy, thereby consolidating the modern (European) imperialist world system (Wallerstein). If plantations had transformed slavery into a mass migration of humans from Africa and Asia for capitalist profit, indentured labour continued the supply of cheap labour for commodity capitalism and imperialism on a global scale in post-slavery contexts. While the Second World War had formally seen the end of empire, travel from the commonwealth to European and American metropolises for study, work and tourism became paradigmatic for citizen–subjects of the postcolonial world. These world-historical events of war and colonialism also resulted in the 'phenomenon' of refugees and displaced people seeking asylum and refuge in economically advanced (former colonising) countries, complicating the term 'migration' in the postcolonial context. In this chapter, we will engage with postcolonial migrations through the lenses of enforced and voluntary travel, suggesting that the word 'migration' has a deep-rooted colonial meaning and use for our times.

Migration, Diaspora and Postcolonial Studies

Thanks to the publication of key works in colonial discourse analysis/postcolonial studies by migrant scholars such as Said, Bhabha and Spivak – often considered the 'holy trinity' of postcolonial studies (Young, *Colonial Desire* 154) – and due to the critical popularity of literary texts by Salman Rushdie, V. S. Naipaul, Doris Lessing, Wole Soyinka and Bharati Mukherjee, who lived away from their 'home' countries for individual or political reasons (to name a few), the diasporic exile of the educated elite and their experiences of negotiating the cultures of their host lands came to broadly define postcolonial migration in the early years of the field. Consider this oft-quoted definition of a postcolonial migrant by Salman Rushdie in *Imaginary Homelands*:

> A full migrant suffers, traditionally, a triple disruption: he loses his place, he enters into an alien language, and he finds himself surrounded by beings whose social behaviour and codes are very unlike, and sometimes even offensive to, his own. And this is what makes migrants such important figures: because roots, language and social norms have been three of

the most important parts of the definition of what it is to be human being. The migrant, denied all three, is obliged to find new ways of describing himself, new ways of being human. (277–78)

This moving definition is able to reflect upon the different kinds of postcolonial migrations I will discuss in the chapter. Rushdie's account takes place against the backdrop of race, culture and blackness debates in the UK and the USA (which we discussed in the previous chapter), enabling a reading of the 'migrant' through cosmopolitan un-belonging and cultural reconstruction. Homi Bhabha's observations in *The Location of Culture* attends to this point. Bhabha writes, 'To live in the unhomely world, to find its ambivalences and ambiguities enacted in the house of fiction, or its sundering and splitting performed in the work of art, is also to affirm a profound desire for social solidarity: "I am looking for the join . . . I want to join . . . I want to join"' (26–27).

Much of the discussion of migration in postcolonial studies, as Andrew Smith argues, has drawn upon Bhabha's concepts of ambivalence, hybridity, ethical migrancy and liminality in literary texts and cultures (Andrew Smith 248–55). However, as we will note, particularly in the final section of the chapter on refugee crisis and the arts, politically, economically and environmentally controlled people in the aftermath of the Second World War and global decolonisation could hardly afford to find either social legitimation of their ambivalent cultures or visible recognition of their traumatic experiences in contemporary postcolonial literary and critical works. While this does not mean their experiences or works did not exist alongside that of the educated elite, it is in the last two decades – thanks to the internet and social media – that new technological means have developed to more visibly address the refugee crisis and its cultural registers. What I will show in the chapter is that slavery was the key driver for colonialism and capitalism in the Americas, followed by the indentured labour diaspora in Euro-America and Asia. Together these constitute the central examples of enforced migration in postcolonial studies. These world-historical practices were also heavily resisted through epochal armed resistances (such as the Haitian Revolution or

Nat Turner's Rebellion), or everyday forms of critique through a reluctance to engage with such systems or escape from plantations to live a life of domesticity and respect. These criticisms and interventions, which are decolonising and anticolonial at heart, were best registered in literary and cultural works such as the ones I will discuss in the rest of the chapter. Rewriting these historical events and emotions allows for the acknowledgement of their ongoing presence in our contemporary world. Hence these new works demand global recognition for their historical decolonising agenda. I will argue in the chapter that historical slavery finds analogous patterns of forced displacement and trauma in the contemporary refugee and asylum crisis. As a corollary, postcolonial migration also means migrating for professional opportunities following capitalist globalisation, more specifically echoing Rushdie's and Bhabha's sentiments above.

I will, thus, read three aspects of postcolonial migration here – slavery, labour diaspora and refugee crisis in postcolonial arts and literature. I contend through Steve McQueen's film, *12 Years A Slave*, that black filmmakers have often used the neo-slave narrative genre to address the contemporary racist climate and history of race violence in America. The two novels by Mohsin Hamid and Chimamanda Ngozie Adichie are able to demonstrate how, despite initiatives of cultural assimilation and (celebratory) claims of migrant cosmopolitanism, religion, race and ethnicity have continued to haunt and racialise ethnic minorities, expressed here through the lenses of Islam in the 9/11 context and post-racial discourses. Finally, I show that the contemporary refugee crisis is linked with colonialism and neocolonialism. Here I engage with the exodus of Vietnamese 'boat people' to America following their being subjected to colonial and imperialist wars through a graphic novel by Thi Bui. My selection of texts, which are either about or written from the USA, is indicative of the fact that the USA has replaced Britain in the post-war, postcolonial period as *the* neo-imperialist superpower either invading countries in the postcolonial world for resource accumulation and global security and giving rise to refugee and migrant conditions, or then attracting migrants with promises of refuge, work and opportunities and continuing to remind them of their racialised inferiority (Ashcroft et al. 2). I have used the genres of film, novel and graphic novel to suggest the extent and breadth of genres artists and writers have used to retrieve and critique colonising moments and to convey their decolonising messages.

SLAVERY, NEO-SLAVE NARRATIVE AND AMERICAN FILMS: STEVE MCQUEEN'S *12 YEARS A SLAVE*

Slavery and colonialism are not interchangeable. Slavery existed much before the modern, capitalist basis of European colonialism. Slavery's most traumatic chapters in modern times took place in the USA. From the early nineteenth century onwards, like most of imperialist Europe, an independent, settler, colonial America started to expand its territories rapidly to the west and south of its borders. Buoyed by national poets like Walt Whitman who spoke of the need for expansion – understood as being predestined for the nation to further the development of its trade, resources, individual liberty, self-sufficiency and territorial security – numerous travelogues and expedition narratives appeared from 1804 onwards to encourage the settler population to travel and explore lands in order to create plantations and settlements (Sundquist 15). This required cheap labour thereby providing encouragement for slavery. When slavery was abolished in Europe, plantation owners and slave traders argued that plantations were a national economic need for which the wide availability of cheap labour was necessary. This was also the time, Arthur Riss writes, when the scientific discourses of ethnography and anthropometry published numerous reports on the human skull, body, bones and skin colour demonstrating that the 'Negro' not only belonged to the lowest rung of human progeny (in which Caucasians were at the top), but also that they were a different species (7). Religious discourses around the period also argued that the 'Negro' was a separate species (9). In economic, scientific, and religious discourses, the African slave was not understood as a human being and thus, did not have rights as enshrined in the 'Declaration of the Rights of Man' (1789). Riss writes that 'to argue for example, race-consciousness represses or twists this identity [based on equal rights] is to attribute to Man, a fixed, immanent meaning, a meaning that racial categories block, a meaning upon which a racist interpretation is forcibly imposed and with which racialist premises inevitably interfere' (5).

The heated pro-slavery arguments for the African slave to be categorised as a different species were countered vociferously in anti-slavery publications such as William Lloyd Garrison's *The Liberator* and *Thoughts on African Colonization*, which attacked colonisation as futile and undemocratic; David Walker's *Appeal . . . to the Coloured Citizens of the World* (1829); and William Jay's *Inquiry* (1835) which criticised 'American Colonisation Society' (Sundquist 139–44). Many of these thinkers, including Walker, resorted to Christian and Calvinist theologies to justify the emancipation of slaves – a point already raised so evocatively in Britain by Olaudah Equiano's *Interesting Narrative* (1789) through the genre of life writing and Frederick Douglass's poignant *Life Narrative* (1845). Between the 1830s and 1860s, Sarah Meer tells us that almost a hundred slave narratives (life writings) were published in the United States that took the form of a 'bondage to freedom journey'. These narratives would describe the tremendous suffering on American plantations; the rigorous routine of cotton picking; being whipped at the whim of the master; the everyday violence on women including rape and torture; and questioning how Americans who constitutionally adopted equality and justice as the supremely cherished values of their free nation could tolerate these atrocities (75–82). Written and published in the north of the country which had declared slavery illegal, these works would implement a mixed narrative genre composed of the white slave narrative, colonial captivity narrative, gothic romance, and sentimental domestic novel (notably by Harriet Ann Jacobs) to present an emotional plea for social justice. If the literature of colonisation was important for the geographical exploration of America and Europe, to follow Sundquist, it is the literature of anticolonialism and slave rebellions that were fundamental to anti-slavery and anticolonial writings (15).[1]

While slavery was abolished in the 1860s, racist discrimination against black people lived on 'in debt peonage; in control of movement; in employment and vagrancy laws; in the forced labour of the chain gang; and in the imposition of arbitrary violence in lynching' (Armstrong 206). The civil rights movements in America in the 1960s, anti-racist demonstrations in universities and the expansion of independent publishing brought slave narratives to the fore once again, expedited by Toni Morrison winning the Nobel Prize in Literature in 1993. This, however, exposed the question of ethics as to who could write on slavery and how to write about it: 'To fictionalize slavery meant to navigate the complex question about the ethics of literary representation. Did authors writing about slavery have unique responsibilities to the forms and substance of the past, or might they enjoy the same aesthetic prerogatives as those who wrote about other topics?' (Rushdy 237). These questions about representation and ethics also came to haunt the cinematic revival of slavery. Tom Dixon's *The Clansman: A Historical Romance of the Klu Klux Klan* (1905), was adapted as a feature-length silent film by D. W. Griffith titled *The Birth of a Nation* (1915). The movie implemented, through different innovative techniques, racist nostalgia and a reductive portrayal of black people in its historical rendition of the American Civil War. Margaret Mitchell's *Gone with the Wind* (1936), adapted for the screen by Victor Fleming in 1939, wallowed in 'miscegenation fantasy' and sentimentalism for the Lost Cause of the Confederacy through long shots and portrayal of the black body, as well as medium and close shots to heighten emotion. Film critic Sharon Willis notes that *Gone with the Wind* popularised the medium with the spectacle of enslavement in its widely popular run: here 'black people were always ready to greet, to observe, and wish the white people well' (226). During the Civil Rights movement era, the ABC-run miniseries *Roots* (1977) brought slavery to television, shifting the focus from nostalgia or black innocence to black perspective and resistance. This constituted a dramatic refusal of the familiar conventions that highlighted the black body as an 'exhibit' and a source of the spectacle of suffering at the hands of white brutality (229).

Questions of dignity, love, humanity, community and intimacy among the enslaved were also widely explored. Once again, the slave narrative genre offered a key stylistic register since, as a mixed genre written for universal social justice, it was a flexible, heterogeneous and temporally stretchable breed. This is also because the aesthetic flexibility of slave narratives is at once historic: 'the aesthetic and the historic are of a piece. That is to say that these are not arguments couched in literary forms; they are arguments inseparable from the literary form itself' (Tawil 7). This point is also raised by Yogita Goyal in *Runaway Genres*. In the current proliferation of the crisis of migrants, refugees, detainees and asylums seekers, writers of testimonio, autobiography and creative fiction have gone back to the slave narrative to make the case that not only is racism still present, but the past of the American South can be recognised in the workings of the present and future of the Global South. Goyal uses the method of 'analogy' while being aware that these are peculiarly specific historical and literary contexts that cannot be conflated with each other (*Runaway Genres* 8–9). While Goyal does not discuss films, her readings of new ideas like diaspora and immigration (which we will discuss in the next section) in neo-slave narrative, black satire and gothic romance are key to my thinking of the revival of slave narrative in literature, the arts and films. Although many of the migratory elements of slavery could be noted in written and visual/performative works about the Middle Passage (most recently by V. S. Naipaul, Caryl Phillips, Daniel Black, Yaa Gyasi or Steven Spielberg) by focusing on the cinematic adaptation of slave narratives, this section will specifically point to the migratory selves of enslaved people who did not have a homeland and stationary life of their own, and how cinema could capture these complex sentiments through its innovative aesthetics.

Steve McQueen's *12 Years A Slave* was released in 2013, almost a hundred years after Griffith's *The Birth of a Nation*. The film is an adaptation of Solomon Northup's memoir about his twelve years of enslavement in New Orleans. Born to a freedman father Mintus and a freewoman, Solomon grew up as a farmer, received a state education and was a violinist settled with his wife and two children in Saratoga, New York. New York had passed a Slave Act effective from 1827 that no black person could be sold into slavery from the state. Northup was led to believe by two businessmen that his skill as a violinist was of great importance to a circus group in Washington where they drugged and sold him to slave traders.

He was taken to a slave pen-holder named James Birch who then sold him to William Ford in New Orleans. Ford, who ran a timber mill on the Red River, leased him to Tibeats and then to Edwin Epps, a man who knew no bounds to torturing slaves on his cotton plantation. After serving Epps for about ten years, Simon Bass, a Canadian carpenter, wrote a letter for Northup to a contact in New York. Word got around and Northup was eventually released from the plantation and freed again in 1853. In the same year, with the help of his amanuensis David Wilson, he published the journey of his life from a freedman to a slave and eventual release. Riding upon the success of Harriet Beecher Stowe's *Uncle Tom's Cabin* (1852), the book became an instant bestseller making him a popular figure who gave lectures on abolition and, interestingly, also aided slaves in escaping through the Underground Railway. Although information about Northup's disappearance and death are unknown (he is said to have taken to drinking), his memoir also disappeared from popular memory in the post-war period. It is in the context of the revival of the slave narrative for reasons mentioned in the preceding section and the rise of anti-racist and Black Lives Matter movements in recent years that McQueen finds great cause for adapting the book to screen (Alonzo Smith 627). I will not pursue the truthfulness of Northup's narrative or of McQueen's adaption (historian Sue Eakin and researcher David Fiske published an authoritative volume on Northup's verifiable documents in 2012 for readers to consult). I am interested instead in exploring three cinematic techniques that McQueen uses – his rendering of women characters; the camera shots of the everyday life of slaves; and his close-ups of Solomon's face – through which, I argue, McQueen attempts to both represent and critique migratory aspects of slave life and attach human qualities of emotion, sexuality, pathos and empathy to them that may be inspired by contemporary events of refugee and humanitarian crises. These sentiments refer back to Fanon's notion of decolonisation as a process of retrieving the humanity and dignity of the colonised and the oppressed.

Like most slave narratives, the film begins with a flash-forward to when Solomon is working under Epps. On a certain night he is approached by a slave woman sleeping next to him in a small room full of other slaves to give her an orgasm; finding no sexual response from him in the act she moves away sobbing (00:04:43–00:05:34). This abrupt sexual experience reminds Northup of his wife in bed, and here we move to the back story of his life as a freedman. This anecdote with the woman's orgasm does not appear in Northup's memoir. As one would expect, such vivid portrayal of sexual activity is uncommon in nineteenth-century writing, especially in slave narratives which had to be highly controlled as a literary form in order to incite sentimentalism and sympathy for justice. Nevertheless, this scene was necessary for McQueen to render the private lives and feelings of enslaved women on screen which were otherwise absent in slave narratives (Carby 40–61). Indeed, the representation of women in the film differs greatly from that of the memoir in this respect. Patsey, a highly efficient cotton-picker whom Epps fancies and Epps's wife hates and tortures, is an example here. In a deeply moving sequence, she asks Northup to kill her and free her from the torture. Northup, a Christian, cannot murder her; even the thought of suicide is a sin (1:19:26–1:20:32). When Patsey returns from the Shaw's with some bars of soap as Mrs Epps denies her clean washing, she is ordered to be beaten by Northup. Interestingly, in the memoir, Northup tells us that he engineered new ways of whipping which would hide the power of the lash. In the film, he whips Patsey but also shouts at Epps 'Thou devil. Thou sinner', to which Epps replies, 'I am pleased to do what I want to my property' (1:52:06–1:52:28). The concept of the slave as property and thus reducible to an object or a (sexual) commodity is repeatedly depicted in the film. In another powerful sequence, as Northup runs to fetch Patsey from Mrs Shaw's house (Mrs Shaw being a black woman married to a white man), he finds tremendous inspiration in Mrs Shaw's authority and confidence as well as her liking for Patsey and tells them that the unfortunate time will be over soon. Tracing Solomon's facts through historical documents, Stephanie Li has argued that Northup received more power from this short sequence than throughout his life as a slave, and thus McQueen wanted to give it more time in the film, although it does not appear as significantly in the memoir (327, 329). Alonzo Smith has further argued that in these scenes, McQueen has produced an infrapolitics of passive resistance that slaves offered on an everyday basis, especially through the tactics of ridicule and an exaggerated use of camera movements and body gestures (623–24). By allowing the women moments in which they hold on to their private lives and desires, their solidarity and resistance to suffering, as well as their humanity and everyday struggles, McQueen offers to 'give us an ensemble of African-American women's experiences during both freedom and slavery that start to complicate this American story and fill in those silences and omissions of the old and new historiographies of slavery' (Tillet 360) in a restorative gesture reminiscent of Brand in the previous chapter.

These rewritings of gender and sexuality also bring to attention the film's rendering of Northup's masculinity. Larry Rohter argues in a *New York Times* review of the film that Northup, through Chiwetel Ejiofor's portrayal, becomes a rare figure of vulnerability ("It's Just How He Carries Himself"). In the beginning of the film, Northup argues with slave traders that he is a free man, after which he cries profusely. He then bickers with a slave woman who cannot console herself at the loss of her children, and looks for opportune moments to escape (25:27, 39:54–41:47). While his survival strategies work, he also resists oppression by attacking Tibeats who beats him for no reason. Chapin, the main overseer, comes to stop the fight and asks Northup to stay put if he wants to survive. But Tibeats and his men come back to hang him. Chapin intervenes to remind them that Northup is Ford's property. As Ford is in debt, killing Northup will pass the debt on to them. Tibeats and his men leave, not fearing for their lives, but the condition of property and debt (00:48:24–00:49:26). Scholars have widely written about chattel slavery as commodity and property (E. Williams 98–107; Wilentz 25–57), but the rest of the sequence is compelling for our current conversation. For about three minutes, McQueen shows Northup on the gallows balanced on the tips of his feet. Chapin does not release him from the gallows; he rather sends for Ford. This sequence has no background score other than insects chirping. We see a hanging Northup from various camera angles as the day passes on. This is contrasted with shots of the beautiful landscape, green vegetation, the neo-Greek architecture of Ford's mansion, and massive oak, willow and cypress trees covered in Spanish moss (00:49:37–00:52:26). Soon we are given to realise this is no cinematic contrast. Suffering and torture are part of the beauty of the landscape which poets and filmmakers of the American South chose not to focus on. Thus, the long shots of beautiful landscape in films like *Gone with the Wind* are challenged in *12 Years A Slave,* signifying that the happy slaves that appeared in the former were also there in the latter; but in some other places in the same garden, not on camera, some slaves were beaten and hanged to death. Indeed, in this sequence as well, as the sun slowly sets, we see slaves coming back from the field; children playing around; a slave mother calling her children back; in the mansion Chapin paces up and down the corridor overseeing them. Although one of the slave women rushes to give Northup water, it is not until late in the evening, when Ford comes back, that he is released.

This scene is tremendously powerful in showing how masculinist violence was a part of everyday life in slave societies recalling Fanon's conjectures that colonialism permanently maims the colonised. Closely reading this scene, Scott Loren argues that the visual artistry and poetic density of McQueen's work achieves the double meaning of the 'incongruities of natural beauty and social atrocities' beyond a melodramatic racial mix: 'What can be seen in the frame is no longer an opposition between society or culture (atrocity) and nature (beauty), but bodies in nature that appear to be beyond sense-making' (348). Violence is permanent in the transitory life of slaves – transitory not only in terms of being sold to different plantations but also of not having a life rooted to a family or a place. Saratoga is Northup's homeland, but he is repeatedly led to believe he is property and thus not free to exercise reason, intellect or will. He will be given the option to have a family and enjoy the semblance of human life, as we noticed about slaves in this sequence, but only on the condition of the fullest exploitation of his commoditised body. If he does not agree to the exploitation, or retorts with reason, he will instantly lose his 'humanity' and be reduced to an object that can be thrown out and broken down in public. This transient and migratory aspect is powerfully captured in the sequence, with his small figure set against the massiveness and the masculinity of the plantation.

The scene looking at Northup's contorted face from afar leads to my third and final point on his close-ups in the film. As Bass and Northup build a wooden house for Epps, Bass asks Northup about his story. Northup cannot believe Bass completely, as in the previous sequence his request to a white servant about posting a letter to New York was reported to Epps. But Bass's countering of Epps's arguments on property and the ills of slavery encourages Northup to tell his story and send the letter through him (1:44:22). After the story, the sequence takes us to a close-up of Northup's face. The afternoon sun falls on the left side of his head. A teary-eyed Solomon looks at the camera and then, turning away, breaks down and wails (1:59:02–2:00:21). The remarkable sequence, again without a background score, deeply expresses Northup's anxiety through his eyes about whether Bass can at all be trusted; whether he would write the letter; and whether at last he could be released. Rohter writes in his *New York Times* article that McQueen thought of Ejiofor because of his eyes, that he could express so much pathos and pity through those sharp and tender eyes – features that McQueen highlights throughout in his rendition of Northup; not a hero like the historic and rebellious Nat Turner, but a survivor, a believer that an opportune moment will arise to 'reclaim' his life ("It's Just How He Carries Himself").

But McQueen also made another important innovation at the end. As Alexander Parker comes from New York to save him, we see Patsey bidding Northup farewell. Northup looks back at her as she faints but cannot do anything. McQueen again provides a long close-up of his contented yet helpless face – a man who feels greatly for Patsey and her resistance. This goes back squarely to the scene of Northup's auctions when his fellow slave is saved from being sold to a plantation by a white owner, and all Northup could do is cry and call for help. This scene like most of McQueen's film, reminds us that slavery continued much after it was officially abolished (as Yaa Gyasi's novel *Homegoing* tellingly captures). That Northup could go back to his family is a rare example of escape. Most slaves would remain on the plantation suffering the tortures meted out to them by their masters. As McQueen said in an interview with Henry Gates Jr. 'Because the story goes on. And the thought I wanted them to leave with was what happened to Patsy and all the other millions of slaves' (Gates Jr.). By reclaiming intimacy, sexuality and pathos in the migratory slave life, McQueen put forth his anticolonial retrieval of 'humanity' in the film. But in allowing the film to be open-ended, he effectively asserted the Fanonian principle that colonialism and slavery did not end with the historical events of abolition and decolonisation. The latter are processes that the world would need to continue to resist.

PROFESSIONAL DIASPORA: ISLAM, POST-RACIAL AND RETURNEE MIGRANTS IN MOHSIN HAMID'S *THE RELUCTANT FUNDAMENTALIST* AND CHIMAMANDA NGOZIE ADICHIE'S *AMERICANAH*

In this section we move from the contemporary rendition of slavery to that of labour diaspora. While slavery was abolished by Britain and the USA in the early nineteenth century, between 1834 and 1914 two million people from Africa, Asia and the Pacific Islands were signed up to migrate as indentured labourers to different parts of the world to further global colonial capitalism (Akyeampong 168). From slave diasporas (Gilroy 36–37) to indentured labour migration, the diasporas of various groups are crucial elements in colonial and postcolonial studies. The diaspora, as scholars argue, has never existed as 'a discrete entity but rather as being formed out of a series of contradictory convergences of peoples, ideas, and even cultural orientations' (Quayson and Daswani 4). Meaning 'scattered across' in Greek due to Greek migration and colonisation, 'diaspora' came to primarily indicate Jewish exile from Israel and stretched its definitive meaning to include global indentured labour migrations post colonialisation, standing for elements of coercion, loss and displacement, and of nostalgia and reimagination of the homeland (Tölölyan 647–49). These different modern meanings of diaspora which arise from 'decentred or lateral connections' in modern times (Clifford 306) have given birth to what Sudesh Mishra calls 'diaspoetics' (7). In the postcolonial context, outside of slavery, diasporic studies gained prominence through Caribbean and Indian writings. As the world's largest diaspora, which was a direct consequence of European colonisation of Asian and African territories and migration of labour forces for production of commodities on a global scale, India provided some of the key examples of diaspora writing. Vijay Mishra writes about two diasporas in Indian writing: while V. S. Naipaul is the architect of the old Indian labour diaspora, Salman Rushdie, M. G. Vassanji and Rohinton Mistry carry forward the new diaspora for professional opportunity (421–22).

I would like to argue in this section that in the latter part of the twentieth and twenty-first centuries, this new diaspora has turned into a global diaspora (Cohen) shaped by the major forces of capitalism, colonialism and nationalism (Koshy and Radhakrishnan 3). Set between 'nation-states' and 'travelling cultures', these diasporas have given rise to the new concepts of transnationalism and transculturalism (Om P. Dwivedi in Bauböck and Faist 13–14). As we argued in the introduction to this chapter, in the post-Cold War period USA emerged as an economic and cultural superpower, taking over from Britain. Like Bharati Mukherjee, Jhumpa Lahiri, NoViolet Bulawayo or Gyasi, new diasporic authors migrated to the US for better opportunities to rewrite their 'slave' or colonial histories differently. However, these new writers have shown that unlike their two diaspora counterparts mentioned by Mishra previously, the protagonists in their works are not bound by filial or professional duties to remain in their host lands. Like their authors who shuttle between two or more nations, their protagonists can return to their homelands and live a comparably secure life thanks to multinational capitalism, thus enabling new imaginaries and routes for diaspora studies (Banerjee 10). I will explore in this section that, despite the rhetoric of cultural assimilation and racial and ethnic diversity, the old colonialist concept of social and cultural otherisation through the means of religion and race continue to haunt the diasporic subject of return. I give examples from two novels – British Pakistani author Mohsin Hamid's *The Reluctant Fundamentalist* (2007) and Nigerian author Chimamanda Ngozi Adichie's *Americanah* (2013) – to discuss the role of Islam and terror, and of the post-racial in the postcolonial context through the metaphors of head and facial hair. I will further argue that these texts broadly deploy a linear and progressive realist chronology of migration marked, however, by heterogeneous narrative forms to accommodate their protagonists' constant 'decolonising' anxieties of settlement and return.

For the Princeton-graduate, Pakistani immigrant Changez in Hamid's *The Reluctant Fundamentalist*, New York is a breath of fresh air: 'moving to New York felt so unexpectedly like coming home' (Hamid 18). Home is not necessarily Lahore and his conservative family for this mobile migrant, but a blurring of identity in multicultural and multinational New York where his skin colour and religious identity do not matter. Changez comments, 'in a subway car, my skin would typically fall in the middle of the colour spectrum . . . I was, in four and a half years, never an American, I was immediately a New Yorker' (18). He can find similar groups of people populating the transport systems of New York who do not give him unusual stares. At the same time, coming from New Jersey, he knows that this is not the 'real America'. New York is a hotchpotch of communities of which migrant workers are a key constituent. He falls in love with a batchmate Erica, the daughter of a top-ranking businessman in New York; gets a job at Underwood Samson, an elite multinational company; and feels like he is living the American dream, until 9/11 occurs and suddenly his Muslim identity comes to the fore, forcing him to go back to Lahore. Changez's flash-forwards to his interview with an unnamed American, which this novel is narratively composed of, are useful here as he can now offer a retrospective view of what worked for him and what he could not see ever existing there: that is, the sedimented thoughts arising from slavery, and years of the racialisation and religious otherisation of Islam.

Claire Chambers argues that since the issuing of the fatwa against Salman Rushdie by Ayatollah Khomeini for *The Satanic Verses* (1988), Islamophobia has entered Anglo-American discourses (Chambers xiv), transforming more recently into 'the focal point of anxieties about citizenship, loyalty, and liberal values' in an increasingly Islamophobic world (Morey 2). Changez experiences these anxieties in the post-9/11 context as his Muslim and 'Other' identities – his skin colour and physical composition – become a matter of constant questioning and uncomfortable stares (othering or foregrounding one's difference from the normative white racist experience and formation has been a key colonialist strategy). Changez goes from being, 'well-liked as an exotic acquaintance'

(Hamid 11) to being compared with a Filipino driver for his Third World background (34). After the 9/11 blast, which he watches on TV in a hotel in the Philippines, the othering is almost complete. An immediate realisation at the airport consolidates his feeling of isolation from the group: 'I was escorted by armed guards into a room where I was made to strip down to my boxer shorts . . . I was as a consequence, the last person to board the aircraft. My entrance elicited looks of concern from many of my fellow passengers' (36). His othering happens so fast that it betrays the hatred and prejudice deeply harboured in white, middle-class America for three centuries, expressed in racist laws and social and religious discriminations against blacks and Asians, the inheritors of a forced labour diaspora (recall *12 Years A Slave* here), which contemporary multinational capital and migration have barely managed to do away with. Here was Changez, a South Asian, Muslim other who was not welcome in white America any longer – a point corroborated in contemporary realpolitik by American President Donald Trump's blanket ban on citizens of seven Muslim-majority countries in West Asia from entering America in 2017 ("Trump's Executive Order").

While the role of religion has been noted, though belatedly, in postcolonial studies (Scott), Islam has received particular critical attention of late, especially in the context of the post-9/11 'war on terror'. Salman Sayyid argues that Islam suffers the 'double decolonization' of anticolonial struggles against (Christian) European colonial powers and the whitewashing of Muslim and non-western communities as racist, backward, patriarchal, and 'terroristic' – though it was European colonialism, and not Islamicate empires, which was based on racist and terroristic laws and practices (132–35). The concept of terror, marked by police torture and state violence, as Stephen Morton has shown, emerged in colonial emergency laws which did not count the colonised as human (based on prevalent scientific and religious discourses as we saw previously). While the US declared a war on terror after 9/11, terrorism was encouraged, supported and maintained by American capital (Lazarus and Gopal 8) and widely suppressed in media discourses until these discourses became necessary in order to unleash historical orientalist and religious prejudice against Arabs as barbaric, illiterate and irrational subjects needing to be civilised or terminated. Terror, thus, has become an important gateway for scholars to think through the question of Islam and its colonialist otherisation marked by rampant Islamophobia in post-imperial and postcolonial communities and spaces (Boehmer and Morton 6–12; Tolan, et al; Goyal, "The Genres of Guantánamo Diary" 69–87). Hamid's narrator makes us see how quickly racism and prejudice permeated white America after the traumatic events of 9/11. On one occasion Changez states, 'once I was walking to my rented car in the parking lot of the cable company, when I was approached by a man I did not know. He made a series of unintelligible noises akwalamalakha . . . and pressed his face alarmingly close to mine' (54). This racist verbal abuse is followed by a man shouting, 'fucking Arab' at him (54). While in the first incident Changez's South Asian brown identity induces racial hatred, the second instance suggests that it does not matter if he was an Arab. It does not matter if he was Muslim or not. All South Asian-looking men and women were now targets of hatred and bigotry by jingoist white Americans. Changez's identity is now displaced and merged into an overarching Arab identity, the archenemy of 'Americans' in post-9/11 New York. Although he tries to resist it, we realise that Changez now represents the other that is not exotic and desirable any longer, but threatening and evil; or because it is exotic, it is not of white America, it is un-American (Hartnell 338).

Sayyid further contends that in the war on terror, terror takes on a socio-somatic form: 'terror is incarnated in the bodies of Muslims, whose very appearance (both in terms of what they look like and that they are present) becomes problematic' (139). The violence over skin colour in the context of slavery has merged here with the historical racialisation of Islam. The novel, however, uses the socio-somatic as a mode of resistance to the 'race making' of the Islamic other. Since Changez was already stereotyped as an Arab and an Other, he decides to grow a beard, a sign of protest against the racism towards South Asian people. As he retrospectively notes, 'traveling on the subway – where I had always had the feeling of seamlessly blending in, I was subjected to verbal abuse by strangers' (Hamid 59). His old New York was now gone, and a crude and hateful America was emerging through the debris of the disaster. As he returns home to Lahore, an increasingly disconnected and isolated Changez fends off strange reactions from family. When his mother warns him to shave before leaving, he feels tremendously resistant to the global acceptance of the American hatred towards a Muslim identity – a hatred that Pakistanis were now swallowing without criticism on their part, recalling again Fanon's classic concept of the guilt and inferiority imposed upon the colonised by the coloniser (*Black Skin, White Masks* 177). His sharp unspoken response is: 'I had not shaved my two-week-old beard it was perhaps, a form of protest on my part a symbol of my identity, or perhaps I sought to remind myself of the reality I had just left behind' (59). Changez's beard, thus, becomes a corporeal and trusted mode of symbolic protest and discursive resistance in 'postcolonial' America and Pakistan. As he becomes popular amongst university students for his radical thoughts and America sends forth search parties to dig out Osama bin Laden, Changez's bearded face invites a comparison with Bin Laden in this interview and the narrative – a comparability that is as absurd as the second person narrative is clever, which I will discuss soon.

Unlike Changez, Ifemelu in Adichie's *Americanah* does not find America suitable to live in and after graduating from university decides to go back to her home country, Nigeria. Begun with flash-forwards, Adichie slowly unfolds the various experiences of racism and gender violence that Ifemelu undergoes in America, similar to our discussion in the previous chapter on Jackie Kay's poetry. Like Hamid, the socio-somatic – that is, hair – becomes both a context for racism in 'post-racial' America and a symbol for Ifemelu's anti-racist protest for Adichie. In the first months after arriving from Nigeria, Ifemelu looks for an economy salon in Trenton. Although within a few kilometres from the upper-middle-class Princeton, New Jersey (where she studies, like Changez), Trenton is a black-majority, working-class area full of government-funded and built social housing for the poor, cracked main roads, dirty streets and 'fat', 'old' men and women waiting at the train station (Adichie 3). In the salon, Ifemelu is treated with curiosity as she wants to keep her hair as it is. She is told that for Africans and African immigrants who run this salon and most other salons in the area, to live and earn in the USA means learning to adapt to the local accent and to the lifestyle and beauty standards in vogue. Ifemelu's hair is a class and race anomaly and needs to be straightened or braided. Later in the novel, Ifemelu witnesses that a white girl is given very different treatment with a majority of white cultural referents in conversation with hairdressers (232). For the Nigerian Ifemelu, this is strange as she soon realises the racialised makeover of her aunt and the moral hypocrisy of her white liberal friends. As Marina Vlahaki argues, these salon conversations and scenes expose 'how colonial and Eurocentric assumptions persist in daily encounters between people of different cultural and racial backgrounds . . . which makes it difficult to establish a two-way conversation and to navigate the space freely' (113).

It is through hair that Adichie indicates the problematics of post-racial America. 'Post-racial' is often used to indicate the period after Barack Obama's 2009 election as the first 'black' president of USA, suggesting that race was less of an obstacle to progress now than it was historically. Race and postcolonial studies scholars such as Brett St Louis, Gilroy and David Theo Goldberg, among others, have variously argued that race was scientifically, ethically and politically 'a false, dangerous and consequently indefensible category' (Paul 703). Reading through their arguments, Joshua Paul contends that 'Post-racialism(s) advocate(s) the excising of race as a necessary political step to (re-)empower anti-racism and to end the cyclical (re) production of race – a prerequisite for racism. Activism, freed from the naturalistic predicates and dubious explanatory frameworks of race, will be able to more effectively battle culturalist racisms' (704). Adichie's 'progressive' novel, however, shows that race and racism, whose life histories manifested most brutally in chattel slavery, are deeply ingrained in the American psyche, whether white, black or Asian. The conversations and different treatments of white and black customers showcase the challenges of a post-racial America – challenges that activists and academics like Kalwant Bhopal, Robin DiAngelo and Karen D. Pyke have variously called out by the use of terms such as 'white privilege', 'white fragility' and 'internalised racism'. Probably, the most significant challenge comes in the novel through the concept of hair in constructing Western ideals of beauty, which proves particularly harmful for African and Asian female immigrants. In the salon, Ifemelu finds beauty magazines in which 'three black women (are shown) in maybe two thousand pages of women's magazines . . . (n)ot one of them is dark' (295). The suggestion here is: if beauty magazines are known for showcasing feminine and beautiful women, they do so by conspicuously making them white and taking out the black and dark-skinned ones. Black is understood to be not as beautiful as white. This is not only true for Ifemelu but is a practice that is rampant in the postcolonial world where beauty standards must follow a white face or whitened face of a brown woman (Hunter; Gill).

Alfred Lopez has demonstrated how whiteness and white ideals borrowed from slavery and colonialist cultures and practices have continued to shape postcolonial lives (13–18). Like several resisting discourses of black as beautiful, this incident of Ifemelu's encounter with the magazine is not only a symbolic protest by Adichie but also a stark reminder that whitening skin colour and straightening hair can seriously harm the body; processes which immigrants are ready to undertake, in their desperate attempt to assimilate in the host land and be part of the ideal order. This point is evidenced in the scene with Ifemelu, in which the African hairstylist comments, 'Just a little burn . . . [b]ut look how pretty it is . . . you've got the white-girl swing!' (Adichie 203). That Ifemelu is asked to undertake the tragic burning of parts of her body in order to attain the ideal standard of beauty (which she knew she would anyway never be able to achieve because of her skin colour) forms the core of her emotional distress and her postcolonial self, configured to imitate the standards set by her colonising and neoliberal masters. Dina Yerima states in a reading of the novel that '[t]his adoption of imperial notions of beauty is rooted in self-loathing' which she links to the historical trauma of colonisation (Yerima 639). This colonial masterstroke of 'internalised racism' towards the postcolonial self's own features is clearly portrayed in Ifemelu's reaction to her natural hair – 'I look so ugly I'm scared of myself' – and Aunty Uju who states that '[t]here is something scruffy and untidy about natural hair' (Adichie 208; 216). That black is beautiful; that one can proudly declare and 'wear' one's identity is not allowed in this colonialist, post-slavery world of beauty standards and subject formation. Multiculturalism and multiracialism are acceptable as long as every culture is made to follow white standards of beauty, conduct, and culture.

Like Changez who decided to return to Lahore after the hostility he encounters post-9/11, Ifemelu also feels she should leave America: 'Nigeria became where she was supposed to be, the only place she could sink her roots in without the constant urge to tug them and shake off the soil' (11). This comfortable feeling, however, changes soon after her return: 'She had the dizzying sensation of falling, falling into the new person she had become, falling into the strange familiar. Had it always been like this or had it changed so much in her absence?' (385). Here is another important trope that both the novels implement, making us wonder about this new migrant and diasporic identity in a globalised world who does not need to settle in the imperial metropolis and can come back to and leave their postcolonial or post-Communist metropolises (Tsuda). Drawing upon Kwame Anthony Appiah, Maximilian Feldner identifies this as Ifemelu's 'rooted cosmopolitanism' (Feldner 197). At the same time, this constant shuttling also makes Ifemelu feel – what Adichie pointedly captures – as the 'strange familiar'. Like Changez's parents and relatives who feel a strange unease with his return, Ifemelu's parents are also concerned if she will be able to cope in Nigeria since America has irrevocably altered her. These instances serve to suggest for our discussion that although migrants can travel between countries now, the impact of never being able to cope anywhere because of the radical transformation of their selves in more progressive pockets of the 'First World' is real and dangerous; something which Changez and Ifemelu will have to negotiate (Galipo; Quayson and Daswani 172–189).

The decolonising anxieties of negotiation and cooperation have a commanding role in the way these narratives are constructed; which bring us to our final thoughts on the section. Consider the beginning of *The Reluctant Fundamentalist*, for instance:

> Excuse me, sir, but may I be of assistance? Ah, I see I have alarmed you. Do not be frightened by my beard: I am a lover of America. I noticed that you were looking for something; more than looking, in fact you seemed to be on a mission,

and since I am both a native of this city and a speaker of your language, I thought I might offer you my services. (Hamid 2) Here is a second person narrator–protagonist who is full of humour, irony and caustic satire commanding confidence in his narrative and making the interviewer feel that this is a dialogue in which the interviewer's questions will appear similar to orthodox (Western) media commentary on the issue. In another reading, this may mean – as Mike Marais argues – that by precluding knowledge about the stranger, the narrator 'safeguards the stranger's strangeness', allowing 'the reader to render him proximate' (91–92). Both for Marais and Mandala White (446), Hamid's use of the narrative properties of uncertainty, allegory and frame-narrative situates and punctures his realist fiction; Hamid himself considers his novel a combination of non-real formal structure and realist narrative (Singh 155). That his narrative begins retrospectively in Lahore indicates that these are memories and can be insidious, and that such a perspective is only possible after a profound realisation, as his life's journey has shown. At the same time, the narrative assumptions and uncertainties also make us think about how far his experience can be believed. Why does Hamid set up such a narrative then? Probably because, as White argues through allegory, it is not Changez's fault that he was abused and forced to leave his dream world. He is a casualty of the Anglo-American (neo)colonialist and neo-conservative media narrative around a Muslim subject as an enabler of terrorism; around Islam propagating hatred and radicalisation; and around the role of the true American patriot being that of ridding society of the other (White 453–55). If lives are in danger because of the polarised representation of Muslim identities in the media, how do we make certain what truth is and what it is not? Hamid's frame-narrative, inventive prose and figurative techniques (such as that of the facial hair trope), which Nazry Bahrawi calls his 'novel strategies', serve to remind us that certain truths are constructed, and thus we will have to find for ourselves which one to follow in a post-truth world (270–73).

Adichie also mobilises a linear realist narrative to understand and capture the actual cases of discrimination and prejudice that dominate white America. However, she also uses a heterogeneous set of narrative techniques to reinforce the constructed element of truth such as the use of a blog, which serves as a counter-narrative to mediatised truth claims. For instance, in the blog entry 'To My Fellow Non-American Blacks: In America, You Are Black, Baby', Ifemelu adds,

> Dear Non-American Black, when you make the choice to come to America, you become black. Stop arguing. Stop saying I'm Jamaican or I'm Ghanaian. America doesn't care. So what if you weren't "black" in your country? You're in America now. We all have our moments of initiation into the Society of Former Negroes. Mine was in a class in undergrad when I was asked to give the black perspective, only I had no idea what that was. So I just made something up. And admit it—you say "I'm not black" only because you know black is at the bottom of America's race ladder. And you want none of that. (220)

These are powerful messages about the post-slavery, colonialist racialisation of bodies in the (former) colonial-imperial metropolis. Narratively speaking, most of these blogs (like Changez's interview) are in second person and full of humour and irony. They are informative and analytical, combined with instructive and accessible prose, leading to widespread engagement and popularity (Isaacs 178–82). By using blogs in the middle of narrative prose, Adichie makes the point that many of our everyday narratives and truths are now controlled and filtered through social and new media. In order to reclaim the voice of the suppressed migrant, it is important to take cognisance of the various alternative archives of digital spaces, sound and music other than those of text and interpretation (Appadurai 561). If mainstream media has fostered standardised opinions of beauty and encouraged discrimination, social media and the blogosphere have allowed for a feminist and emancipatory potential to write about personal and community injustice and to instruct and educate a wider population, as Christine Cruz-Gutiérrez (67–68) and Fiona Darroch (143) argue.

This goes back to the question of neo-diaspora, or 'digital diasporas' (Ponzanesi) heralding that narratives will have to be hybrid yet retain narrative emotions and conventional storytelling techniques in this age of information.[2] Caroline Levine points out that by creating a sense of realist defamiliarisation through these blogs, Adichie shows that race needs to be talked about in a straightforward and plain manner rather than through a challenging and destabilising narrative of modernist nuances (594–95). We are certainly not in a post-racial world. Race, following slavery, imposed a painful order in the US, and people need relatable and palpable stories to hear and see in order to counter this grand narrative. Adichie both retains the narrative elements through her realist prose and stretches narrative elasticity to bring contemporary means of storytelling within it, through social and new media. What characterise Hamid's second person interview style and Adichie's blog techniques are the notions of mobility and diaspora – something that McQueen's cinematic adaptation of an earlier narrative form adequately responds to. That, in a world of statistics, theory and ready-made marketisation of beauty and terror, postcolonial stories need to travel across time and space to evoke a comprehensive and inclusive way of narrating a comparative history and furthering the call for global justice through their decolonising tactics.

FORCED MIGRATION, REFUGEES AND POSTCOLONIAL MEMORY: THI BUI'S *THE BEST WE COULD DO*

The concept of rights and justice is probably most robustly present in the case of forced migration in the contemporary moment. Indeed, in the inaugural editorial of *Diaspora*, Tölölian claimed that the term diaspora 'now shares meanings with a larger semantic domain', which includes 'immigrant, expatriate, refugee, guest-worker' (4). Following this vein, Caren Kaplan argued for 'historicizing the refugee experience . . . through the inclusive mantle of the term "diaspora"' (121). While these observations appropriately point to the double elements of displacement and nostalgia associated with the term diaspora, the 'hierarches of mobility' within postcolonial studies cannot be ignored, as David Farrier usefully cautions us. For Farrier, the 'convivial cosmopolitanism' that is often understood to be a part of postcolonial migratory culture, too readily includes the displaced who often desire the opposite: territorial sovereignty, citizenship and rights (4). Agnes Woolley follows Farrier in arguing that refugees and asylum seekers cannot afford to participate in a postcolonial cosmopolitan community of marginality, contending the existence of 'domineering narratives' in civic society: 'when it is that very society that has the power to legitimate their presence' (15). Indeed, the ambiguous and ambivalent ties of migrants with their home nations that Rushdie or Bhabha echo in the introduction to this chapter, or that Changez and Ifemelu practice, may not be viable for refugees and asylum seekers because 'to admit the continuance of such ties to a home nation is potentially to jeopardize the success of the asylum claim, which requires that the individual be unable to return home' (17). The problems of legitimation and failed asylum (creating illegal subjectivities) also contest, Woolley continues (16), any notion of ethnic homogeneity or 'culturally determined solidarities' for the displaced (Gikandi 26). Like the enslaved in slave-narratives, refugees are compelled to speak of their experiences in a linear, progressive and bureaucratic fashion that is acceptable to the nation-state in which they are seeking refuge, in order to establish the authenticity of their claims. For Woolley, as for Farrier, fictionalised narratives appear in this context as 'a site of contestation which offers alternative, non-coercive, narrative forums in which to explore the condition of statelessness' (20). This section will critically engage with the complex questions of forced migration, displacement and narrative in refugee crises through the historical antecedents of slavery and colonialism that are embedded within it. It will read a Vietnamese-American graphic novel to further argue why refugee writers have often used the graphic novel form to convey their harrowing experiences of suffering, shame and sanctuary, as well as resistance and narrative justice.

'Refugee' as a term goes back to seventeenth-century France when the Protestants fled France after the revocation of the Edict of Nantes, which had granted them religious liberty and civil rights (OED). Hannah Arendt tells us that the massive refugee influx in the aftermath of the Second World War was a 'great shock' for Europeans as the two remedies of repatriation and naturalisation had not worked for the uncountable 'stateless' people (Arendt 281–83). So wide and deep was human displacement globally, added to by decolonisation and the ensuing civil wars in ex-colonised territories, that soon the United Nations Conventions Relating to the Status of Refugees (1951) was established. The Refugee

Convention defined a 'refugee' as a person who had a 'well-founded fear of being persecuted for reasons of race, religion, nationality, membership of a particular social group, or political opinion' (qtd. in Cox et al. 8). But as Aimé Césaire acidly cautioned in *Discourse on Colonialism* (1950), the racial purity demanded by Hitler and Nazism was engineered in the colonies through scientific discourses of racism and implemented through the unimaginable use of violence, stripping citizen–subjects of their rights and duties to life and place of birth (Césaire 3–4). The unprecedented and 'morally justified' use of violence to repress the subjects of the colonised world then enables the decolonised subject–ruler, who is inevitably the elite that profited from colonialism, to retain power and governance through violence in the postcolonial period. Achangkeng Fonkem notes in the African and Middle Eastern context,

> Political repression in postcolonial settings of Africa and the Middle East goes back to the colonial rule and its legacy. Colonial rule was the antithesis of democracy, because it was premised on the usurpation of the fundamental right of self-determination . . . Colonial rule never raised the issue of good government. The only issue was power and that remained the tradition of politics the new leaders in Africa and the Middle East took to independence in their respective nations. (56–57)

These new leaders not only retained state power but also continued to reinforce it through authoritarian and violent means leading to conflicts, refugees and forced migration. Fonkem gives the example of the Assad family in Syria and the many years of civil war in that country that led to a wide refugee crisis in the Middle East and Europe. On the other hand, in the Global South (mostly in oil generating countries in the Middle East and East Africa) the post-war postcolonial period saw a sharp scramble for power between the USA and the USSR, known largely as the Cold War. What is understood as terrorism and the 'war on terror', historically goes back to the contexts/doctrines of colonialism, imperialism and neocolonial resource extractivism which mainstream literary and arts media in (neo)imperialist countries have ideologically kept hidden from their population. This contributed to an otherisation and exoticisation of the colonised subject (which we noted in

Hamid's *The Reluctant Fundamentalist*) in, what Derek Gregory appropriately calls, 'the colonial present' (17; see also Khalidi). Indeed, the complex condition of the refugee or asylum-seeking does not end after being granted refuge. Refugees and asylum seekers are kept under surveillance either by the state or by civil society, courting endless detentions and a persistent feeling of second-class citizenship (Einashe). What these observations suggest is that while colonialism and neocolonialism played a key role in forcing citizen-subjects into becoming refugees and asylum seekers in foreign lands, the refugees' different nomenclatures and physical compositions (from the normalised 'white' in white majority/Euro-American nations granting refuge) prevent them from becoming 'insiders enough' (Hilario, et al. 213, 216; Ferracioli 202).

This is an important point for our discussion of refugee representation in postcolonial arts and literature – that refugee and forced migration, colonially bred, are as much a problem during the crisis of seeking refuge as it is after settlement in a new country. Such a complex and *longue durée* condition of life and living puts particular pressure on the narrative forms and styles of representing asylum. Like Woolley, who considers narrative a site of contestation for an alternative genealogy and value of truth for refugees, Anna Bernard also finds that approaching refugee writing through the prism of genre and literary craft asks us to go beyond the bureaucratic impulse of overt politics and didactic messaging in the works and welcome literature as a site where competing claims 'might be received with openness rather than suspicion, and the reader might be willing to act as an ally rather than a judge' (67). These resonate with Claire Gallien's prescient argument that postcolonial studies is uniquely placed to talk about the refugee crisis not only because of its colonial roots but also because of the urgent need to respond to 'politically, ethically, and ideologically problematic modes of representation of forcibly displaced people' (721). For Gallien, there is a 'narrativizing imperative' in refugee literature, as if refugees were obliged to be testimonial in their discourse and speak coherently about their violent experiences. While the novel, as Lyndsey Stonebridge contends, is the premier medium through which the bourgeois values of democracy, rights and justice were enshrined in European writing, the violence of decolonisation and postcolonial dictatorships created urgent pressures on these discourses, breaking open possibilities within the genre of the novel (Stonebridge 26, 38–39). Recently, the graphic novel form has been widely used to address refugee rights and discourses in the post-colony (Nayar). The graphic novel, to follow Bernard, is marked by a 'synthesis of visual and narrative conventions for representing the figure of the refugee, and [a] reliance on the quest narrative, which both endorses and interrogates the idea of the refugees' ultimate redemption as a citizen of the host country' (67). Postcolonial scholars have widely explored the 'refugee subject' in the graphic novels of Art Spiegelman, Joe Sacco, Marjane Satrapi and Leila Abdelrazaq, among others, from the Middle East, Africa and South Asia, and raised the urgent question of the representation of trauma – which is otherwise largely understood, via Holocaust studies, as 'unrepresentable' – through the palpability of word and image (Mehta and Mukherji; Knowles; Davies and Rifkind 8), to which we will resort in the next chapter on 'Traumas'. I want to shift the narrative to Southeast Asia and the French-Vietnamese anticolonial war which led to the US-Vietnam War in the late 1960s, making it clear that imperialism was far from over. This example also offers a chance for us to note how the colonising powers of Europe and America worked within an imperial world-system to implement comparable practices and discourses in the colonised world. We will see in this work that Thi Bui offers a portrayal of three generations of rooted/migrant life and diasporic subjectivity to showcase how her family went from being Vietnamese citizens to refugees in offshore camps; then from refugees to immigrants in the US; and then from immigrants to naturalised citizens, interrogating the anticolonial notion of citizenship and the right to land as we noted in the previous chapter on minorities. My discussion of the novel will be based on two key features: its rendering of the colonial historicity of forced migration, and its artistic representation of the refugee condition through faded colours and panels which I will argue is Bui's decolonising agenda.

Born in Vietnam three months before the end of the Vietnam War in 1975, Bui migrated to the United States in 1978 as part of the historic 'boat people' wave of refugees from Vietnam and Southeast Asia (Vo). As she writes in her 'Preface', Bui began working on the novel in 2002 during her graduate programme, which included an assignment on oral history in which she transcribed the journeys of her own family. Part of a new wave of American-Vietnamese autobiographical narratives, such as G. B. Tran's comic *Vietanamerica* (2010) and Viet Thanh Nguyen's novel, *The Sympathizer* (2016), Bui's 'Illustrated Memoir' – or what Gillian Whitlock calls 'autographics' (84) – follows a non-linear format in which Bui's giving birth resonates with her mother's painful birthing of her brother in a refugee camp. Bui, thus, often creates a dissonant yet connected temporality for her historical narrative. In the middle of the memoir, we come across a couple of panels detailing the Vietnam War, from its anticolonial struggle against the French during the Second World War to the Fall of Saigon and the mass migration of Vietnamese people from the South to neighboring countries like Cambodia and Malaysia, and to the USA. Bui uses here what Sally McWilliams calls a 'cotemporal parallel' to exhort her readers to imagine how their family's personal journeys were, in essence, the traumatic and collective journeys of the nation. As Bui grows up in San Diego, she frequently faces racist attacks from her peers. In one of these episodes, white American children hurl a racial slur at her and spit at her father's cheek. Bui shows that the spit takes the shape of the Vietnam peninsula (67). Through this imagery, Bui – as delineated by Sayyid's theory on terror's psychosomatic impact in Hamid's use of facial hair in his novel – conjures the double alienation and trauma of losing one's homeland and continuing to be racialised in the host land. As McWilliams continues, 'The memoir creates a cotemporal parallel between the moribund fatigue of slow death experienced by the first-generation Vietnamese refugees in their attempts to assimilate to U.S. liberal society's racialized taxonomy and the lingering shadow of slow death in their children's lives' (323).

Like McQueen, Adichie or Hamid, who suggest that racism is never over in the postcolonial world, Bui writes to counter the domineering colonialist narratives of the American presence in Vietnam as beneficial, heroic and masculine. The war was probably over for Americans in 1975, but it continued to rage in diasporic and refugee life through memories and intergenerational trauma, largely excluded from dominant western representations of the war. Thus, in revisiting the 'event trauma' of the forced exodus, Bui cannot abandon the 'insidious trauma' of everyday life that her family has inhabited, intergenerationally reconstructing the very notion of family itself (Brown 197). Bui's poignant reminder is, 'family is now something I have created and not just something I was born into' (21). The question of a constructed sense of family and intimacy directly echoes McQueen's thematic innovations in *12 Years A Slave* giving Northup and Patsey the warmth of humanity and dignity which, I argued through Fanon, is a decolonising tactic for postcolonial art. Echoing these suggestions, Stella Oh writes that Bui's narrative 'illustrates intimate memories of women and families often disregarded as unimportant and recuperates these memories, affirming their importance in understanding history and cultural identities shaped by such exclusions' (77). Family, nation and memory are, thus, strategically used to build and recuperate the anticolonial and anti-imperialist historicity of the memoir.

The juxtaposition of temporalities through different media has been discussed widely in comics and graphic novels (Kukkonen; Baroni). What Bui particularly adds here is to both write an intimate history of her family and fictionalise this history through a 'bildung' that is as linear as it is frozen in time (P. Williams 9–10). Such a strategy offers a different understanding of diasporic subjectivity that is suspended between a nostalgic yet disconnected homeland and the 'historylessness' of an adopted host land. The strategy is best represented in the sequence where Bui visits Vietnam with her parents – their ancestral street; their relatives and neighbors – and gathers data for research. She soon realises the pathos and pity in the lives of her parents who continue to hold their Vietnamese/homeland traditions close in America and yet know that they cannot return to the abandoned land; that they would not fit in, that the memories are too traumatising and disorienting for them (Bui 180–181). In a similar yet markedly different suggestion from Adichie and Hamid, Bui shows that even a first generation, displaced migrant finds the homeland unaccommodating. Cultural critic Lan Duong writes that the cotemporality of time and space for Vietnamese refugees in America dispels the myth that diaspora is singularly about the diasporic migrants' feeling of exile, affect, and nostalgia (3). It may rather be the everyday challenges of memorialising place and relations in a homeland that once was and the new social and cognitive relations that the host land offers, making it difficult for later generations to envision the *longue durée* of trauma emotionally and aesthetically, or feel the ethical urgency to do so.

Viet Thanh Nguyen writes about the role of memory in the Vietnam War; that 'all wars are fought twice, the first time on the battlefield, the second time in memory' (4). In order to represent the double historicity of war and memory, Bui makes a strategic use of colour and style, which is her decolonising aesthetic. Throughout the novel, Bui uses a faded saffron colour alongside black and white. The faded saffron adds a sepia sense to the narrative, that she is talking of a past which is not very far away. This is directly taken from photographic art. 'Photographs', Marianne Hirsch writes, 'are precisely the medium connecting first and second-generation remembrance, memory and postmemory . . . They affirm the past's existence and, in their flat two-dimensionality, they signal its unbridgeable distance' (Hirsch 23). It is also through the use of photography that, Elisabeth El Refaie writes, the documented and 'authentic' trials of refugees are persuasively presented in graphic novels (158). But graphic art uses spaces differently; through gaps, gutters, voices, erasures and interruptions (Chute 17). Drawing upon it, Candida Rifkind adds, 'This faith in comics' ability to represent the unimaginable, even the seemingly unrepresentable, fits with many recent refugee and migrant comics projects that use the form to interrupt static media images with the plenitude, fragmentation, and unruliness of the comic's page' (649).

These scholarly observations come alive in Bui's rendering of historical details about the Vietnam War, merged in two pages full of scribbles against cartoons characters which resembles a notebook entry. This act, much like Adichie's use of blogs in *Americanah*, indicates the actual and painstaking scholarly journey of digging out notes from buried sources in libraries and archives and furnishing them with the task of synthesising and making meaning for her art. This style, which is clearly about situating the author's narratorial consciousness or 'positionality' (following Lazarus in the first chapter), is important for the narrative. She could have used this narrative widely in the first half of the story which is about her parents' life in Vietnam instead. However, she chooses to set it up together in quick succession because this part is important as historical background for readers. But the war actively shapes their family lives too. So, the information cannot be entirely in the background. It needs to have its own substantive agential presence. Bui thus offers a unifying narrative of a thirty-year-old struggle against war and colonialism in these pages, suggesting that these events are so massive in their impact that they will continue to reappear in glimpses throughout the narrative. She also uses a different colour to describe their escape from the war and the journey of her parents on the sea. In a panel, we see her describing the refugees as ants who are crawling underneath the ground as a huge hand is about to fall on them. In another panel, she shows the worried faces of her mother and siblings huddled in the narrow space of a boat on the sea as her father counts the tides. Here, Bui uses black and white and sharp facial expressions which serve to suggest the refugees' existential anxiety and the will to live. This black and white is contrasted with the sepia and black of Bui's imagining of the sea, as all of these are now memories to be reconstructed with faithfulness and empathy. These are then followed by their refugee or ID photos (taken when they entered the country) juxtaposed with painted photos of the family which showcase their continuous anxiety and exhaustion with the process of migration; of losing members and feeling insecure for their future (Bui, 236-238, 267). This creates, what Eyal Weizmann calls, a 'forensic aesthetic' of tracing refugee subjectivity through the photography of human remains, or what is left embodied in the world of loss (qtd. in Viljoen 12–13).

This narrative style has echoes of the 'plain talk' about racism in Adichie's blogs, or of the zooming in and out technique in McQueen's film to suggest the slow and long-term violence of slavery. Although the contexts of slavery, professional migration and refugee migration are categorically different, these artistic comparabilities (or 'analogies', according to Goyal) point to the fact that these episodes are part of the metanarrative of colonialist violence. Hence, their contemporary artistic treatment warrants a resonance with narratorial consciousness and the building of a decolonising agenda in order to re-humanise the dispossessed body.

So, for instance, in the episode where Bui contrasts the protest campaigns against the Vietnam War in America with the killing campaigns in Vietnam, the panels are strategically implemented. The sequence begins with a close-up of the contorted face of a political leader in Vietnam. This panel is then juxtaposed with that of young American men and women sloganeering and offering roses to stern looking soldiers. The same panel then offers an elongated frame of the close-up of the political leader who is about to be assassinated. Here, the writing captures how the Saigon Execution made anti-war sentiments popular but adds the crucial sentiment that 'I think a lot of Americans forgot that for the Vietnamese, the war continued whether America was involved or not' (Bui 209). It is through such panels that Bui makes a narrative critique of America's colonial–imperialist involvement in the war through military and civic means. As Harriet Earle shows through a reading of films and comics about the war, the world hardly knew of what was happening in Vietnam other than narratives that were filtered through American media. Discourses of racial discrimination or empathy were constructed by the hugely popular global American media, which completely forgot to hear or see the Vietnamese voice (89–90, 99–101). The American representation of Vietnam is so deeply entrenched in war that it disregards all complexities and nuances: As sociologist Karin Aguilar-San Juan writes, 'If they want to be seen and acknowledged as anything other than ghosts of war, Vietnamese Americans have no choice but to counter with their own strategic memory narratives' (San Juan 128–29).

Bui is among a handful of artists and writers who have begun to question not only the historic reasons of colonialism and US imperialist involvement in Vietnam, but also the deeply damaging impact of being refugees in a host country that has systematically taught its citizen–subjects to never trust and instead hate different-looking people, black or Asian. The continuous marginalisation of refugees, immigrants and citizen–subjects in America, whose imperialist intentions in the post-war period were understood as the fulcrum of postcolonial studies by Ashcroft et al., thus gives us the unique opportunity to understand migration and colonialism through the arguments raised here. This includes how colonialism and neo-imperialism have 'produced' refugees; turned them away;

and when these refugees have been embraced, ensured that they have been reminded that they are the other who would hardly be able to save themselves from the wrath of a white (majoritarian) supremacy, regardless of whether they were immigrant or citizen. Here, Bui's graphic novel achieves the decolonising act of retrieving suppressed histories and carries out the ethical role of 'witnessing' through its complex narration of family and history, its strategic use of photography and panels, and its ethico-political and aesthetic demand on the reader to feel the everyday trauma of a not-so-far-away violent past along with the author. Together, these have managed to produce what Sidonie Smith calls a rehearsal of 'a form of rescue of the other' through 'alternative engagements of witnessing, memory, loss, and recovery in graphic form' (66).

While refugee and forced migrations bring back the political and aesthetic contours of slavery and slave narratives that Goyal insightfully captures in *Runaway Genres*, I would like to conclude the chapter by noting that slavery has continued in modern times through other forms such as human, organ and sex trafficking, or stringent labour laws where, in the name of work and obligation, workers' visas and passports are seized, preventing them from going home, and taking sick leave or getting decent wages (Kara). McQueen's *12 Years A Slave* thus finds popular and critical resonance in the modern world, as does Bui's memoir. What is obvious in these literary–artistic examples is that colonialism is certainly not over. There may have been an official end to it through political independence, but as long as (neocolonial) capitalism remains the key method through which to achieve growth and development in the postcolonial world, or as long as Indigenous peoples, tribals, Dalits and ethnic minorities are understood to be obstacles to 'progress' narratives, the demonisation of the migrant will continue. In this demonising climate, the emigrés who can choose to go back to their homelands, such as Hamid's Changez and Adichie's Ifemelu, are not spared either. While they could go back, in the current discourse of hostility against migrants (Goodfellow), they will never know if they are going to be banned from travelling to their own countries in the name of the 'war on terror' and national security. Migration, thus, offers a compelling prism through which to understand the persistence of colonialism. It forces an equivalent narrative form to emerge in the literary–artistic work that can capture the elasticity of colonialism and the decolonising tactics of re-humanising the dispossessed. Thus, the neo-slavery narrative of close-ups finds resonance in the refugee narrative that uses panels and photography, thereby building the logic of critical awareness and social justice in narratives which together offer a migration-for-profession narrative of postcolonial othering an aesthetic arc that it can either draw from or fracture.

NOTES

1. In this context, see Priyamvada Gopal's *Insurgent Empire. Anticolonial Resistance and British Dissent*.

2. Remember how the forms of slave narrative and McQueen's neo-slavery cinema had to offer a convincing case for social justice and critical awareness. One can look for comparative techniques in the section on refugee representation.

REFERENCES

12 Years A Slave. Directed by Steve McQueen, Regency Enterprises, 2013.

Adichie, Chimamanda Ngozi. *Americanah*. 4th Estate, 2013.

Akyeampong, Emmanuel. "Slavery, Indentured Labour, and the Making of a Transnational World". *A Companion to Diaspora and Transnationalism*, edited by Ato Quayson and Girish Daswani, Wiley-Blackwell, 2013, pp. 163–71.

Appadurai, Arjun. "Traumatic Exit, Identity Narratives, and the Ethics of Hospitality". *Television and New Media*, vol 20, no. 6, 2019, pp. 558–65.

Arendt, Hannah. *The Origins of Totalitarianism*. 1958. Harcourt Brace Jovanovich, 1979.

Armstrong, Tim. "Slavery and American Literature 1900-1945". *The Cambridge Companion to Slavery in American Literature*, edited by Ezra Tawil, Cambridge UP, 201, pp. 204–218.

Ashcroft, Bill, et al., editors. *The Empire Writes Back: Theory and Practice in Post-colonial Literature*. Routledge, 1989.

Bahrawi, Nazry. "Mohsin Hamid's War on Error: *The Reluctant Fundamentalist* as a Post-Truth Novel". *CounterText*, vol. 4, no. 2, 2018, pp. 256–80.

Bailyn, Bernard. *The Barbarous Years: The Peopling of British North America – The Conflict of Civilizations, 1600–1675*. Vintage, 2013.

Banerjee, Sukanya. "Introduction: Routing Diasporas". *New Routes for Diaspora Studies*, edited by Sukanya Banerjee, et al., Indiana UP, 2012, pp. 9–17.

Baroni, Raphaël. "(Un)natural Temporalities in Comics". *European Comic Art*, vol. 9, no. 1, 2016, pp. 5–23.

Bauböck, Rainer, and Thomas Faist, editors. *Diaspora and Transnationalism: Concepts, Theories and Methods*, Amsterdam UP, 2010.

Bernard, Anna. "Genres of Refugee Writing". *Refugee Imaginaries: Research Across the Humanities*, edited by Emma Cox, et al., Edinburgh UP, 2020, pp. 65–80.

Bhabha, Homi K. *The Location of Culture*. Routledge, 1994.

Bhambra, Gurminder K. "The Current Crisis of Europe: Refugees, Colonialism, and the Limits of Cosmopolitanism". *European Law Journal*, vol. 23, no. 5, 2017, pp. 395–405.

Bhopal, Kalwant. *White Privilege: The Myth of a Post-Racial Society*. Policy Press, 2018.

Boehmer, Elleke, and Stephen Morton. *Terror and the Postcolonial*. Blackwell, 2010.

Bui, Thi. *The Best We Could Do: An Illustrated Memoir*. Abrams Books, 2017.

Carby, Hazel V. *Reconstructing Womanhood: The Emergence of the Afro-American Woman Novelist*. Oxford UP, 1987.

Césaire, Aimé. *Discourse on Colonialism*. Translated by Joan Pinkham, Monthly Review Press, 1973.

Chambers, Claire. *Making Sense of Contemporary British Muslim Novels*. Palgrave Macmillan, 2019.

Chute, Hillary L. *Disaster Drawn: Visual Witness, Comics, and Documentary Form*. Belknap Press, 2016.

Clifford, James. "Diasporas". *Cultural Anthropology*, vol. 9, no. 3, 1994, pp. 302–38.

Cohen, Robin. *Global Diasporas: An Introduction*. Routledge, 2008.

Cruz-Gutiérrez, Cristina. "Hair Politics in the Blogosphere: Safe Spaces and the Politics of Self-representation in Chimamanda Adichie's *Americanah*". *Journal of Postcolonial Writing*, vol. 55, no. 1, 2019, pp. 66–79.

Darroch, Fiona. "Journeys of Becoming: Hair, Blogosphere and Theopoetics in Chimamanda Ngozi Adichie's *Americanah*". *Text Matters*, vol. 10, 2020, pp. 135–50.

Davies, Dominic, and Candida Rifkind, editors. *Documenting Trauma in Comics: Traumatic Pasts, Embodied Histories, and Graphic Reportage*. Palgrave Macmillan, 2020.

DiAngelo, Robin. *White Fragility: Why It's So Hard for White People to Talk About Racism*. Beacon Press, 2018.

Duong, Lan P. *Treacherous Subjects: Gender, Culture, and Trans-Vietnamese Feminism*. Temple UP, 2012.

Dwivedi, Om Prakash. *Tracing the New Indian Diaspora*. Brill, 2014.

Earle, Harriet E. H. "A New Face for an Old Fight: Reimagining Vietnam in Vietnamese-American Graphic Memoirs". *Studies in Comics*, vol. 9, no.1, 2018, pp. 87–105.

Einashe, Ismail. "The Struggle to be British: My Life as a Second-class Citizen'. *The Guardian*, 2 March, 2017, https://www.theguardian.com/uk-news/2017/mar/02/struggle-british-life-as-second-class-citizen#:~:text=In%201948%2C%20the%20British%20Nationality,no%20blacks%2C%20no%20dogs%E2%80%9D. Accessed 29 March 2022.

El Refaie, Elisabeth. *Autobiographical Comics: Life Writing in Pictures*. UP of Mississippi, 2012.

Equiano, Olaudah. *The Interesting Narrative of the Life of Olaudah Equiano, or Gustavas Vassa, the African*. Cambridge UP, 2014.

Fanon, Frantz. *Black Skin, White Masks*. 1952. Translated by Constance Farrington, Grove Press, 1994.

Farrier, David. *Postcolonial Asylum: Seeking Sanctuary Before the Law*. Liverpool UP, 2011.

Feldner, Maximilian. "Return Migration in Chimamanda Ngozi Adichie's *Americanah* (2013)". *Narrating the African Diaspora: 21st Century Nigerian Literature in Context*. Palgrave Macmillan, 2019.

Ferracioli, Laura. "Refugees, Rescue, and Choice". *The Political Philosophy of Refuge*, edited by David Miller, and Christine Straehle, Cambridge UP, 2020, pp. 193–210.

Fiske, David. *Solomon Northup: His Life Before and After Slavery*. Createspace Independent Publishing, 2012.

Fonkem, Achankeng. "The Refugee and Migrant Crisis: Human Tragedies as an Extension of Colonialism". *The Round Table*, vol. 109, no. 1, 2020, pp. 52–70.

Galipo, Adele. *Return Migration and Nation Building in Africa: Reframing the Somali Diaspora*. Routledge, 2018.

Gallien, Claire. "'Refugee Literature': What Postcolonial Theory has to Say". *Journal of Postcolonial Writing*, vol. 54, no. 6, 2018, pp. 721–26.

Gates Jr., Henry. "Steve McQueen and Henry Louise Gates Jr. Talk *12 Years A Slave*". *The Root*, 24 December 2013, https://www.theroot.com/steve-mcqueen-and-henry-louis-gates-jr-talk-12-years-a-1790899438. Accessed 8 April 2022.

Gikandi, Simon. "Between Roots and Routes: Cosmopolitanism and the Claims of Locality". *Rerouting the Postcolonial: New Directions for the New Millennium*, edited by Janet Wilson, Cristina Sandru, and Sarah Lawson Welsh, Routledge, 2009, pp. 22–35.

Gill, Tiffany M. *Beauty Shop Politics: African American Women's Activism in the Beauty Industry*, U of Illinois P, 2010.

Gilroy, Paul. *After Empire: Melancholia or Convivial Culture?* Routledge, 2004.

Goldberg, David Theo. *The Threat of Race: Reflections on Racial Neoliberalism*. Wiley-Blackwell, 2008.

Goodfellow, Maya. *Hostile Environment: How Immigrants became Scapegoats*. Verso, 2020.

Gopal, Priyamvada. *Insurgent Empire. Anticolonial Resistance and British Dissent*. Verso, 2019.

Goyal, Yogita. "Africa and the Black Atlantic". *Research in African Literatures*, vol. 45 no. 3, 2014, pp. v–xxv.

---. *Runaway Genres: The Global Afterlives of Slavery*. New York UP, 2019.

---. "The Genres of Guantánamo Diary: Postcolonial Reading and the War on Terror". *The Cambridge Journal of Postcolonial Literary Inquiry*, vol. 4, no. 1, 2017, pp. 69–87.

Gregory, Derek. *The Colonial Present: Afghanistan. Palestine. Iraq.* Wiley-Blackwell, 2004.

Hamid, Mohsin. *The Reluctant Fundamentalist.* Penguin, 2007.

Hartnell, Anna. "Moving through America. Race, Place and Resistance in Mohsin Hamid's *The Reluctant Fundamentalist*". *Journal of Postcolonial Writing,* vol. 46, no. 3–4, 2010, pp. 336–48.

Hilario, Carla T., et al. "'Just as Canadian as Anyone Else'? Experiences of Second-Class Citizenship and the Mental Health of Young Immigrant and Refugee Men in Canada". *American Men's Health,* vol. 12, no. 2, 2017, pp. 210–20.

Hirsch, Marianne. *Family Frames: Photography, Narrative, and Postmemory.* Harvard UP, 1997.

Hunter, Margaret L. *Race, Gender, and the Politics of Skin Tone.* Routledge, 2005.

Isaacs, Camille. "Mediating Women's Globalized Existence through Social Media in the Work of Adichie and Bulawayo". *Safundi,* vol. 17, no. 2, 2016, pp. 174–88.

Juan, Karin Aguilar-San. *Little Saigons: Staying Vietnamese in America.* U of Minnesota P, 2009.

Kaplan, Caren. *Questions of Travel: Postmodern Discourses of Displacement.* Duke UP, 1996.

Kara, Siddhartha. *Modern Slavery: A Global Perspective.* Columbia UP, 2017.

Khalidi, Rashid. *Sowing Crisis: The Cold War and American Dominance in the Middle East.* Beacon Press, 2010.

Knowles, Sam. "The Postcolonial Graphic Novel and Trauma: From *Maus* to Malta". *Postcolonial Traumas: Memory, Narrative, Resistance,* edited by Abigail Ward, Palgrave Macmillan, 2015, pp. 83–96.

Koshy, Susan, and Rajagopalan Radhakrishnan, editors. *Transnational South Asians: The Making of a Neo-Diaspora.* Oxford UP, 2008.

Kukkonen, Karin. "Space, Time, and Causality in Graphic Narratives: An Embodied Approach". *From Comic Strips to Graphic Novels: Contributions to the Theory and History of Graphic Narrative,* edited by Daniel Stein and Jan-Noël Thon, De Gruyter, 2013, pp. 49–66.

Lazarus, Neil, and Priyamvada Gopal. "Editorial: After Iraq". *New Formations,* no. 59, 2006, pp. 7–9.

Levine, Caroline. "The 'Strange Familiar': Structure, Infrastructure, and Adichie's *Americanah*". *Modern Fiction Studies*, vol. 61, no. 4, 2015, pp. 587–605.

Li, Stephanie. "*12 Years A Slave* as a Neo-Slave Narrative". *American Literary History*, vol. 26, no. 2, 2014, pp. 326–31.

Lopez, Alfred J., editor. *Postcolonial Whiteness: A Critical Reader on Race and Empire*. State U of New York P, 2005.

Loren, Scott. "An American Odyssey of Suffering: Aesthetic Strategies in Steve McQueen's *12 Years A Slave*". *Anglia*, vol. 132, no. 2, 2014, pp. 336–51.

Marais, Mike, "Hospitality, Reading, and the Aesthetics of Uncertainty: Mohsin Hamid's *The Reluctant Fundamentalist*". *Journal of Narrative Theory*, vol. 51, no. 1, 2021, pp. 84–103.

McWilliams, Sally E. "Precarious Memories and Affective Relationships in Thi Bui's *The Best We Could Do*". *Journal of Asian American Studies*, vol. 22, no. 3, 2019, pp. 315–48.

Meer, Sarah. "Slave Narratives as Literature". *The Cambridge Companion to Slavery in American Literature*, edited by Ezra Tawil, Cambridge UP, 2016, pp. 70–85.

Mehta, Binita, and Piu Mukherji, editors. *Postcolonial Comics: Texts, Events, Identities*. Routledge, 2015.

Mishra, Sudesh. *Diaspora Criticism*. Edinburgh UP, 2006.

Mishra, Vijay. "The Diasporic Imaginary: Theorizing the Indian Diaspora". *Textual Practice*, vol. 10, no. 3, 1996, pp. 421–47.

Morey, Peter. *Islamophobia and the Novel*. Columbia UP, 2018.

Morton, Stephen. *States of Emergency: Colonialism, Literature and Law*. Liverpool UP, 2013.

Nayar, Pramod K. *The Human Rights Graphic Novel: Drawing it Just Right*. Routledge, 2020.

Nguyen, Viet Thanh. *Nothing Ever Dies: Vietnam and the Memory of War*. Harvard UP, 2017.

Northup, Solomon. *Twelve Years a Slave*. 1853. U of North Carolina P, 2011.

Oh, Stella. "Birthing a Graphic Archive of Memory: Re-Viewing the Refugee Experience in Thi Bui's *The Best We Could Do*". *MELUS: Multi-Ethnic Literature of the U.S*, vol. 45, no. 4, 2020, pp. 72–90.

Paul, Joshua. "Post-racial Futures: Imagining Post-racialist Antiracism(s)". *Ethnic and Racial Studies*, vol. 37, no. 4, 2013, pp. 702–18.

Ponzanesi, Sandra. "Digital Diasporas: Postcoloniality, Media, and Affect". *Interventions: International Journal of Postcolonial Studies*, vol. 22, no. 8, 2020, pp. 977–93.

Pratt, Mary Louise. *Imperial Eyes: Travel Writing and Transculturation*. Routledge, 2007.

Pyke, Karen D. "What is Internalized Racial Oppression and Why Don't We Study It? Acknowledging Racism's Hidden Injuries". *Sociological Perspectives*, vol. 53, no. 4, 2010, pp. 551–572, https://doi.org/10.1525/sop.2010.53.4.55. Accessed 18 October 2024.

Quayson, Ato, and Girish Daswani, editors. *A Companion to Diaspora and Transnationalism*. Wiley-Blackwell, 2013.

'Refugee'. *Oxford English Dictionary*, https://www.oed.com/search/dictionary/?scope=Entries&q=Refugee. Accessed 22 June, 2021.

Rifkind, Candida. "Refugee Comics and Migrant Topographies". *a/b: Auto/Biography Studies*, vol. 32, no. 3, 2017, pp. 648–54.

Riss, Arthur. *Race, Slavery, and Liberalism in Nineteenth-Century American Literature*. Cambridge UP, 2006.

Rohter, Larry. "'It's Just How He Carries Himself': Chiwetel Ejiofor's Stature Carries *A Slave*". *New York Times*, 3 January 2014, https://www.nytimes.com/2014/01/05/movies/awardsseason/chiwetel-ejiofors-stature-carries-12-years-a-slave.html. Accessed 6 April 2022.

Rushdie, Salman. *Imaginary Homelands: Essays and Criticism, 1981–1991*. Granta Books, 1991.

Rushdy, Ashraf H.A. "Slavery and Historical Memory in Late-Twentieth-Century Fiction". *The Cambridge Companion to Slavery in American Literature*, edited by Ezra Tawil, Cambridge UP, 2016, pp. 236–49.

Sayyid, Salman. "Empire, Islam, and the Postcolonial". *The Oxford Handbook of Postcolonial Studies*, edited by Graham Huggan, Oxford UP, 2013, pp. 127–41.

Scott, Jamie S. "Religion and Postcolonial Writing". *The Cambridge History of Postcolonial Literature*, edited by Ato Quayson, vol. 2, Cambridge UP, 2011, pp. 739–70.

Singh, Harleen. "Deconstructing Terror: Interview with Mohsin Hamid on *The Reluctant Fundamentalist* (2007)". *ARIEL: A Review of International English Literature*, vol. 42, no. 2, 2011, pp. 149–56.

Smith, Alonzo. "Adapt and Resist: Infrapolitics in McQueen's *12 Years A Slave*". *The Journal of Popular Culture*, vol. 54, no. 3, 2021, pp. 613–33.

Smith, Andrew. "Migrancy, Hybridity and Postcolonial Literary Studies". *The Cambridge Companion to Postcolonial Literary Studies*, edited by Neil Lazarus, Cambridge UP, 2004, pp. 241–61.

Smith, Sidonie. "Human Rights and Comics: Autobiographical Avatars, Crisis Witnessing, and Transnational Rescue Networks". *Graphic Subjects: Critical Essays on Autobiography and Graphic Novels*, edited by Michael A. Chaney, U of Wisconsin P, 2011, pp. 61–72.

St Louis, Brett. "Post-race/post-Politics? Activist-intellectualism and the reification of race". *Ethnic and Racial Studies*, vol. 25, no. 3, 2002, pp. 652–75.

Stonebridge, Lyndsey. *Writing and Righting: Literature in the Age of Human Rights*. Oxford UP, 2020.

Sundquist, Eric J. *Empire and Slavery in American Literature 1820–1865*. U of Mississippi P, 1995.

Tawil, Ezra. "Introduction". *The Cambridge Companion to Slavery in American Literature*, edited by Ezra Tawil, Cambridge UP, 2016, pp. 1–15.

Tillet, Salamishah. "'I Got No Comfort in this Life": The Increasing Importance of Patsey in *12 Years A Slave*'. *American Literary History*, vol. 26, no. 2, 2014, pp. 354–61.

Tolan, Fiona, et al. *Literature, Migration and the 'War on Terror'*. Routledge, 2012.

Tölölyan, Khachig. "The Nation-State and Its Others: In Lieu of a Preface". *Diaspora: A Journal of Transnational Studies*, vol 1, no. 1, 1991, pp. 3–7.

"Trump's Executive Order: White House Stands Firm over Travel Ban". *BBC*, 30 January 2017, https://www.bbc.com/news/world-us-canada-38790629. Accessed 28 March 2022.

Tsuda, Takeyuki, editor. *Diasporic Homecomings: Ethnic Return Migration in Comparative Perspective*. Stanford UP, 2009.

---. "When the Diaspora Returns Home: Ambivalent Encounters with the Ethnic Homeland". *A Companion to Diaspora and Transnationalism*, edited by Ato Quayson and Girish Daswani, Wiley-Blackwell, 2013, pp. 172–89.

Viljoen, Jeanne-Marie. *War Comics: A Postcolonial Perspective*. Routledge, 2020.

Vlahaki, Marina. "Braiding Worlds: Disharmonious Encounters in Mariama's African Hair Salon in *Americanah* by Chimamanda Ngozi Adichie". *Research in African Literatures*, vol. 52, no. 1, 2021, pp. 108–125.

Vo, Nghia M. *The Vietnamese Boat People, 1954 and 1975–1992*. McFarland, 2006.

Wallerstein, Immanuel. *The Modern World-System III: The Second Era of Great Expansion of the Capitalist World-Economy, 1730s–1840s*. U of California P, 2011.

White, Mandala. "Framing Travel and Terrorism: Allegory in *The Reluctant Fundamentalist*". *Journal of Commonwealth Literature*, vol. 54, no. 3, 2019, pp. 444–59.

Whitlock, Gillian. "Protection". *We Shall Bear Witness: Life Narratives and Human Rights*, edited by Meg Jensen and Margaretta Jolly, U of Wisconsin P, 2014. pp. 80–97.

Wilentz, Sean. *No Property in Man: Slavery and Antislavery at the Nation's Founding*. Harvard UP, 2018.

Williams, Eric. *Capitalism and Slavery*. U of North Carolina P, 1944.

Williams, Paul. *Dreaming the Graphic Novel: The Novelization of Comics*. Rutgers UP, 2020.

Willis, Sharon. "Moving Pictures: Spectacles of Enslavement in American Cinema". *The Cambridge Companion to Slavery in American Literature*, edited by Ezra Tawil, Cambridge UP, 2016, pp. 219–35.

Woolley, Agnes. *Contemporary Asylum Narratives: Representing Refugees in the Twenty-First Century*. Palgrave Macmillan, 2014.

Yerima, Dina. "Regimentation or Hybridity. Western Beauty Practices by Black Woman in Adichie's *Americanah*". *Journal of Black Studies*, vol. 48, no. 7, 2017, pp. 639–50.

Young, Robert J. C. *Colonial Desire: Hybridity in Theory, Culture and Race*. Routledge, 1995.

---. *Empire, Colony, Postcolony*. Wiley-Blackwell, 2015.

Chapter Four

Traumas

GENOCIDE, SEXUAL VIOLENCE, EXILE AND SOLIDARITY IN RAIHAN, NOTTAGE AND DARWISH

The readings of refugees and asylum through Thi Bui's graphic novel in the previous chapter have set the stage for a discussion on violence, trauma and solidarity in the postcolonial context. Critic Achille Mbembe writes that the postcolonial world (which he calls the 'postcolony') has institutionalised colonial violence through corporate and political machinery and the fetish of 'commandment'. Since colonial forms of law, governance, social and cultural codes, and linguistic and educational standards are still followed by formerly colonised nations, the postcolonial is marked by a continuation of colonial violence, corruption and spectacle (Mbembe, *On the Postcolony* 102–03). What is particularly noticeable about 'postcolonial violence' is that unlike a 'foreign' occupation (for example, a European colonising presence in non-European majority territories) against whom an anticolonial and anti-imperialist nationalist campaign could be launched, in the postcolonial period the perpetrators and victims of state and ethnic violence are postcolonial citizen–subjects themselves. Mahmoud Mamdani has argued that since postcolonial violence draws from the originary colonialist binary of native and settler, it is marked by a deliberate making of an 'alien' settler out of a citizen: in the Rwandan case, alien settler Tutsis; in the Indian case, alien Muslims; in the Nigerian case, alien Igbos et cetera. In this form of violence one's neighbour, teacher or husband can all of a sudden vanquish their peer (Mamdani, "Making Sense of Political Violence in Postcolonial Africa" 133–34; 140).

The nature and appeal of this violence is different from anticolonial violence, though. In the latter, anticolonial leaders such as M. K. Gandhi, Patrice Lumumba, Kwame Nkrumah or Sukarno invoked commonalities among colonised people, despite differences in religion, language or ethnicity, in their bid to unify the nationalist fight against European colonialism. In the post-colonial context, these markers of historical unity – which were always fractured and discontinuous even during anticolonial struggles and a clever management of which allowed the discourse of unified campaigns to continue – are now broken into neat social categories to carve out a persistent settler–native paradigm in order to support ethnonationalist causes. Thus, Hitler's Nazi Party identified Jews as alien settlers – and the root cause for Germany's humiliating defeat in the First World War – who needed to be exterminated (through the Holocaust) for the nation's renewed rise. Similarly, Tutsis, Muslims or Igbos – in different contexts – are now ascribed the same denomination, making enemies out of neighbours, friends and family.

Whereas critical and literary writings on anticolonialism could glorify violence for the nobler cause of national liberation (Fanon), the depiction of violence in postcolonial literature is full of trauma born out of unbelievably tragic events. This is not to say that colonial violence is bereft of trauma. However trauma in the postcolonial context, now divided and imagined through smaller groups in a nation (or transnationally), may continue for generations and destroy both body and soul in the form of 'insidious trauma' (Brown 197). To write about trauma arising out of a partition of national territory, of war between citizens/neighbours, or of sexual violence in a civil war is to not only write about these tragic events but also about the bizarreness of their happening in postcolonial societies, especially when evoked through the causes of patriotism, nationalism and faith. In this chapter, I will read trauma through the interconnected lens of civil war and genocide (which are only two specific enablers of postcolonial violence). I will show through a reading of a documentary film on the Bangladesh War of Liberation, a play on rape and female solidarity in the Democratic Republic of the Congo, and poetry on the Israel–Palestine conflict that individual and historical trauma has pervaded postcolonial societies. Recovery from such pervasive trauma is imagined through acknowledging the resilience of people living in its aftermath and the decolonising solidarity they offer each other through fellow feeling, cultural memory and an aesthetic imagining of togetherness.

Genocide, Trauma Studies and Postcolonial Studies

Trauma studies is historically linked with the genocide that was the Holocaust. The term 'genocide' was officially used by the United Nations in 1948, in the aftermath of the Second World War, to refer to crimes 'committed with intent to destroy, in whole or in part, a national, ethnical, racial or religious group' (*UN*). Lasse Heerten and A. Dirk Moses observe that the field of genocide studies did not exist until the 1980s and 1990s (181). The Armenian, Bosnian, Rwandan, Cambodian, Yugoslavian, Biafran and East Pakistani instances of genocide in contemporary decades compelled scholars to rethink the analytical framework through which genocides are studied, thereby calling for an extension of its meaning to apply to a situation 'where there is an actualized intention, however successfully carried out, to physically destroy an *entire* group' (Katz 28; emphasis in the original). These 'global' genocides have also called for an exploration of the relationship between genocide and war (Shaw). As Heerten and Dirk Moses further note, 'the intention to defeat a state militarily can co-exist with an intention to destroy a group's social power and ability to resist, indeed destroy it as a group—consistent with Shaw's point about the hybridity of war and genocide' (191).

The frequency of civil war and genocide in the postcolonial world has also encouraged scholars to explore the concept from colonial and imperialist angles. Probably the most compelling argument on genocide's colonial–imperialist basis comes from Aimé Césaire's *Discourses on Colonialism* (1950) in which he argued that Nazism and the Holocaust were results of European colonialism – a form of capitalism that preached pseudo-humanism and justified vanquishing peoples, animals and resources for the sake of progress and civilisation (3). For Fanon, as for Césaire, 'Nazism turned the whole of Europe into a veritable colony' (101). Following Césaire, Hannah Arendt wrote powerfully about how race and bureaucracy had laid the ground for imperialism to enter the age of totalitarianism, and for the concepts of refugees and statelessness to happen (207–10). In the last two decades, scholars have more forcefully set up the connections between these ideologies and practices. Separating 'colony' from colonialism, Dirk Moses writes, 'the greater the intensity of colonial rule, the greater the likelihood that it is genocidal' (22–3). Patrick Wolfe adds that since the invasion for conquest and the annexation of land and people work through the 'logic of elimination', settler colonialism is marked by 'structural genocide' (102–03). Genocides have not ended with the 'official' end of colonialism and imperialism per se. Philip Spencer usefully reminds us that 'The logic of violence set in motion by imperialist annexation can continue to play itself out as previously oppressed groups turn upon those who were either their colonial tormentors or colluded with them' which is known as 'genocides by the oppressed' (612). This chapter will primarily attend to 'genocides by the oppressed' in which postcolonial populations have turned on each other in the name of religion, ethnicity, power, caste, race or other issues best understood through the poignant title of Mamdani's book *When Victims Become Killers*. It will further show that many of these genocides are conditioned by neocolonial, neoliberal and imperialist forces indicating that colonialism and its violent agenda are far from over.

Like scholarly studies of war and genocide, trauma studies also began in the 1980s and 1990s, primarily through the prism of the Holocaust. In her foundational work *Unclaimed Experience* (1996), Cathy Caruth argues that 'the language of trauma, and the silence of its mute repetition of suffering, profoundly and imperatively demand' a 'new mode of reading and of listening' (7). She adds, 'the most direct seeing of a violent event may occur as an absolute inability to know it; that immediacy, paradoxically, may take the form of belatedness' (91–92). Caruth has asked to read this new mode of the belatedness and incomprehensibility of trauma as its unrepresentability in narratives. On the other hand, psychiatrist and scholar Judith Herman observes that 'the victim must be helped to speak the horrifying truth of her past – to speak of the unspeakable' (179). Postcolonial scholars of trauma have relied upon these observations on silence and speech and on Dominic LaCapra's contention that trauma theory indiscriminately generalises historical specificity through Freudian readings (xi–xii). Drawing upon Geoffrey Hartman's insightful exhortations that trauma theory include the chronic and collective experience due to its 'emphasis on acts of violence like war and genocide' (546), postcolonial critics have argued that the scope of the field needs to be broadened from the narrow and 'unique' circumstances of the Holocaust to account for the long-term, historical and collective nature of trauma in colonial and imperialist contexts and to situate them in their specific historical–cultural contexts (Craps and Buelens 4; Baxter 22). Irene Visser, for instance, has pointed towards keeping an 'openness to indigenous belief systems and their rituals' for 'trauma, its aftermath, and possible resolution' ("Decolonizing Trauma Theory: Retrospect and Prospects" 262) – a topic I raise specifically through an examination of gender, voice and resistance in Lynn Nottage's play later.

Michael Rothberg cautions us that postcolonial scholars do not uncritically homogenise trauma, as slavery, Holocaust and colonialism have variously drawn from each other's violent historical and aesthetic frameworks. 'A decolonized trauma studies', Rothberg warrants, 'should attempt to demonstrate the internal heterogeneity of Europe, North America, and Australia at the same time that it draws attention to the frequent non-fit between the categories of colonizing nations and those of the societies they have colonized' (228). He further suggests that an attentive reading of complicity is important to think through the question of ethical responsibility: 'Attention to hybridity and heterogeneity need not distract from hierarchies of power' (228–29). These features of heterogeneity, collectivity, multiplicity, specificity and ethical responsibility have allowed critic Abigail Ward to understand postcolonial trauma in the plural sense: 'there is not one homogeneous postcolonial trauma, such as a unified trauma of colonisation' (8) but rather postcolonial traumas – a line of argument that I pursue in this chapter.

As genocide and postcolonial trauma are argued to have long-term, insidious and chronic effects on individuals and communities, the question of recovery becomes challenging. In his path-breaking essay 'Colonial Trauma/Postcolonial Recovery?', David Lloyd offers an insightful reading of recovery through the Folkloric Commission's report on the Great Irish Famine, in which 'the dehumanization of the colonized, the denial to them of an interest in the future that is the index of human subjectivity' is replaced by 'the collective reaction to eviction that refuses to assent passively to humiliation' signifying 'the stirrings of resistance and the determination to survive in altered states' (227). For Lloyd, postcolonial scholars must take note that the future of a genocidal catastrophe is changed and subdued, but not subjected, selves and communities which can be indicated by literary and cultural narratives. This is a point that Ogaga Ifowodo raises; that recovering colonised trauma is also about recovering postcolonial identity and beginning to think about healing (2–3) – a perspective that applies strongly to Zahir Raihan's documentary on the Bangladesh War of Liberation. The question of recovering (from) the suppressed, a clear decolonising strategy, was notably raised in the context of the Holocaust by Shoshana Felman and Dori Laub in *Testimony* (1992) in which they argued for the usefulness of the transmissibility of trauma by including readers' affective responses. Trauma needs to be listened to and engaged with through empathy and speech – a point, Visser shows, literary scholars have drawn upon and expanded. But for Visser, the question of transmissibility needs specific attention to social, cultural and historical specificities ("Trauma Theory and Postcolonial Literary Studies" 275) as indicated previously and which Lloyd has helpfully maintained as well.

Reading these contexts, Hamish Dalley has argued for framing trauma and solidarity through the lens of narrative form. Contrary to scholarly suggestions, Dalley continues, realism has aesthetic strategies built into it to not only forge cross-cultural communication – a key point in trauma solidarity – but also to assert the ambivalence in such practices. He instructs, 'Trauma theory will only be effective for postcolonial analysis if it is supplemented by a critical materialism that pays attention to the specificities of setting, and which is attuned to the power hierarchies that differentiate experiences and make what is progressive in one context regressive in another' (Dalley 389). While this point goes back to Craps, Visser and others previously mentioned, it is helpful to remember Craps's suggestions in *Postcolonial Witnessing*: that narratives do not always offer cross-cultural solidarity for resolution but rather for 'the ethico-political practice of anamnestic solidarity with the oppressed of the past and the present' to 'open up a space of remembrance in which historical losses' are 'constantly re-examined and re-interpreted' (60). This is most tellingly evoked in my reading of Mahmoud Darwish's poetry on the Israel–Palestine conflict in the final part of the chapter. Scenes of anamnestic solidarity, as Zoë Norridge confirms through a reading of Rwandan non-fictional, testimonial genocide writing, are universally marked by 'the unified desire to write against its violent consequences' (241) which can be applied to all of my subsequent examples.

What I have tried to establish through these scholarly conversations on trauma, recovery and narrative style is that postcolonial trauma writings on war and genocide are marked by their specific long-term, historical contexts; their ethical intent to address and assuage the grief of their 'victim communities' (often overlooked by national and international media); their aesthetic styles of anticolonial opposition; and empathetic communicability for creating solidarity – even if by fragmented narration – which I will show filmmakers, playwrights and poets have implemented in their art forms. Here, the question of genre is important for two particular reasons. By using the means of documentary filmmaking, an artist can often reach a wider audience to forge postcolonial solidarity. By dramatising sexual violence in war-torn Congo, a play can viscerally put across a sharp comment on trauma and transnational solidarity. By evoking the pain and sorrow of statelessness and exile through the imagistic genre of poetry, poets can often move us in their call for universal humanity. As I have been arguing in the book, recovery, retrieval, humanity, dignity and solidarity address the crucial process of decolonising mind and society. By taking a multi-genre approach, we can also continue to question our over-reliance on the genre of the novel in trauma narratives and postcolonial literature.

THE BANGLADESH WAR OF LIBERATION: CIVIL WAR, TRAUMA AND FORCED MIGRATION IN ZAHIR RAIHAN'S *STOP GENOCIDE*

This section will address the colonial and genocidal underpinnings as well as the trauma-induced anticolonial cinema of the Bangladesh war of liberation, beginning with a quick history of the topic. After the Partition of British India into India and Pakistan in 1947, West Pakistan implemented Urdu as the official state language for the new country which East Pakistan, with a Bengali majority population, refused to follow. The crisis culminated in a violent 'Bhasha Andolon' or Language Movement in 1951. Throughout the next two decades, East Pakistan (or modern-day Bangladesh) accused West Pakistan of socially, economically and militarily neglecting the East, and collaborating with the East's Urdu-speaking elite to extract resources and capital away to the West. The 1960s also saw the stellar rise of East Pakistan's major party, the Awami League, and its leader, Sheikh Mujibur Rahman. When Cyclone Bhola made landfall in the East in 1970, killing half a million people and resulting in a huge loss of property, lives, livestock and resources, West Pakistan's delayed and inefficient recovery programme invited widespread criticism in the East. This was followed by a massive victory for Rahman in the parliamentary elections. Rahman then famously issued a six-point programme calling for devolved administration in the East, which was denied by West Pakistan, leading to his call for an indefinite strike and courting subsequent military retaliation from the West. The civil war began in March 1971 and ended in December, turning into a South Asian geopolitical war (van Schendel Parts II & III; Beachler 471–74).

Throughout the war, the term 'genocide' was used both in Bangladesh and internationally. In a high voltage piece in *The Sunday Times* which brought international attention to the war, Anthony Mascarenhas wrote in chilling, passionate language about the systemic and planned killing of Bengali people by the Pakistani army, titling the piece 'Genocide' (1971). Gary Bass later showed through declassified data on 'the Blood Telegram,'[1] that the US, which supported its Cold War-ally Pakistan in the war, had known about the atrocities being perpetrated in East Pakistan and exchanged information using the term 'genocide' although it never acknowledged the term publicly (11). Others such as Rounaq Jahan (Totten et al.), Donald Beachler and Azra Rashid have subsequently read this violent episode as genocide. I show that the artistic foundation for this political categorisation was efficiently laid by Zahir Raihan's 1971 documentary, *Stop Genocide*.

One of the key characteristics of twentieth century wars is the use of digital/audio-visual technology and documentary filmmaking to keep records. The American invasion of Vietnam, as we suggested in the previous chapter, is one of the most documented wars in film and television history (Shaughnessy; Anderegg). Dusty Sachs and Michaël Weill's *Winter Soldier* (1972) was a documentary made about the Vietnam War which collected testimonies of war veterans on the atrocities committed in the war. Peter Davis's *Hearts and Minds* (1974) and Neil Davis's *Frontline* (1979) had a wide impact on the genre of war documentary filmmaking, offering a trenchant critique of imperialism, war crime and human society. Raihan's *Stop Genocide* falls into this category of films and also significantly expands the genre. His landmark *Jibon Theke Neya* (1970; 'Taken from Life') based on the Language Movement and critical of the dictatorship of Ayub Khan, was, in the words of prominent film-maker and activist Alamgir Kabir, 'the first filming expression to the rising tide of Bengali nationalism that became the living spirit behind the War of National Liberation less than a decade later' (Kabir 45). Raihan directed *Stop Genocide* while in exile in Kolkata, India. Kabir and other exiled artists and intellectuals gathered support for this English language documentary from The Motion Pictures Association of Bengal and the Bangladesh Liberation Council of Intelligentsia because of its potential global reach. In a remarkable close reading of the film, Fahmida Akhter tells us that Raihan went into exile in Kolkata to collect documents and resources related to the war and to secretly travel to the border and 'liberated zones' to 'shoot the processions of displaced refugees, their plight and suffering, and the training and combative actions of the Bengali guerrillas' (Akhter 237).

The 'revolutionary conjuncture' within which the film was made in a month using found footage, newsreels, video clips and secret travels ushered in a new era of documentary filmmaking on war by exiled auteurs (Akhter) which may be termed as 'Third Cinema' following Solanas and Getino (237). James Leahy notes that Raihan's work was deeply influenced by the Cuban documentary film-maker Santiago Alvarez who made *Hasta la Victoria Siempre!* (1967) in forty-eight hours using newsreels and found footage of Fidel Castro's public meeting announcing the death of Che Guevara. As Leahy comments, 'It's not just their subject matter that makes these films remarkable, but the skill with which the filmmaker structures and deploys his material' ("Films that Make a Difference"'). I will argue in this section that Raihan uses an experimental cinematic style that draws from revolutionary socialist–realist cinema to address the collective trauma of the nation and his call for international solidarity. Drawing upon a work from 1971 for a book on 'postcolonialism now' will also be able to suggest two further aspects for us: that Raihan's use of the documentary, a genre that has been used more widely in the context of genocide of late, is a breakthrough for the genre's historical genealogy and for postcolonial cinema; and that watching the film in retrospect also makes us face the complex question of the ethics of trauma representation in postcolonial art and culture.

Raihan begins the film with an image of Lenin and a quote from *The Right of Nations to Self-Determination*: 'To accuse those who support freedoms of self-determination, i.e., freedom to secede, of encouraging separatism, is as foolish and hypocritical as accusing those who advocate freedom of divorce of encouraging the destruction of family ties' (Stop Genocide, 00:07:00). This is an important quote in the film's context for two reasons. Lenin was the first high-profile revolutionary and philosopher in 'western' Marxism to acknowledge that colonialist imperialism was the highest stage of capitalism, and who recognised the need to eradicate colonialism and mobilise support for anticolonial nationalism, democracy and the right to self-determination through which nations would be able to move to socialism. He further wrote that secession did not mean fragmentation of the nation-state into smaller parts but a consistent expression of struggle against all forms of national oppression (Lenin 417–25). These relevant statements allow Raihan the expositional instructive vantage point of describing the atrocities committed by the Pakistani army as genocide; thus the revolutionary struggle for self-determination which the film ends with can be seen as an urgent ethical need. The second important element is the analogy of secession with divorce. Secession is not seen as the destruction of family values but rather a decision reached through consensus by family members followed by a careful management of common wealth and duty towards a child. As Jing Lu comments, the comparison was an innovation from Lenin: 'If secession should be treated as a divorce the bilateral character and procedural character of secession must be recognised' (103). By using Lenin's quote, Raihan also posited his socialist and secular belief in secession, suggesting that national self-determination is needed not only to give expression to the national struggle but also to free one's mind and thought from orthodox and fundamentalist (Islamic) ideologies and practices.

However, this provocative beginning is juxtaposed with two uneven sequences: scenes of peaceful, rural Bengal with lush vegetation and labouring women husking rice and cooking, followed by three striking images on war and violence from 20 July 1971 in New York, Saigon and Bongaon, Bengal. These uneven juxtapositions are important for the film's postcolonial basis: while in New York the UN charter documents equal rights for men and women and the right of humans to live with dignity and respect, scenes of aerial bombing of the Vietnamese people and a long procession of refugees in Bongaon suggest the opposite. Here, Raihan seems to point to the irony that not only have the UN declarations not been followed by the US in Vietnam, but that the fate of the people of Vietnam and East Pakistan is also similar, making a case for the creation of solidarity through the spectacle of suffering by works on trauma, as Caruth and Craps have indicated previously. In these stylistically innovative sequences, Raihan makes clear his socialist and realist beliefs. He also adds to the scene a background voice-over by Kabir who dexterously employs pitch, language and tempo to evoke the horrors of the war, producing a Brechtian theatrical alienation for his viewers. While the language for the Vietnam bombing, delivered in a sombre and fast tempo, is about sexual violence and the 'rape' of humanity, the language used for the Bongaon refugees is more dramatic. Here the tempo is slower, almost insidious in its suggestion that their long walk is 'natural': 'It was not difficult to find them. They were coming like an endless procession of sleepwalkers, as if instinctively they moved on' (*Stop Genocide* 00:03:22). This image of their walk is followed by a freeze-frame with the repeated telegrammatic inscription 'Stop' (00:03:24; 00:03:28; 00:03:34), indicating both the fragmented nature of a long narrative and the injustice of the war on innocent people now rendered homeless.

Reminding us of Bui's use of the juxtaposition of photography and art in *The Best We Could Do* in the previous chapter, the freeze-frame saying 'Stop' reappears throughout the film as a declaration that this genocide must stop. Here the background score is ironic: a veena tune evoking peaceful, romantic conjugal life; a life of stability and vitality. The contradictoriness of these aesthetic accessories seems to evoke the incomprehensibility of the situation for the viewers as the narrator asks, 'For what crimes must they go through this terrifying ordeal? They did not know. Neither did we' (00:03:58). This inquisitive pathos follows a more direct and robust question: 'How long must the world allow Yahya and his accomplices to go on committing genocidal crimes against such innocent people?'. Pointing out the Pakistani army and its East Pakistani collaborators inflicting such crimes on humanity, the narrator throws this question of responsibility, of conscience, to the world. These scenes end with the camera focusing on the faces of the refugees as one of them declares that by killing the innocent people of Bangladesh, raping its women and looting its wealth, Yahya Khan has become an invader–emperor akin to Nader Shah, Timur and Mahmoud of Ghazni. He is then compared with Mussolini and finally, in a roaring thunderous call, with Hitler (00:04:13). This scene is deeply suggestive as Yahya Khan, the then Prime Minister of Pakistan, is understood as an 'alien' who has no interest in this part of the world; whose sole job is to plunder, loot and rape, and who does not have any claim to the people and the land of Bangladesh (the term 'Bangladesh' and not 'East Pakistan' is already mentioned in this frame), recalling Mamdani's formulations of the alien settler versus the native in mobilising support for civil war or 'national' liberation in the postcolonial contexts. What is also important is linking war crimes with fascism and Nazism. Indeed, Hitler is shown in a number of freeze-frames with images of concentration camps and detention camps juxtaposed with refugee camps and the dead bodies of people and animals. Through these close-ups, Raihan then constructs a broad historical narrative of invasion, looting and atrocities of fascism and Nazism to which Yahya's methods and crimes claim a genealogy. Ending the comparison with Hitler also serves to remind the viewer that this systemic destruction of the Bangladeshi people is a genocide and needs to be recognised as such.

While these aesthetic styles and political messages echo the socialist–realist tradition of Third Cinema, Raihan's distinct use of history and genealogy merits attention. Third Cinema began in Argentina and South America as revolutionary Marxist cinema which was aimed at the masses, using limited technical means and rich experimental techniques. Solanas and Getino called it 'guerrilla cinema', which was not meant to be produced only by and for the Third World (6). Raihan probably draws from this new cinematic form, as Leahy suggests, but he is located in the postcolonial 'Third World' – a concept that gained prominence post the 1955 Bandung conference (in the beginning of the Cold War) as referring to the shared experiences of colonial and capitalist exploitation as well as anticolonial revolutionary political and creative energies. Furthermore, the hope of freedom from British colonialism in Raihan's country was confronted with imminent disillusionment due to religious, linguistic and ethnic violence, culminating in a genocide. Finally, Bengal's history of being exploited went back at least a thousand years to Muslim invaders, British colonialism and the unique contemporary condition of political independence commingled with the religious, social and moral subjection of East Pakistan. These specific experiences called for a cinematic mode that could draw from the revolutionary tradition of socialist realism and Third Cinema but focus on the historical and cultural specificities of the region and its people (the 'conjunctural cultural front' that Sunderason and Hoek point to in *Forms of the Left in Postcolonial South Asia*, 9–10). The short experimental documentary format suited

Raihan both for the paucity of technical means required because of his exile (which also meant implementing experimental techniques) and for the mode's didactic efficacy in the context of genocide. As Adam Tyson writes on genocide documentary, 'Interventions through film cause ripple effects and have the power to move political questions or strategic goals such as transitional justice into the visual sphere' (178). Considering that the Bangladesh or Cambodian instances were not officially read as genocides in the early usages of the term, the film's documentary production and its brave call for recognition of the episode as genocide was stunningly forward-looking.

The question of refugee and gender is important in this context for the specific postcolonial and ethical dimension of the film. Bengal, like Punjab, had encountered one of the most harrowing instances of human suffering in 1947 when India and Pakistan wrested independence from colonial rule. Communal riots and the Partition caused millions of people from the province of Bengal, now divided into India and East Pakistan along religious lines, to forcibly migrate from one country to another resulting in a massive refugee crisis for the newborn countries (Murshid; Datta). The refugee crisis continued throughout the 1950s and 60s, and thus the scenes of refugees in processions or huddled in camps were not new for Raihan. This is why Kabir's voice-over ironically calls this tragedy 'natural' – 'as if instinctively' (00:03:14) – as this was meant to be the tragic fate of colonial and postcolonial nations calling for self-determination. However, what Raihan does here is juxtapose the procession scenes with close-ups of a flailing old woman and a silent girl (00:05:12–00:05:41). Here, the voice-over is about the vulnerability of the population having to take up this nightmarish ordeal of walking and living through the trauma of sexual violence (harkening back to the impossibility of voice and language that Caruth referred to in the context of the Holocaust). Instead of taking recourse to sensational melodrama – a mode that has a long-term tradition in South Asian cinema and theatre – the narrative soon shifts to a declamatory demand for the perpetrators of the genocide to be punished. This aspect creates an opportune moment to showcase the film's postcolonial character while underscoring the traumatising gendered element of the genocide. The close-ups of violated and fragile women are meant to be an axiomatic opposite of the shots of the loving and idyllic women in the beginning of the film – that is, a metaphor of the violation of the mother goddess. There is also the exclusionary side of this strategic representation: by not giving women a voice in the narrative and imposing his political narrative on them, Akhter argues that Raihan strips them off their agency and tragedy (244–45; following Gayatri Chakravorty Spivak's classic argument that the gendered subaltern cannot speak). Looking at these representations outside of the violent contexts of its production (the film is now available on *YouTube*), we may also feel a sense of constructed sympathy for the women which seems to defeat Raihan's political purpose. This is probably the opposite of what McQueen wanted to do through close-ups in *12 Years A Slave*, to humanise and construct empathy for the enslaved. Echoing Craps's and Visser's interventions in the ethics of trauma representation, Raihan, probably against his will, appears to make sensational use out of his female 'victims'; they are vessels and objects for a political cause incapable of wielding aesthetic and political agency. The obvious masculine element in this film, or for that matter in Third Cinema in general, which uses formulaic 'narrative patterns' to invisibilise women characters has already been noted (Yekani 34). Scholars have, thus, called for a 'post-thirdist' critical culture or 'fourth cinema' in which 'women's gazes and voices would not be assimilated to the political programmes of their male counterparts' (Ponzanesi and Waller 5; Khanna; Shohat and Stam).

However, it could be argued that by not focusing on particular characters but on the conditions that produce the endless march of refugees, on their homelessness and camp life, Raihan makes a notable statement on the characteristic postcolonial conditions of civil war and statelessness which are traumatising for a population as a whole. Unlike McQueen's drama, this is not a full-length feature film retrospectively made in a relatively peaceful time, but rather a quick production to gather momentum, propagate the evils of war, and collect sympathy from all over the world. In juxtaposing images of the beauty and idyllic charm of Bengal alongside images of what has been forever lost to the displaced populace, Raihan was capturing live what Laura Marks calls a 'haptic visuality' (the sense of touch evoked visually) that the refugees and the diaspora are now left with in their host lands (something that Bui's graphic novel in the previous chapter so powerfully captures through the white boy's spit on Bui's father's cheek taking the shape of the Vietnamese peninsula). In these scenes portraying the collective trauma of the population due to genocide, and in reminding us of the peculiar historical genealogy of Bengal's violent rule, Raihan displays a complex artistic acumen in capturing postcolonial trauma.

The ending of the film asserts that this collective trauma will remain for a long time, but we can attempt to redress it through anticolonial international solidarity. Like Jackie Kay's use of Angela Davis in 'Black Bottom' to evoke racial solidarity, Raihan's remarkable comparison, in blurred, negative photo-vision, creates an overlapping narrative that mentions Paris, Haiti and Algeria. If the French Revolution gave voice to the oppressed majority in their demand for equality and fraternity, it is France as the colonising country that denied Haiti and their enslaved population the same human rights of equality and self-determination which the Haitians earned through a bloody thirteen-year-long war in 1804. The French colony of Algeria saw another bloody campaign for independence in 1967 – a campaign in which the French soldiers used inhuman and illegal methods to crush the anticolonial struggle. Here, one can hardly miss the distant echo of Fanon and of Gillo Pontecorvo's *The Battle of Algiers* (1966) used for building revolutionary anticolonial and postcolonial cinema (Weaver-Hightower 1). Using English language in the film and bringing the oppressed and colonised together in one frame, Raihan also asks global viewers and readers to recognise both the long-term demands for human rights of these people and the specific human struggles in colonised nations for national self-determination. This goes back to Dalley's thoughts on narrative materialism as an important tool for an anticolonial recovery of postcolonial solidarity. When Raihan's narrator mentions Palestine, South Africa, Congo, Auschwitz and Spain in one frame in an 'analogous' manner (recall Goyal in the previous chapter), we get the sense that whenever leaders of fascist or colonising powers have committed atrocities, people have taken up arms to protect their dignity and fought for their existence. He ends the film with snippets of the new guerrilla Muktibahini (Liberation Front) in Bangladesh and their campaigns calling for global solidarity with their war:

> Neither is their heroic resistance an isolated happening. It is indeed an integral part of their relentless struggle being waged by working men and women for their democratic right to choose their own destiny. In the interests of this international solidarity, freedom-loving people of the world must fight alongside the people of Bangladesh and do everything on their part to bring to an end this grisly campaign of genocide. (*Stop Genocide*, 00:18:37–00:19:17)

Naeem Mohaiemen writes that the next documentary/film to be made on this topic, after Raihan's secular and progressive example, arrives more than two decades later in the form of Tareque and Catherine Masud's *Muktir Gaan* (1995; *Song of Liberation*) because of the country's turn to religious fundamentalism and the people's uneasy negotiations with their immediate trauma (37). In the absence of the visual, depictions of the war and the genocide took the verbal– imaginative route through stories, narratives and memoirs. However, as Yasmin Saikia raised, reconciliatory tasks in the aftermath of the war could not be an individual-oriented (private-reading) matter as the Truth and Reconciliation Commission aimed to do. An entire community was subjected to routinised violence. In bringing out survivors' memories and stories, she asked for 'a way of developing shared responsiveness for allowing transformation within the self while simultaneously acknowledging the interconnectedness with others' (Saikia 8). A significant example of this communal sharing of grief is the Liberation War Museum. Reading the objects, memorials, and photographs in the Museum, Nayanika Mookherjee shares that revisiting pain and suffering through objects and linking them to global contexts creates a 'genocidal cosmopolitanism'. This cosmopolitanism is marked by conscience: 'Individuals are meant to have a conscience and act according to it. Conscience is predominantly understood to be an ability through which one determines whether one's actions are right or wrong, a faculty which informs moral judgement' (Mookherjee S85). Like the war museum which strikes at our conscience, like the shared element of grief that Saikia raises, Raihan's documentary film is the first to outline such a reconciliatory task of anticolonial solidarity and contributes effectively to creating what Mookherjee calls 'a cultural and historical public' in its dialectic of the local and the cosmopolitan and in its sensitive and aesthetically innovative recording of the genocidal suffering of Bangladeshi people (S83).

WAR, SEXUAL VIOLENCE AND FEMINIST SOLIDARITY IN LYNN NOTTAGE'S *RUINED*

If Raihan's documentary failed to focus on the resilience and fighting voices of women in the genocide, Lynn Nottage's Pulitzer Prize-winning play, *Ruined* (2009), based on the civil wars in the Democratic Republic of the Congo (henceforth DRC) addresses this absence excruciatingly. There has been a long debate in the fields of feminist, social and cultural studies as to whether representing rape perpetuates sexual violence and retraumatises the violated (Virdi 266). To follow Tanya Horeck, representing rape plays an important role 'as a scenario through which questions are posed about masculine and feminine identity, sexuality and sexual difference, and the origins of culture' (9). None of these issues, however, are alien to postcolonial societies. Indeed, colonisation is often compared to the rape of land and culture. Noting this problematic analogy in Seamus Heaney's poem 'Act of Union', Zoë Brigley Thompson and Sorcha Gunne comment, 'For second-wave feminism the primary objective was to put rape on the agenda in an effort to prevent it from occurring. Now what is at stake is not just whether we speak about rape or not, but how we speak about rape and to what end' (17), following up on the question of ethics in representing sexual violence that we raised for Raihan's work. In the postcolonial world, they continue, writers and artists have repeatedly shown 'how narrative can work to subvert and transcend dominant hegemonies, refusing the category of victim' (17). In Nottage's play, victims or victimisation are not central to the action. What she dextrously weaves is a narrative in which sexual violence is linked with war and resource-grabbing but which also makes a strong case for bonding between women who refuse to submit to military or ethnic violence.

The use of the genre of theatre is strategic here. While reports and data developed by academics, funding bodies and NGOs routinely discuss the brutal condition of sexual violence in the DRC, they often sensationalise, objectify and reduce the complex fabric of Congolese society to stereotypes in order to negotiate for aid. As Ngwarsungu Chiwengo notes, rhetoric, genres and styles determine the framework of human rights discourse on justice and the appeal for justice, in which the rapes and genocide in the DRC routinely go unnoticed in comparison with those in Rwanda:

> The Congolese woman is commodified and delineated as a mere object in the market economy. Her sexuality becomes capital, since she willingly gives herself in exchange for money. The horrible mutilations and disfigurements, which no other women have been subjected to, images of which have been distributed through the Internet and made subject to voyeurism, thus lose their centrality; the violence, discrimination, and promiscuity inherent in their society displace the act of rape and normalize it. (89)

Writing memorial narratives of violence and rape is, thus, a monumental challenge as they are far from being neutral or universal. Chiwengo ends her 2008 article with the longing and the hope that the women of the Congo receive a complex and historically aware treatment of their pain and suffering – which I will argue Nottage's 2009 play duly responds to. Nottage wrote this play after a stint of community work in Uganda where she interacted with Congolese refugee women; a narrative she thought 'might call attention to the crisis' (x). Unlike NGO discourses and narrative styles, the play hardly depicts sexual violence; neither does it make stereotypes out of Congolese women. Unlike in Raihan where trauma leads to silence, Nottage (echoing Judith Herman) offers strong, vocal characters who build female solidarity through trauma. Here, the feminist aesthetics of theatre add a self-reflexive and compelling tone to the narrative, determined to restore agency and dignity to Congolese women. In this sense, the play is less about the graphic nature of rape and sexual violence than what Patrick Cannon, reading through various local solidarity and storytelling networks of women in the DRC, calls 'a feminist resistance to rape' (481). I will discuss here the (post)colonial conditions that have led to war and sexual violence and the ethics of anticolonial solidarity built through the character of Mama Nadi and through the theatrical conventions of dialogue and stylistics used in the play.

The play begins with a travelling salesman, Christian, soliciting two rescued women at Mama Nadi's bar. These women, Salima and Sophie, were raped by government military personnel and enslaved by a regiment from which they have subsequently escaped. Although Mama initially refuses to take them in, she soon realises that Salima's rustic innocence and Sophie's charm and singing talent will work well for her entertainment 'business'. We then discover both rebel and government soldiers drinking, eating and flirting with women at the bar, and claiming to be the rightful rulers of the DRC. Mama is too prudent to trust any of them; she has a business to run and mouths to feed. She thus liaises with both parties, until the Commander gets to know of the rebel soldiers gathering in her establishment and assaults Mama and her women. A pregnant Salima dies in the end declaring 'you will not fight your battles on my body any more' (Nottage 94), while Mama and her girls stand resolute against their attack. The intersections of sexual violence and resource wars are at the forefront of the play. Christian informs us in the beginning that 'Things are gonna get busy, Mama. All along the road people are talking about how this red dirt is rich with coltan. Suddenly everyone has a shovel and wants to stake claim' (13). The diamond merchant, Mr Harari, tells her, 'in this damnable age of the mobile phone it's become quite the precious ore, no? And for whatever reason God has seen fit to bless your backward country with an abundance of it' (25). These discussions make clear that this war is as much about who should rightfully rule the Congo as it is about who has better claim to its rich mineral resources. As Commander Osembenga, a military leader in the ruling government, suggests, the rebel leader Jerome Kisembe and his 'careless militias wage a diabolical campaign . . . And remember the land he claims as his own, it is a national reserve, it is the people's land, our land' (44). To this, Kisembe's response later is that the soldiers brought in from Uganda by the government drive them out of their homes and make them refugees, then call them criminals when they try to protect themselves: 'How can we let the government carve up our most valuable land to companies in China. It's our land' (74). These discussions insightfully set up the play's broader contexts – that it is a neoliberal, neocolonial war aimed at grabbing land and resources and lending them out to economic superpowers such as the USA or China for 'development' and 'democracy'.

These sociopolitical contexts of the play are, however, not new. Since the establishment of the Congo Free State by King Leopold II of Belgium in 1885 to develop and 'civilise' the territory through infrastructural projects, colonialism in the Congo, was widely marked by brutal imperialist military violence in which rape was used as a weapon of war to crush dissent – as poignantly shown by Adam Hochschild in *King Leopold's Ghost* (1998). After the Belgian government took over in 1908, rape, looting and killing continued in the resource-rich Congo and worsened in the postcolonial period under the dictator Joseph Mobutu and most prominently during the civil wars (Hunt). The civil wars were led by rebel leader Laurent-Désiré Kabila with support from Ugandan, Rwandan and Burundian military forces. After Kabila won the war and thereafter snapped ties with international forces, a second civil war began in which Mayi ayi, Interahamwe and other rebel forces such as FLDR based in the eastern DRC fought with government soldiers – FARDC – now led by the assassinated Kabila's son, Joseph Kabila, who became president of the DRC in a democratic election in 2007 thereby ending the civil war (Nzongola-Ntalaja; Stearns). Despite his constitutional pledge to curb sexual violence, the issue has not been addressed adequately. As several reports suggest, Kabila works as a neocolonial ruler, more of a CEO of the mining companies in the Congo rather than a president of the nation (Goddeeris 441). Nottage's strategic use of soldiers as characters and their selfish interests in land and resources is able to suggest this *longue durée* (neo)colonial history of the country.

Nottage has further shown that the neocolonial rapacity of the current government is sexually driven. Dr Denis Mukwege, renowned director of the Panzi Hospital in the eastern DRC's provincial capital Bukavu, calls this war a 'gynocide' in which rape is used as a tool to 'tear the bonds of a community apart and facilitate access to mineral wealth'. He further broods, '[a] century ago, the world needed rubber for tyres and ten million people died in King Leopold's plantations. Now it wants coltan ore for the microchips of phones and gadgets' (Duval Smith). In two of the most distressing scenes in Nottage's play, Salima poignantly establishes this link between sexual violence and resources. Seeing government soldiers at the bar, she remembers the harrowing experience of being raped and taken to a military regiment: 'I lay there as they tore me to pieces, until I was raw ... Five months. Chained like a goat. These men fighting ... fighting for our liberation' (Nottage 68). She heard from a soldier that they shot fifteen farmer-miners dead in the pit and split one miner's belly with a machete because he stuffed coltan into his mouth to prevent 'the soldiers from stealing his hard work' (Nottage 31). After this, the soldier had sex with Salima and then cried on her lap for consolation. What comes across from these tormenting remembrances is that raping unarmed, rural women is a display of masculine prowess – a declaration that soldiers can take the land and break the sanctity of family and household at any time; it is a means to emasculate family and society (Baaz and Stern 498–99; 510). Shelly Whitman, among others, has argued, 'Sexual violence is not just an unfortunate aspect of war, but a deliberate tactic used as a weapon of war' (136). Whitman shows that the demand for electronics in which coltan is used spiked radically after 2000 leading to an unprecedented surge in rape in the DRC (141). While these may suggest a simplistic reading of what Anne Laudati and Charlotte Mertens call the 'rape-resources narrative' (59), Salima's experience and the narrative of the soldier's actions as well as the immediate and historical contexts of rape and resources may indicate that Nottage has done a very careful job in weaving these complex narratives of looting, killing, rape and violence, guilt and catharsis together in this two-act play.

Postcolonial critic Anne McClintock writes that 'race, gender and class are not distinct realms of experience, existing in splendid isolation from each other' (5). They are interdependent 'if in contradictory and conflictual ways' (47). While Nottage establishes the interdependence of economy, resources, class, race and gender in the discussions above, she further offers a snippet of how women have to tackle the question of violence and yet continue to survive through bonds of solidarity which, following Thompson and Gunne, may be understood as an attempt at subverting their narrative beyond victimisation (and as a multidimensional reading of totality that we suggested in the first chapter of the book). Although the play is titled *Ruined*, despite rape, mutilation and ruin – like Bama's Dalit women in *Karukku* – women emerge strong, most expressly in Mama Nadi's character. She is a strong-willed woman who has survived several traumas including most harrowingly of being raped and her vagina being mutilated (from which the play's title is derived). From family history, she knows all too well the value of paperwork; she says to Mr Harari that she wants a piece of paper powerful enough that she can 'cut down forests and dig holes and build to the moon if I choose . . . But tell how does a woman like me get a piece of land, without having to pick up a gun?' (Nottage 27). This statement makes clear her anti-war sentiments and her historical experiential knowledge. Indeed, as Christian points to the postcolonial and racialised character of the Congo in his statement about the murder of a white missionary indicating that their lives mean nothing, Mama's matter of fact response is: 'a dead pastor is another dead man, and people here see that every day' (57).

In these examples, Mama appears as a postcolonial survivor who understands the importance of land and bureaucracy more than anything – that colonialism has made paperwork more important than tribal beliefs, and that diamonds and resources are finite and less valuable than legal contracts. This is the world built by white men who have brought only misfortune to the wealthy Congo, and thus their death does not perturb her. Throughout the play she continues to stand her ground against soldiers and militants, asking them to leave their guns with her and their 'bush laws' outside of the bar. She uses cunning and presence of mind to preserve her bar and livelihood from their wrath. As she whispers to Christian who is reluctant to drink with Osembenga: 'He can help us, or he can cause us many problems. It's your decision.' (49). Here, Mama is a pragmatic character. Wounded, yet determined to survive the bloody war, she shatters the girls' romantic longing to elope and go back to their families. It is ironic that the play ends with Mama softening towards Christian, a poet and an idealist, whom she has always liked from a distance. Like in Dionne Brand's poetry in *No Language is Neutral*, love, despite being poisonous and burdensome, offers her a relief and embrace that is much needed to survive. It is the same love and care for her girls that makes her give away her most valued object, a raw diamond, to Mr Harari to take Sophie away from the mess and find a hospital for her wounded vagina. In these examples of protection, protest and offering provisions to live, Mama builds the strongest example of anticolonial resistance and solidarity out of the ruined landscape of the Congo. This is where 'ruin' receives a historical and hopeful side. Following Ann Laura Stoler's reading of Walcott's ruinous imagination in *Omeros* as a celebration of survival, one may argue that through Mama 'we might turn to ruins as epicentres of renewed collective claims, as history in a spirited voice, as sites that animate both despair and new possibilities, bids for entitlement, and unexpected collaborative political projects' (Stoler 14).

This historic, hopeful aspect of ruin is corroborated by the theatre's effective techniques of speech, dialogue and stage building to decolonise trauma writing and render a voice to the 'subaltern'. While themes of rape and sexual violence have engaged feminist postcolonial theatre (Canning 152), critics such as Lauren Love and Joanna Townsend-Robinson have identified hysterical performance as a means of using gesture to undermine dramatic dialogue. Nottage's play, however, removes hysteria from its repertoire and, like Raihan above, is astonishingly lacking in sentimentality. Lisa Fitzpatrick further argues that 'Dramaturgical and performance strategies that maintain the audience's sympathetic focus on the woman's experience tend to attempt a phenomenological or morphological response to the violence of rape, often avoiding realistic or naturalistic representation entirely' (89). Conversely, the play offers a compelling realist take on sexual violence instead, giving voice to its characters and encouraging a postcolonial feminist resistance (as Herman and Visser have suggested). For instance, consider the opening stage directions of the play, 'A bar, makeshift furniture and a rundown pool table. A lot of effort has gone into making the worn bar cheerful. A stack of plastic washtubs rests in the corner. An old car battery powers the audio system, a covered birdcage sits conspicuously in the corner of the room' (Nottage 5). This bar is built through an assortment of discarded and makeshift materials. They are worn out yet valuable. In this worn-out and 'ruined' space, Mama and her girls stage their most resilient feat against the soldiers. Throughout the play, there is no escape from the bar (like there is no escape from action in the single room accommodation of Manjula Padmanabhan's play explored in the next chapter on 'Futures'). Nottage builds a very tight, contained setting to suggest that this play is not about the graphic nature of violence, war or patriotic glory. It is about living through the war, surviving and restoring oneself from its wounds. It is to recover humanity and dignity from the horrors of the war (the decolonising agenda), fought by local, domestic forces that are enabled by international forces and in which no one knows which side is good and which is bad. What matters is survival and living with respect, which Mama aims to do and which Nottage successfully addresses for postcolonial recovery.

Further, despite being a play based on sexual violence and trauma it contains hardly any monologues. It is full of dialogues, interspersed with songs, proverbs and dance. Countering Caruth and early trauma theories' stress on 'fragmented narratives', this play uses full-blooded, coherent, articulate dialogues to bring out the energy, enthusiasm and vitality of people talking and reaching out, even with banter and sarcasm. Dialogues are also important strategically because the play is not about the trauma arising out of colonising–patriarchal violence but about building anticolonial bonds through words, songs and cunning. What is particularly remarkable in the play is its use of songs. While there are ample references to the Americanisation of music and culture in the Congo, Sophie sings songs which have narratives and prose-like elements in them; very close to the African-American musical traditions of blues and jazz. Thus, in one of her songs, she reminds the soldiers,

> Cuz you come here to forget
> You say drive away all regret,
> And dance like it's the ending
> The ending of the war. (Nottage 30)

In another song, she uses the metaphor of a bird to express the paradoxical condition of searching for comfort and recognition and the consequences of capture and torture:

> To be seen is to be doomed,
> It must evade, evade capture
> And yet the bird
> Still cries out to be heard. (38)

Interestingly, there is a bird at the bar – a parrot which was given to Mama by the last of the Pygmies who had taught the parrot a few of the tribe's words for linguistic survival. While the parrot is mostly silent and bites people, forcing Mama to consider selling it, it remains with her throughout. The final lines of the play are spoken by the parrot, which utters 'Mama, Primus, Mama Primus'. Primus is a Congo-brewed beer that Mama sells. It is the beer that brings people together in her bar making them forget the war. Primus also means the head or lead Bishop of the Scottish Episcopal Church (*OED*). Mama is the leader here. While we do not know if the parrot can recall a single Pygmy word, it will certainly remember Mama and her bar which refused to give in to the violence of the soldiers; where everyone took care of each other through affective solidarities against sexual violence and brutality. It is through the tangible aesthetics of the play that *Ruined* attains a decolonising restorative element from the trauma of colonisation and the brutality of colonising violence and establishes an ethics of care between humans which is also extended to non-humans.

CONFLICT, EXILE AND THE TRAUMA OF STATELESSNESS IN MAHMOUD DARWISH'S *A RIVER DIES OF THIRST*

In Raihan's documentary, we encountered the key issue of exile and statelessness for postcolonial populations embroiled in civil wars. In Nottage, we noted the possibility of ethical bonding through the 'ruined' landscapes of war. In Mahmoud Darwish's poetry on the Israel–Palestine conflict, the phenomenon of statelessness and ethical bonding is rendered into an example of evocative and haunting tragedy, from which restoration may only lie in an imaginative reconciliation with the land and its people. Stan Smith writes that the displaced is the paradigmatic figure of twentieth century history and poetry. Displacement is 'not simply an external, geopolitical phenomenon. It is also an internal process, in which the subject is cast out from its own history and culture, sometimes from the very language in which it has been constituted. Yet, oddly, it continues to be the carrier and medium through which that culture comes to know itself' (Smith 10). The odd connotations of the displaced – absent and present in their homeland at the same time – appears evocatively in Darwish's poetry on the conflict. The Israel–Palestine conflict, broadly speaking, is centred around Israel as the Jewish 'Promised Land' in Israel which was ideologically built through the Zionist Congress and the Balfour Declaration in the early-twentieth century. This led to Jewish settlement in the region known as Palestine in the wake of the Second World War and the first Israel–Palestine War in 1947, which, however, proved catastrophic (known as 'nakba') for the Palestinians. In the following years, as a Jewish Israel settled on Arab lands, Palestinians lost their statehood, citizenship as well as humanity, suspended in their own homeland as exiles and the displaced (Robinson; Caplan). Darwish's poetry is marked by this loss of land and nation and is often read as a form of 'national narration' (Barnard). 'Poetry in the Palestinian context', Charlotta Salmi opines, has 'maintained a capacity to not just bring people together but to consolidate local as well as national allegiances' (59).

Darwish's first noted poem, 'Identity Card' written in the tumultuous period of the 1960s, caused an uproar amongst both Israeli and Palestinian people resulting in an unceasing forced exile for Darwish in Lebanon, Russia, the USA and elsewhere. Although he visited Palestine and Israel on various occasions, much of his poetry is about distorted, bifurcated identities in which his self contemplates the loss of his land and people, the disjunctive beings that he must live with, as well as about the beauty and eternity of love in nature that is lost to him forever – what Ifowodo, following Fanon, calls the psychopathology of the post/colonial subject (24). My discussions here will draw from his 2007 anthology *A River Dies of Thirst: Journals*, and focus mainly on the question of trauma as experienced through the loss of land and self.

The titular poem sets up the question of how land and resources of the Palestinian people have been hijacked and destroyed by armed forces.

> A river was here
>
> And it had two banks
>
> And a heavenly mother who nursed it on drops from the clouds (36)

The diction and imagery as well as lack of punctuation in the poem's beginning evoke a sense of pristine innocence and the untenable beauty of the river and its surrounding environment. The river is nursed by the clouds and the rain, and meanders through the nearby villages and tents 'like a charming lively guest', bringing 'oleander trees and date palms' to the valley and gurgling songs to the 'nocturnal revellers'. These images introduce us to the immense role this river plays in the valley, helping humans and non-humans draw life-nourishing sustenance from it and participate in the joy of its heavenly presence. Critics have duly noted the abundance of environmental imagery in Arab/Palestinian poetry, especially in Darwish, the 'national poet of Palestine' (R. Spencer; Boast).

The romantic Keatsian imagery of a world sustained by humans and nonhumans alike is then disrupted by the reminder of its past existence. The past tense of the poem gains momentum here, suggesting we are approaching an uncertain, probably tragic end to the tale of this river:

> But they kidnapped its mother
>
> So it ran short of water
>
> And died, slowly, of thirst. (36)

Unlike the Keatsian romance with nature, Darwish employs heavy war-related imagery of kidnapping. While kidnapping has been a key strategy in postcolonial civil wars where armed groups have forcefully taken away civilians, women and children from the land or resources that sustain them, the term has longer roots in the discourses of slavery and colonialism. Kidnapping means abduction and holding someone captive for ransom. The word began to be used in the seventeenth century, roughly coinciding with the emergence of European slavery in Africa (*OED*). Indeed, a number of scholars have written widely about postcolonial abduction especially in the context of indigenous displacement (Hulme; Sen). Abduction, thus, becomes a key trope through which the atmosphere of fear, power and threat is built. It is also worth noting here that postcolonial scholarship has long raised Israel's existence in the Arab world (like India or Pakistan in Kashmir), as an occupier and a settler–coloniser working, through genocide, forceful displacement, abduction and slaughter of Indigenous people and occupation of their lands and resources, such as has happened in Canada, Australia or Latin America (Zureik; Shafir). 'Kidnapping the clouds' in this sense refers to the occupation of the sky or the heavens, for war, seizing its abundance and generosity – meaning the natural relations between clouds, water and the growth of the vegetational world are lost. The inevitable consequence is the absence of water for the river. The final line is alarming here: 'a river is dying of thirst'. A river is known by its waterbody; without it, the river becomes dry and meaningless. Not only is it unable to sustain a natural world around it, but it loses its main resource of vitality or its existential meaning. Hannah Boast reads these lines as 'hydropolitical': the poem is about the colonial abduction of land and humanity as well as about River Jordan drying up and its course being forcibly diverted, proving catastrophic for the local population who are dependent on it for their survival (279). What is remarkable about the imagery of the river drying up is its oxymoronic nature: a river does not live without water. Without water not only does it lose ontological significance and dies of thirst, metaphorically, this longing for water also makes the oxymoron (ironically) complete – which suggests that the vitality it brought to the valley is also gone. This is the larger meaning of the extinction of life that Darwish suggests war brings forth, producing through this poem and imagery an 'archive of ecological trauma' (Mortimer-Sandison 342) in the postcolonial world.

Trauma, thus, begins with the feeling of constantly being at war and in exile. The past tense in the poem already evokes a sense of loss, which is consolidated through the loss of a single, unitary self and the constant fear of forgetting and death. In the prose poem 'The law of fear', Darwish offers how fear of a pre-emptive strike is the cause of the current catastrophe:

> The killer looks at the spectre of the dead man, or into his eyes, without regret. He says to those around him: 'Don't blame me. I'm afraid. I killed because I'm afraid, and I'll kill again because I'm afraid.' (*A River Dies of Thirst* 38)

Naomi Klein writes that one of the key reasons behind man-made disasters in West Asia is pre-emptive strikes from richer nations in the West. While these strikes seem to be about defending and protecting national sovereignty, they are often conducted in order to instil a deep sense of neocolonial fear and submission in the target populations. Klein writes, 'this fundamentalist form of (deregulated) capitalism has consistently been midwifed by the most brutal forms of coercion . . . escalating levels of violence and ever larger disasters are required in order to reach the goal' (18–9). These observations resonate well with the colonising sentiments of the killer in the poem. The conversational structure of the prose poem (note that Darwish's collection is subtitled 'journals') – renders explicit the 'logical' sentiment in murdering subjected and displaced populations. As the poem progresses, we notice that this sentiment is institutionalised through a psycho-juridical endorsement from the public – that 'He's defending himself' – followed by their drumming up politico-economic support for it:

> Others, admirers of the idea that progress is superior to Morality, say 'Justice emanates from the generosity of power. The victim should apologise for the trauma he has caused the killer'. (*A River Dies of Thirst* 38)

With remarkable poise and integrity, Darwish here exposes the frailty of 'trauma theory' in besieged lands. Here victims are blamed for causing the killing. Victim-blaming, or what is technically known as DARVO (Deny, Attack, and Reverse Victim and Offender), is a widely present technique in psycho-trauma theory which has been used for 'curing' perpetrators of violence, especially soldiers, since the US invasion of Vietnam (Figley). The trauma of the victim or survivor of being raped, killed, abandoned, robbed of land and family or surviving will not matter here as social, legal and economic institutions have established themselves through the means of victim-blaming. What is striking about Darwish here is that, like Hamid in *The Reluctant Fundamentalist*, he draws upon the corrosive nature of irony to expose the murderous logic that allows a killer state to absolve itself of all its crimes. The perpetrators in the poem, thus, offer foreign tourists – much like Changez's second-person narrator to the interviewer – the logic behind murdering children, women and trees/nature because they will grow up and frighten the already frightened. But we know that this is a very different living condition from Hamid or Adichie, as the latter's protagonists can at least return to their 'homeland' to feel alienated and choose to move further elsewhere. For Darwish, there is no land to return to; Palestinians are perpetually exiled. Thus, women will give birth only to memories (a compelling metaphor for the displaced, strikingly tied up with children growing) and birds will sit on trees and sing songs of loss, beauty and joy. Even then, these human and natural conditions will need to be terminated with pre-emptive strikes. As Darwish writes in 'The law of fear', 'The spectre of the dead man appeared to them from a cloudless sky and when they opened fire on him they did not see a single drop of blood, and they were afraid'. Just before this action, the populace supporting pre-emptive strikes shouted that 'fear, not justice, is the basis of power' (*A River Dies of Thirst* 38). What is suggested in this frightened defence is the birth of absolute biopower – where the sovereign can decide on the death of its citizens and enemies only to protect itself, turning people into displaced, stateless refugees (Cohen). In his noted essay 'Necropolitics', Achille Mbembe called this settler-colonialism of Israel 'necropolitical'. For Mbembe, a necropolitical state

> allows a modality of killing that does not distinguish between the external and the internal enemy. Entire populations are the target of the sovereign. The besieged villages and towns are sealed off and cut off from the world. Daily life is militarized. Freedom is given to local military commanders to use their discretion as to when and whom to shoot. ("Necropolitics" 28)

The fearful neocolonial state in Darwish has killed everyone it considers enemies. Its enemies are now all the spectres of dead people, conjuring an image of the enemy which however cannot be killed any longer. This fear further terrifies the 'neocolonial necropolitical' state (Motyl and Arghavan) with the imminent coming of a spectral army. The image and the thought process are both haunting and traumatising in its calm prosaic language and its sense of never-ending terror evoked by the use of free verse.

While fear runs through many of the poems in the collection, they also lead to a sense of modernist disjunction of the self, mediated through the means of free verse. Because the victim or Darwish's poet–narrator (or subject–protagonist) is either dead or displaced, there is a constant sense of longing and forgetting in the poems – a kind of modernist anticolonial healing for Ifowodo. Ifowodo writes that Fanon's concept of 'occult instability' merges the psychological and the political trajectories of revolutionary anticolonial politics where 'the oppressed people dwell and their souls are crystallized'. This is 'where we must come to do any meaningful work of reconstituting the fragmented identity of the postcolonial subject— with the realm of postcolonial trauma' (Ifowodo 14). 'Occult' here refers to both the supernatural and that which is excluded from normal and standardised reality. Darwish's poems on the dead dwell on the 'occult' for building an anticolonial understanding of forgetting and remembering, to decolonise postcolonial identities. For instance, while in 'Identity card', an anguished Darwish declared that the oppressed was hungry and angry and might eat the flesh of the oppressor, in 'Beyond identification' he points to a schizophrenic self which is not able to identify itself in the multitude of selves:

> I sit in front of the television, since I can't do anything else. There, in front of the television, I discover my feelings and see what's happening to me. Smoke is rising from me and I reach out for my severed hand to pick up my scattered limbs from many bodies. (*A River Dies of Thirst* 7)

Many of the poems are written in free verse resembling a thought process – a rambling monologue without expected punctuation (they could easily belong to Mama Nadi if Nottage had allowed that in *Ruined*). In 'Beyond identification' the thought process has a specific rhythm and appeal – it is about the narrator discovering their limbs and body parts scattered elsewhere. Evocative of war and the dismemberment of bodies, the poem continues to create an expansion of the self in which the narrator can empathise with or rather own the many bodies and parts lost and dismembered in wars. This is where lyrical poetry differs from a dialogue-based play in terms of reflecting on the ruined body and state, which for Nottage or Raihan is more of a call for gathering momentum and solidarity.

In 'A sort of loss' for instance, another free verse prose poem, the poet-narrator believes that he and his shadow are two different beings – again modernist in its ethos of social and psychological disjunction and yet deeply realist in its depiction of and reasoning through postcolonial war. While he is interested in seeing the sea from the highest point of the hill, his shadow is 'entangled in a thorn bush and is injured but not bleeding' (57). While he tries to free it, he is pricked by a thorn. He continues upward and can manage to behold the sea which however 'has been taken prisoner in one of the wars'. These themes of a constant sense of loss, disjunction of identity and dismemberment return to Darwish throughout his career, as in these evocative lines in *Memory for Forgetfulness*: 'I am the one walking in the funeral procession, and the one whose funeral procession it is' (647). In the prose poem, 'In the empty square', for instance, Darwish offers a vivid picture of loss and the absence of people and animals in a space that was previously ceaselessly busy with sounds: 'An empty square. Flies, midday heat and a fig tree keeping nobody company' (*A River Dies of Thirst* 92). In this empty square, dryness is compared to 'a piece of metal' again conjuring up the imposing ambience of war. The poet tells us that once there was life here 'that came from the narrow alleys to take the sun or have a breath of air or prove what was possible' (92). The thriving alley is now full of snakes, a metaphor for evil and treachery leading to one's doom. For the poet, this is now a nightmarish reality. As the empty square enlarges magically, the poet remembers 'the words I had not spoken, remembered them and forgot them' (92). Remembering and forgetting are fundamental to being in exile, in which one has to live two lives – one of adaptation and the other of longing. In the poem, 'Exile', Darwish wrote,

> The outside world is an exile,
> And the inside world is an exile
> So who are you between the two? (*If I Were Another* 185)

Reading the theme of exile and forgetfulness in Darwish's writing, Lucy Perry comments, 'Darwish narrates the state of exile not just as a physical or geographical state of dislocation and dispossession, but a temporal one. Without the redemption of a homeland, a disavowal of the present and the resurrection of the past through reminiscence and imagination become the sole means through which identity is recovered and preserved' (102). A dislocated imagination and a blurred and intense gathering of memory are at the heart of postcolonial exile. These words recall Edward Said's poignant thoughts on the topic: 'For an exile habits of life, expression or activity in the new environment inevitably occur against the memory of these things in another environment. Thus, both the new and the old environments are vivid, actual, occurring together contrapuntally' (186). Remembering is thus necessary for engaging with loss and negotiating trauma, but so is forgetting. Forgetting, as Darwish mentions in several of his poems, is the most natural consequence of displacement, in which images arise in disrupted consequences. As Ifowodo mentions, it is remembering and forgetting together, 'a poetics of amnesia', that acts as 'a precondition for individual and communal healing' for postcolonial authors (77).

As readers may note, almost all of Darwish's poems are intensely spatial. They continuously allude to material and metaphorical objects such as land, bird, river, food, people, language and dialogue – all from a Palestine that is no longer there. It is with, what Raymond Williams in another context calls the 'resources of hope' (1989), that Darwish is able to build a sense of solidarity with his long-suffering homeland. I conclude the discussion here with a brief note on love in the poem 'At the top of the cypress trees'. Like Brand's 'Hard against the Soul', this is a lyrical poem about love and sexual inscription in nature. The South African-Australian writer, J. M. Coetzee once stated that apartheid South Africa was so racialised that love, the most natural of all social phenomena, was muffled here; South African literature was a 'literature of bondage' (98). For Darwish, an exile writing on the apartheid of his homeland, however, love is all he can think of and conjure up as a moment of restoration from the chaos and suffering of contemporary life. In his poems, lovers meet and discuss trifling matters, quarrel, love and share intimacies. In the poem 'At the top of the cypress trees' is also a lover who writes a poem to his beloved. For the lover, it was a dream, a song for her, in which the joy and beauty of the valley was compressed and extended: 'Life is short and beautiful' and meant to be enjoyed with love and passion. They both realise then that they are no longer alive, but rather are ghosts at the top of the cypress trees; to which their immediate response is: 'perhaps ghosts can converse like souls' (*A River Dies of Thirst* 85). As noted before, ghosts, spectres and apparitions populate Darwish's spatial imagery; the 'occult instability' of the post/colonised. These are what war has turned a thriving population into. But unlike the previous poem, soldiers cannot kill them any longer. Thus, they can finally converse in the trees. Darwish does not write of humans here. In using 'souls', apart from alluding to the spectral aspect of the conversation, it seems to me that he further recognises (in a Fanonian decolonising gesture) that what makes humans human is their soul and their ability to be kind and generous to each other, which is missing from the current disposition in which humans are understood as enemies and disposable bodies. Critics have argued that love for Darwish is a love for the collective, for national liberation, for an exile's return to their nation (Jayyusi). While this is true, love is also personal and restorative for Darwish, 'genuinely private' as another noted Palestinian poet Mourid Barghouti suggested of his work (146; see also Cohen-Mor's work on Darwish's 'Rita' poems). Through these poems and his evocation of a tangible homeland from a distance, like Salmi I argue that Darwish's work offers a more critical task akin to Said's definition of the critic: 'he is both rooted in the national community and capable of distancing himself from it' (Salmi 63). This is where Darwish's poetry achieves a rare case of Saidian 'critical solidarity', or what Craps terms 'anamnestic solidarity' – of expressing love for his homeland and its lost moments of everyday intimate affairs from afar and being alert to the problematic contingencies that could lead to ethno-nationalist desperations.

In the end, it is useful to note that it is love and fellow feeling that all of these works invoke in the face of brutal postcolonial wars, sexual violence, genocide and exile. This is precisely what literature and imaginative works can offer. Unlike short-term fixes or objective analyses of the situation for quick mitigation, these works point to the heart of the suffering and pain of postcolonial populations. They show that many of these wars are legacies of a colonial past and thus long-term and never-ending, inducing a chronic and collective nature of trauma. A meaningful anticolonial recovery from this lies in listening to the stories of people, sharing their pain and (even if figuratively) standing by them in their endless global struggles. Raihan's documentary film uses the trauma of children and women as a mode with which to reach out towards anticolonial international solidarity. Lynn Nottage's theatre of civil war and sexual violence in the DRC propagates care, bonding and resistance in nationally turbulent times. In Darwish's poetry on the loss of land and resources, recovery is sought through allusions to the divided self and the endless desire to be loved, taken care of and brought to being with one's language, land and self. Overall, these three literary and cultural works through their specific generic properties are able to capture both the broad, sweeping and collective call for solidarity (Raihan) and offer variations on the theme of close-ups (Nottage and Darwish) to build fast (urgent) and slow (reflective) modes of representing and recovering from postcolonial trauma.

As we move to the next chapter on ecology, these conversations on war and postcolonial environments set us up for 'colonialist' questions of scarcity, epidemics and resilience that postcolonial nations complexly negotiate, and in doing so echo the key argument in the book on the interconnectedness of conceptual rubrics and thematic topics in the postcolonial world.

NOTES

1. Archer Blood was US Consul general in Dhaka when the military crackdown was launched. He sent several telegrams to then US president, Richard Nixon, and Secretary of State, Henry Kissinger,

about needing US intervention to stop the genocide and restore democracy in East Pakistan. But the US supported West Pakistan to open diplomatic relations with China and did nothing to stop the violence

REFERENCES

Akhter, Fahmida. "Zahir Raihan's *Stop Genocide* (1971): A Dialectical Cinematic Message to the World". *South Asian Filmscapes: Transregional Encounters*, edited by Elora Halim Chowdhury and Esha Niyogi De, U of Washington P, 2020, pp. 233–49.

Anderegg, Michael, editor. *Inventing Vietnam. The War in Film and Television*. Temple UP, 1991.

Baaz, Maria Eriksson, and Maria Stern. "Why Do Soldiers Rape? Masculinity, Violence, and Sexuality in the Armed Forces in the Congo (DRC)". *International Studies Quarterly*, vol. 53, no. 2, 2009, pp. 495–518.

Barghouti, Mourid. "The Servants of War and their Language". *Autodafe: The Journal of International Parliament of Writers*, Seven Stories P, 2003.

Barnard, Anna. *Rhetorics of Belonging: Nation, Narration, and Israel/Palestine*. Liverpool UP, 2013.

Bass, Gary J. *The Blood Telegram: Nixon, Kissinger and a Forgotten Genocide*. Alfred A. Knopf, 2013.

Baxter, Katherine Isobel. "Memory and Photography: Rethinking Postcolonial Trauma Studies". *Journal of Postcolonial Writing*, vol. 47, no. 1, 2011, pp. 18–29.

Beachler, Donald. "The Politics of Genocide Scholarship: The Case of Bangladesh". *Patterns of Prejudice*, vol. 41, no. 5, 2007, pp. 467–92.

Boast, Hannah. "'A River without Water': Hydropolitics and the River Jordan in Palestinian Literature". *Journal of Commonwealth Literature*, vol. 51, no. 2, 2016, pp. 275–86.

Brown, Laura S. "Not Outside the Range: One Feminist Perspective on Psychic Trauma". *Trauma: Explorations in Memory*, edited by Cathy Caruth, Johns Hopkins UP, 1995, pp. 100–12.

Canning, Charlotte. *Feminist Theaters in the USA: Staging Women's Experience*. Routledge, 1996.

Cannon, Patrick. "A Feminist Response to Rape as a Weapon of War in Eastern Congo". *Peace Review*, vol. 24, no. 4, 2012, pp. 478–83.

Caplan, Neil. *The Israel-Palestine Conflict: Contested Histories*. Wiley-Blackwell, 2011.

Caruth, Cathy. *Unclaimed Experience: Trauma, Narrative, and History*. Johns Hopkins UP, 1996.

Césaire, Aimé. *Discourse on Colonialism*. Translated by Joan Pinkham, Monthly Review Press, 1973.

Chiwengo, Ngwarsungu. "When Wounds and Corpses Fail to Speak: Narratives of Violence and Rape in Congo (DRC)". *Comparative Studies of South Asia, Africa and the Middle East*, vol. 28, no. 1, 2008, pp. 78–92.

Coetzee, J. M. *Doubling the Point: Essays and Interviews*, edited by David Attwell, Harvard UP, 1992.

Cohen, Hella Bloom. *The Literary Imagination in Israel-Palestine: Orientalism, Poetry, Biopolitics*. Palgrave Macmillan, 2016.

Cohen-Mor, Dalya. *Mahmoud Darwish: Palestine's Poet and Other as the Beloved*. Palgrave Macmillan, 2019.

Craps, Stef, and Gert Buelens. "Introduction: Postcolonial Trauma Novels". *Studies in the Novel*, vol. 40, no. 1/2, 2008, pp. 1–12.

---. *Postcolonial Witnessing: Trauma out of Bounds*. Palgrave Macmillan, 2013.

Dalley, Hamish. "The Question of "Solidarity" in Postcolonial Trauma Fiction: Beyond the Recognition Principle". *Humanities*, vol. 4, no. 3, 2015, pp. 369–92.

Darwish, Mahmoud. *A River Dies of Thirst: Journals*. Translated by Catherine Cobham, Archipelago Press, 2009.

---. *If I Were Another*. Translated by Fady Joudah, Farrar, Straus and Giroux, 2009.

---. *Memory for Forgetfulness: August, Beirut, 1982*. Translated by Ibrahim Muhawi, U of California P, 1995.

Datta, Antara. *Refugees and Borders in South Asia: The Great Exodus of 1971*. Routledge, 2013.

Dirk Moses, A., editor. *Empire, Colony, Genocide: Conquest, Occupation, and Subaltern Resistance in World History*. Berghahn Books, 2008.

Duval Smith, Alex. "The Doctor who Heals Victims of Congo's War Rapes". *The Guardian,* 14 Nov. 2010, https://www.theguardian.com/world/2010/nov/14/doctor-mukwege-congo-war-rapes. Accessed 14 May 2022.

Fanon, Frantz. *The Wretched of the Earth.* Translated by Constance Farrington, Grove Press, 1963.

Felman, Shoshana, and Dori Laub. *Testimony: Crises of Witnessing in Literature, Psychoanalysis, and History.* Routledge, 1992.

Figley, Charles R. *Encyclopaedia of Trauma: An Interdisciplinary Guide.* Sage, 2012.

Fitzpatrick, Lisa. *Rape on the Contemporary Stage.* Palgrave Macmillan, 2018.

'Genocide.' *The United Nations Office of Genocide Prevention and the Responsibility to Protect,* https://www.un.org/en/genocideprevention/genocide.shtml. Accessed 11 April 2022.

Getino, Octavio, and Fernando Solanas. "Toward a Third Cinema". *Cineaste,* vol. 4 no. 3, 1971, pp. 1–10.

Goddeeris, Idesbald. "Postcolonial Belgium: The Memory of the Congo". *Interventions: International Journal of Postcolonial Studies,* vol. 17, no. 3, 2015, pp. 434–51.

Gunne, Sorcha, and Zoë Brigley Thompson, editors. *Feminism, Literature and Rape Narratives: Violence and Violation.* Routledge, 2010.

Hartman, Geoffrey H. "On Traumatic Knowledge and Literary Studies". *New Literary History,* vol. 26, no. 3, 1995, pp. 537–63.

Heerten, Lasse, and A. Dirk Moses. "The Nigeria–Biafra War: Postcolonial Conflict and the Question of Genocide". *Journal of Genocide Research,* vol. 16, no. 2–3, 2014, pp. 169–203.

Herman, Judith Lewis. *Trauma and Recovery: From Domestic Abuse to Political Terror.* Pandora, 1994.

Hochschild, Adam. *King Leopold's Ghost: A Story of Greed, Terror and Heroism in Colonial Africa.* Houghton Mifflin Harcourt, 1999.

Horeck, Tanya. *Public Rape: Representing Violation in Fiction and Film.* Routledge, 2004.

Hulme, Peter. *Colonial Encounters: Europe and the Native Caribbean, 1492-1797.* Routledge, 1992.

Hunt, Nancy Rose. *A Nervous State: Violence, Remedies and Reverie in Colonial Congo.* Duke UP, 2016.

Ifowodo, Ogaga. *History, Trauma and Healing in Postcolonial Narratives: Reconstructing Identities*. Palgrave Macmillan, 2013.

Jahan, Rounaq. "Genocide in Bangladesh". *Century of Genocide: Eyewitness Accounts and Critical Views*, editors Samuel Totten, William S. Parsons and Israel W. Charny, Garland Publishing, 1997, pp. 291–316.

Jayyusi, Salma Khadra. "Mahmoud Darwish's Mission and Place in Arab Literary History". *Mahmoud Darwish, Exile's Poet: Critical Essays*, editors Hala Khamis Nassar and Najat Rahman, Olive Branch Press, 2008.

Kabir, Alamgir. *Film in Bangladesh*. Bangla Academy, 1979.

Katz, Steven T. *The Holocaust in Historical Context*. Vol. 1: *The Holocaust and Mass Death before the Modern Age*. Oxford UP, 1994.

Khanna, Ranjana. "*The Battle of Algiers* and *the Nouba of the women of Mont Chenoua*: From Third to Fourth Cinema". *Third Text*, vol. 12, no. 43, 1998, pp. 13–21.

'Kidnap'. *Oxford English Dictionary Online*, https://www.oed.com/dictionary/kidnap_v?tab=meaning_and_use#40158323. Accessed 27 January 2024.

Klein, Naomi. *The Shock Doctrine: The Rise of Disaster Capitalism*. Penguin, 2007.

LaCapra, Dominick. *Writing History, Writing Trauma*. Johns Hopkins UP, 2001.

Laudati, Ann, and Charlotte Mertens. "Resources and Rape: Congo's (Toxic) Discursive Complex". *African Studies Review*, vol. 62, no. 4, 2019, pp. 57–82.

Leahy, James. "Films that Make a Difference…: Santiago Alvarez and the Politics of Bengal". *Sense of Cinema*, no. 23, 2002, https://www.sensesofcinema.com/2002/cteq/alvarez_ciclon/. Accessed 19 April 2022.

Lenin, Vladimir I. "The Right of Nations to Self-Determination". *Collected Works*, Vol. 20. Translated by Bernard Isaacs and Joe Fineberg, Progress Publishers, 1972.

Lloyd, David. "Colonial Trauma/Postcolonial Recovery?". *Interventions: International Journal of Postcolonial Studies*, vol. 2, no. 2, 2000, pp. 212–28.

Love, Lauren. "Resisting the 'Organic': A Feminist Actor's Approach". *Acting (Re)Considered*. 2nd ed., edited by Phillip Zarrilli, Routledge, 2002, pp. 277–90.

Lu, Jing. *On State Secessions from International Law Perspectives*. Springer, 2018.

Mamdani, Mahmood. *When Victims Become Killers: Colonialism, Nativism, and the Genocide in Rwanda*. Princeton UP, 2001.

---. "Making Sense of Political Violence in Post-colonial Africa". *Socialist Register*, vol. 40, 2003, pp. 132–51.

Marks, Laura U. *The Skin of the Film: Intercultural Cinema, Embodiment, and the Senses*. Duke UP, 2000.

Mascarenhas, Anthony. "Genocide". *The Sunday Times*, 21 June 1971, Reprinted in *The Daily Star*, 22 March 2021, https://www.thedailystar.net/supplements/victory-day-special-2017/genocide-1505440. Accessed 19 April, 2022.

Mbembe, Achille. *On the Postcolony*. U of California P, 2001.

---. "Necropolitics". *Public Culture*, vol. 15, no. 1, 2003, pp. 11–40.

McClintock, Anne. *Imperial Leather: Race, Gender, and Sexuality in the Colonial Context*. Routledge, 1995.

Mohaiemen, Naeem. "Simulation at War's End: A 'Documentary' in the Field of Evidence Quest". *BioScope*, vol. 7, no. 1, 2011, pp. 31–57.

Mookherjee, Nayanika. "'Never again': Aesthetics of 'Genocidal' Cosmopolitanism and the Bangladesh Liberation War Museum." *The Journal of the Royal Anthropological Institute*, vol. 17, 2011, pp. S71–91.

Motyl, Katharina, and Mahmoud Arghavan. "Writing against Neocolonial Necropolitics: Literary responses by Iraqi/Arab writers to the US 'War on Terror'". *European Journal of English Studies*, vol. 22, no. 2, 2018, pp. 128–41.

Murshid, Navine. *The Politics of Refugees in South Asia: Identity, Resistance, Manipulation*. Routledge, 2013.

Norridge, Zoë. "Writing against Genocide: Genres of Opposition in Narratives from and about Rwanda". *Postcolonial Poetics: Genre and Form*, edited by Patrick Crowley and Jane Hiddleston, Liverpool UP, 2013, pp. 241–61.

Nottage, Lynn. *Ruined*. 2009. Nick Hern Books, 2012.

Nzongola-Ntalaja, Georges. *The Congo from Leopold to Kabila: A People's History*. Zed Books, 2002.

Perry, Lucy A. "The Poetics of Dispossession in Mahmoud Darwish's 'Exile'". *Journal of Palestine Studies* vol. 49, no. 4, 2020, pp. 91–108.

Ponzanesi, Sandra, and Marguerite Waller. "Introduction". *Postcolonial Cinema Studies*, edited by Sandra Ponzanesi and Marguerite Waller, Routledge, 2011, pp. 1–16.

"Primus". *Oxford English Dictionary Online*, https://www.oed.com/dictionary/primus_n?tab=meaning_and_use#28369695. Accessed 27 January 2024.

Rashid, Azra. *Gender, Nationalism, Genocide: Naristhan/Ladyland*. Routledge, 2019.

Robinson, Shira. *Citizen Strangers: Palestinians and the Birth of Israel's Liberal Settler State*. Stanford UP, 2013.

Rothberg, Michael. "Decolonizing Trauma Studies: A Response". *Studies in the Novel*, vol. 40, no. 1/2, 2008, pp. 224–34.

Said, Edward. *Reflections on Exile and Other Essays*. Harvard UP, 2000.

Saikia, Yasmin. *Women, War, and the Making of Bangladesh: Remembering 1971*. Oxford UP, 2011.

Salmi, Charlotta. "A Necessary Forgetfulness of the Memory of Place: Mahmoud Darwish's Poetry of No Return". *Interventions: International Journal of Postcolonial Studies*, vol. 14, no. 1, 2012, pp. 55–68.

Sen, Satadru. *Savagery and Colonialism in the Indian Ocean: Power, Pleasure and the Andaman Islanders*. Routledge, 2009.

Shafir, Gershon. *A Half Century of Occupation: Israel, Palestine, and the World's Most Intractable Conflict*. U of California P, 2017.

Shaughnessy, C. A. "The Vietnam Conflict: 'America's Best Documented War'?" *The History Teacher*, vol. 24, no. 2, 1991, pp. 135–47.

Shaw, Martin. *War and Genocide: Organized Killing in Modern Society*. Polity Press, 2003.

Shohat, Ella, and Robert Stam, editors. *Multiculturalism, Postcoloniality, and Transnational Media*. Rutgers UP, 2003.

Smith, Stan. *Poetry and Displacement*. Liverpool UP, 2007.

Spencer, Philip. "Imperialism, Anti-imperialism, and the Problem of Genocide, Past and Present." *History: The Journal of the Historical Association*, vol. 98, no. 4, 2013, pp. 606–22.

Spencer, Robert. "Ecocriticism in the Colonial Present: The Politics of Dwelling in Raja Shehadeh's *Palestinian Walks: Notes on a Vanishing Landscape*". *Postcolonial Studies*, vol. 13, no. 1, 2010, pp. 33–54.

Stearns, Jason K. *The War that Doesn't Say Its Name: The Unending Conflict in the Congo*. Princeton UP, 2021.

Stoler, Ann Laura, editor. *Imperial Debris: On Ruins and Ruination*. Duke UP, 2013.

Stop Genocide. Directed by Zahir Raihan, Bangladesh Chalachitra Shilpi-O-Kushali Swahayak Samity and Bangladesh Liberation Council of the Intelligentsia. 1971.

Sunderason, Sanjukta and Lotte Hoek. "Introduction: Forms of the Left in Postcolonial South Asia". *Forms of the Left in Postcolonial South Asia: Aesthetics, Networks and Connected Histories*, edited by Sanjukta Sunderason and Lotte Hoek, Bloomsbury, 2022, pp. 1–32.

Townsend-Robinson, Joanna. "Expressing the Unspoken: Hysterical Performance as Radical Theatre". *Women's Studies*, vol. 32, no. 5, 2003, pp. 533–57.

Tyson, Adam. "Genocide Documentary as Intervention". *Journal of Genocide Research*, vol. 17, no. 2, 2015, pp. 177–99.

van Schendel, William. *A History of Bangladesh*. Cambridge UP, 2009.

Virdi, Jyotika, "Reverence, Rape—and then Revenge: Popular Hindi Cinema's 'Women's Film'". *Killing Women: The Visual Culture of Gender and Violence*, edited by Annette Burfoot and Susan Lord, Wilfrid Laurier UP, 2006, pp. 251–72.

Visser, Irene. "Decolonizing Trauma Theory: Retrospect and Prospects". *Humanities*, vol. 4, no. 2, 2015, pp. 250–65.

---. "Trauma Theory and Postcolonial Literary Studies". *Journal of Postcolonial Writing*, vol. 47, no. 3, 2011, pp. 270–82.

Ward, Abigail, editor. *Postcolonial Traumas: Memory, Narrative, Resistance*. Palgrave Macmillan, 2015.

Weaver-Hightower, Rebecca. "Introduction: New Perspectives on Postcolonial Film". *Postcolonial Film: History, Empire, Resistance*, edited by Rebecca Weaver-Hightower and Peter Hulme, Routledge, 2014.

Whitman, Shelly. "Sexual Violence, Coltan and the Democratic Republic of the Congo". *Natural Resources and Social Conflict: Towards Critical Environmental Security*, edited by Matthew A. Schnurr and Larry A. Swatuk, Palgrave Macmillan, 2012, pp. 128–51.

Williams, Raymond. *Resources of Hope: Culture, Democracy, Socialism*. Verso, 1989.

Wolfe, Philip. "Structure and Event: Settler Colonialism, Time, and the Question of Genocide". *Empire, Colony, Genocide: Conquest, Occupation, and Subaltern Resistance in World History*, edited by A. Dirk Moses, Berghahn Books, 2008, pp. 102–32.

Zureik, Elia. *Israel's Colonial Project in Palestine: Brutal Pursuit*. Routledge, 2016.

Chapter Five

Ecologies

EXTRACTION, HUNGER, EPIDEMICS AND CARE IN DEVI, MPE AND SENIOR

Defined by the *Oxford English Dictionary* (*OED*) as a 'branch of biology that deals with the relation of organisms to one another and with their physical surroundings', 'Ecology'– as a field of research – came into existence during the high tide of European imperialism in the late nineteenth century. Ecology developed from early European discussions on taxonomy, genetics, mutation and natural selection offering studies into ecosystems, that is, the dynamic relations between humans, nonhumans and the biosphere. Scholars have pointed to the colonial–imperialist context of the foundations of the 'natural' or 'ecological' sciences and their contribution to the development of the controversial topics of eugenics and scientifically justified racism. Maria Louise Pratt, for instance, has commented that 'Linnaeus' system alone launched a European knowledge-building enterprise of unprecedented scale and appeal' (25). Richard Grove has subsequently shown that European tropical island colonies were used as laboratories for scientific and sociocultural experimentation from the mid-seventeenth century onwards; often, paradoxically, through the 'environmentalist' discourses of 'paradise' and 'exotica' (229–30). Such research has been crucial in interrogating colonial impact on ecology and environment in the post/colonial periods, thereby establishing the term's second *OED* meaning of 'political movement and advocacy regarding human impact on the environment,' or what is geologically known as the

Anthropocene.[1] If colonisation had originally meant settling on 'foreign' territories and cultivating land, colonialism was turned into a culturally hegemonic doctrine through science and education, in which everything European or western – often shorn of their contexts – came to be understood as civilisational and 'modern'. Anticolonial struggles and decolonisation campaigns, as we noted in the first chapter, were aimed at claiming back land and culture from colonising rulers and their discourses. As Fanon observed in *The Wretched of the Earth*, 'For a colonized people the most essential value, because the most concrete, is first and foremost the land: the land which will bring them bread and, above all, dignity' (9). There is no dignity, humanity, and humanness without reclaiming land stolen or disowned by colonisation.

In this chapter, I will read 'postcolonial ecologies' as a relational concept standing for forms of colonialist resource extraction and their anticolonial resistance. As Elizabeth DeLoughrey and George B. Handley remark, 'to speak of postcolonial ecology is to speak of the historical process of nature's mobility, transplantation, and consumption' as well as of resistance and care, 'the aesthetics of the earth' (13). I will consider three specific themes around the aesthetic of the earth through which authors have represented postcolonial ecologies – hunger, epidemics and planting trees. I will argue that postcolonial nations have often acted upon colonial methods of resource extraction and exploitation resulting in racial or casteist segregations of land and commons, and widespread conditions of hunger and precarity. Postcolonial writers have offered not only methods of fighting back through ingenious aesthetic uses of imaginative, cultural and literary matrices but have also propagated crucial and vital philosophies of care for the planet through these matrices and through activism.

Environment, Ecocriticism and Postcolonial Studies

While literary and cultural studies of the environment known as 'ecocriticism' began in North America in the last decades of the twentieth century (Buell; Glotfelty and Fromm; Garrard), anticolonial movements against neocolonial capitalism such as Green Belt, anti-Green Revolution, or anti-Shell campaigns had already made visible the cogency of conceptual terms such as 'environmentalism of the poor' in academic and activist circles (Maathai; Siro-wiwa; Shiva; Martínez-Alier). By the late 1980s, Ramachandra Guha, among others had exposed the loopholes in the European environmental movement of 'deep ecology' pointing to its dehistoricising bio-centric focus on the purity of nature and its consumerist conservation-logic of 'wilderness' (75–82). These criticisms set up the contexts for Rob Nixon's influential essay on 'Environmentalism and Postcolonialism' in *Postcolonial Studies and Beyond* (2005). In this essay, Nixon observed that these two fields were as dependent on each other as they were indifferent to or distrustful of each other (233). 'Postcolonialism', for him, was interested in the concepts of hybridity, displacement, and translational and cosmopolitan practices, while 'ecocriticism' preferred the values of emplacement, national and purity-based readings. For Nixon, the various environmental impacts of mining, oil drilling and deforestation during colonial and postcolonial periods had a *longue durée* impact on postcolonial and post-imperialist nations and cultures which need to be acknowledged and studied through attending to the wide spectrum of postcolonial comparative works that had engaged diligently with these issues (247–49).

In their book, *Postcolonial Ecocriticism* (2010), Graham Huggan and Helen Tiffin offered a compelling context for such reading which is worth quoting at length here:

> Postcolonial studies has come to understand environmental issues not only as central to the projects of European conquest and global domination, but also as inherent in the ideologies of imperialism and racism on which those projects historically – and persistently – depend. Not only were other people often regarded as part of nature – and thus treated instrumentally as animals – but also they were forced or coopted over time into western views of the environment, thereby rendering cultural and environmental restitution difficult if not impossible to achieve. Once invasion and settlement had been accomplished, or at least once administrative structures had been set up, the environmental impacts of western attitudes to human being-in-the-world were facilitated or reinforced by the deliberate (or accidental) transport of animals, plants

and peoples throughout the European empires, instigating widespread ecosystem change under conspicuously unequal power regimes. (6)

For Huggan and Tiffin, 'Postcolonial ecocriticism preserves the aesthetic function of the literary text while drawing attention to its social and political usefulness, its capacity to set out symbolic guidelines for the material transformation of the world. To that extent, it can be seen as an interventionist or even activist enterprise' (6). This point of reading as an activist intervention, which echoes our early conversations on 'reading for decolonising' in the first chapter, is suggestively raised in DeLoughrey and Handley's use of 'postcolonial ecologies', mentioned in the preceding section. Following Édouard Glissant's concept of 'relational interdependence of all lands, and of the whole earth' and Gayatri Chakravorty Spivak's use of planetarity which embraces 'an exhaustible taxonomy' of alterity, DeLoughrey and Handley call for a politics of care for the Earth that must come from demanding notions of totality and otherness that cannot be possessed. The chief aim of this politics is to establish 'a discourse of transformative self-conscious disruption that calls attention to the universalizing impulses of the global' (28). Considering how the 'exact' sciences and technological innovations have led to global environmental degradations and their disproportionate impact on the poorest regions of the world, the need of the hour is to combine them with the 'inexact' sciences of listening, reading, writing, interpretation and ethics for critique, narrative and accountability, DeLoughrey and Handley argue.

To this end, postcolonial critic Upamanyu Pablo Mukherjee, in *Postcolonial Environments* (2010), has developed a useful critical framework of 'eco-materialism' through which to study literary and cultural texts not as issues separate from the environment but rather produced by it. Mukherjee argues that material environment is the enabling factor for all human labour including cultural labour, such as writing a novel or painting a picture. However, material environment is not a constant globally. In postcolonial territories and the Global South, access to material environment is deeply uneven. Drawing upon Trotsky's theory of 'uneven and combined development' (60) which points to the correlation between 'stylistic moves and the uneven penetration of capitalism into the spatial and physical spaces of postcolonial societies' (80), Mukherjee contends that eco-materialism compels us to think of the differentiated conditions of the production of cultural forms within the larger trajectory of the historical development of capitalist colonialism. Instead of 'attempting to locate aesthetic value in the exotic uniqueness of cultural form, we can look for it in the stylistic and formal moves employed there as a result of a relationship with other cultural forms inhabiting similar environmental matrices' (80). Such a framework allows us to see how differential cultural forms have historically developed in close conversation with specific material environmental conditions and enable a decolonising, historical materialist method which remains true to the cultural and geopolitical specificities of literary and cultural works.

In this chapter, I will draw from Mukherjee's historical materialist framework to analyse works produced broadly on the postcolonial ecologies of catastrophe, vulnerability and sustainability. Extraction, disaster, hunger, poverty, disease, epidemics, precarity – all forms of 'social violence' – are routine elements of postcolonial life in the Anthropocene. Nixon has influentially written on slow and spectacular forms of violence by which he means the frequency of earthquakes, cyclones, floods and other 'natural' disasters, as well as those of toxic drift, biomagnification, malnutrition and climate change in the postcolonial world. While spectacular disasters draw tremendous media attention, slow disasters put media presenters, artists and activists under considerable duress as to how to represent something that is routine and continuous (2–3). His temporality-oriented reading through literary style is useful for a postcolonial eco-materialist approach. Mark Anderson and Pablo Mukherjee have further asked us to consider the spatial aspects of ecological violence, that is, how different *kinds* of violence have resulted in different genres of literary aesthetics in their specific sociohistorical contexts, otherwise understood as 'disaster geographies' for the prevalent imperialist discourses of the tropics and colonies as places of disaster, famine, disease and savagery (Mukherjee, *Natural Disasters and Victorian Empire* 24). These conversations have enabled postcolonial critics to read through the colonising ecological agenda in literary and cultural works and to decolonise them by offering histories and imaginative practices of reclaiming land and forests from neocolonial extractivism, as in Mahasweta Devi's short story, 'Mahadu: Ekti Rupkatha'. They also offer a counter-narrative of healing from colonialism-led epidemics and social segregation as in Phaswane Mpe's novel, *Welcome to Our Hillbrow*, or foreground the anticolonial and planetary consciousness of planting trees and gardening in Olive Senior's poetry in *Gardening in the Tropics*. These conversations across the chapter will also be useful to indicate the emerging interdisciplinary fields of environmental, medical and plant humanities and their dialogues with postcolonial studies.

EXTRACTION, HUNGER, ADIVASI STRUGGLE AND THE POSTCOLONIAL STATE: MAHASWETA DEVI'S 'MAHADU: EKTI RUPKATHA'

We start the discussion with a focus on postcolonial India, specifically West Bengal. Although the formal end of colonialism pointed to a new future of equality and social justice, in a postcolonial nation such a future could hardly be materialised soon. The everyday problems of unemployment, landlessness, poverty and hunger continued for the majority of the populace as the ruling powers had just changed hands – from white masters to their 'native', upper-class, elite counterparts. In India, a country that had seen numerous famines in the nineteenth and early-twentieth centuries culminating in the devastating 1943 Bengal Famine which killed more than three million people, the food crisis in the immediate aftermath of liberation from colonial rule in 1947 was severe. The Bengal Famine was followed by a tribal-peasant uprising in Bengal demanding two-thirds of the share of harvests known as the Tebhaga Movement (1946), while in the states of Punjab, Bihar and Telangana there were several peasant insurgencies. Indeed, in Bengal, numerous food movements broke out in the 1950s and 1960s led by Communist Party outfits and working-class and peasant organisations (Dhanagare). As we have seen in Bama's *Karukku*, the impact of hunger is severe in tribal-majority states. Writing in 2000 about Kalahandi's poverty and hunger in the postcolonial period, Bob Currie notes that the widespread perception that electoral democracy and free speech along with 'Famine Codes'[2] had reduced hunger and famines in postcolonial India was simply not true. Odisha, an eastern state in India, which saw a massive famine killing millions in 1866 under colonial rule due to reasons of administrative neglect, continued to see massive mortality rates relating to hunger and poverty in the Adivasi dominated areas of Kalahandi (Adivasi meaning 'original inhabitants' and understood as referring to tribal/Dalit/Indigenous people in India). '(I)naction and neglect', Currie writes, 'on the part of government officers were central to explaining why people died from starvation related causes in several instances in Kalahandi and Bolangir during the 1980s' (5).

Currie mentions the Odia literary stalwart, Fakirmohan Senapati's autobiography in which he raised the topic of hunger and state neglect. Another writer who has consistently raised the postcolonial state's neglect of the welfare of Adivasis and peasants is Mahasweta Devi. Devi began living with Adivasis in Bengal and Jharkhand from the 1970s onward as a journalist and social worker while simultaneously editing her magazine, *Bartika*, to highlight state neglect of Adivasi welfare and state encroachment in Adivasi forest-oriented lives for material development. Indeed, as Jennifer Wenzel has commented, 'Much of Mahasweta Devi's fiction helps to document India's forest crisis' which she sees as an 'ecological crisis' that is inextricably related with 'narrative conflicts' (138). I will read her short story, 'Mahadu: Ekti Rupkatha' ('Mahadu: A Fairy Tale'; my translation),[3] where like Senapati above, Devi raises the question of state neglect but adds new postcolonial strands of NGOs and scientific innovation to it, none of which, however, are able to help the causes of starvation among Adivasis. Devi uses an ingenious aesthetic by structuring the text as a collage of episodes intermixed with content from other texts. This allows for a style that aims to capture the unreality of narrative realism by interrogating its linearity and the popular perception of the 'myth' that Adivasis have begun to denounce food for religious reasons.

'Mahadu' is about a teenage boy Mahadu of the Korku tribe, which flourished in the forest regions of central India, now the Indian state of Madhya Pradesh. The narrative shuttles between

Mahadu's birth and the current time when he is sixteen years old. It is divided into nine parts. The bulk of the narrative is about governmental and non-governmental researchers and organisations who repeatedly remind the reader that the Korkus have refused to eat. Administrative officers maintain that the government has tried many methods of feeding them, including distributing food grains to encourage them to cultivate staple food, but to no avail because they had built a 'wall of resistance': 'Their mind is controlling their body, they are getting sick of food because they have decided not to eat what they never had eaten' ("Mahadu" 294). When Dr Apte, a food and nutrition specialist researching malnutrition and hunger amongst the Korkus, asks Brij Kapoor, an IAS officer who previously worked with the tribe, if they are violent, Kapoor responds, 'They are resisting through truth and nonviolence. No, no, they are very civilised, gentle, and peaceful, they speak little. No violence . . . They've just decided to die as a race'. When Dr Apte seeks the reason, Kapoor dismisses it as nothing serious. They are not eating because once, 'in the pre-historical times, the British had cut off a few thousand segun trees from their jungle' (295).

In the next part, Devi balances this hurried and light-touch conclusion with historical reasons behind the Korkus's refusal to eat. These reasons are embedded in the act of cutting segun trees for the railways in the 1850s. This part begins with the introduction of the railways in India in 1853, and the wood needed for its construction and to fire the engines were supplied from the plains and jungles at the foothills of the Himalayas. This huge programme of colonial deforestation drove the Korkus off their lands and out of their forests rendering them homeless and gradually non-existent. Consider Devi's narration below:

> Segun or saga trees are their god, their protector, Korkus are married around segun trees. ... How fast were these trees disappeared and turned into ... sleeper trains. When the Nasik-Howrah train had first left the station, people were cracking coconuts on either side of the tracks . . . The Korkus were also there, far away from this spectacle, like stones unmoving. The uprooted segun had now merged into their bodies. This is why one can see in the lifeless eyeballs of dead Korkus the

flowery, leafy segun tree. Korkus are a myth; Korkus have begun to give up control of their life and living. (295–96)

Like the crucial close-up scene of a tied-up Northup in McQueen's *12 Years A Slave*, we can also use this passage to make three key arguments in the section: colonial, ecological and stylistic elements present in such texts. Starting with the 'colonial' elements: through the above references Devi successfully invokes here the *longue durée* of colonial–capitalist and imperialist histories of resource extraction and environmental damage in global peripheries. Environmental historian Jason W. Moore argues that the Capitalocene tracks the long histories of primitive accumulation and agricultural revolution starting from the fifteenth century, behind the origins of the ecological crisis. For Moore, capital accumulation worked by making humans and nature 'cheap' – that is, both cheap extraction at a global scale and reduction of value embedded in 'matter' (600). Building upon this and echoing Marian Aguiar's work on the railways and Andreas Malm's research on fossil fuel capitalism, Pallavi Das shows that the building of fossil capital and the cheapening of nature due to 'the resource extracting enabling' project of the railways led to widespread deforestation in India, especially in the foothills of the Himalayas. Since the trains were to be made following the models of sleeper trains in England, expensive sal, segun, teak and deodar trees, understood to be resilient to insects, were cut down, doing incalculable environmental damage to the country. Das writes, 'The construction and operation of railways which was primarily designed to enable efficient resource extraction from India, itself depleted the natural resources of India. Thus, the metropole's economic exploitation of the colony had ecological costs in the form of deforestation which cannot be ignored' (42).

While this long history of accumulation and resource extraction, globally and colonially, finds an appropriate registration in Devi's brief example, what Das and other researchers above have not followed is the immediate and direct impact of deforestation on the forests' tribes.[4] This is what the second argument of 'ecological' elements in the passage above point to: segun trees and Korku lives are socially and biologically intertwined. They build their houses with segun branches and leaves, eat vegetables and animals that grow and live around these trees, and worship the trees as their god and protector. In an evocative passage, Devi's narrator tells us,

> Humans and snakes have lived together for ever.... However, their ancestral knowledge and experience were dissevered a hundred years ago when the first axe was brought down upon saga and segun trees. Segun had gone, so Korkus had to go too because the carpet of reori grass had dried up... Thus, their means of knowing the world also stopped a hundred years ago. ("Mahadu" 292)

What this passage indicates is the robust ecosystem of humans and non-humans who depend on each other – the ecological life that colonialism and modernisation have irreversibly damaged. The key factor here is the trees which have protected and allowed for multiple life systems to develop around them. Indigenous and postcolonial scholars have long written on Indigenous life's rooted dependence on land and trees which were taken away from them for imperialist resource extraction and greed (Gadgil and Guha; Beinart and Hughes; Wenzel). Indeed, as Wenzel writes for another of Devi's story, 'Dhowli', Dhowli's 'culturally mediated relationship to the forest is at odds with the narrative's muted depiction of it as a site of resource extraction' (141). Devi comes back to this ecological relationship and social points of crisis repeatedly in her work. The rise of colonial modernity, through railways and dams, is also the demise of forests and lives (human and non-human) based on the forested ecosystem. This is the beginning of a monstrous machine reality of the Anthropocene which announces itself thunderously, cheered on by mainstream societies. The Korkus here are far-away onlookers because their lives had stopped with the rise of the machine monster. Also important here is the question of epistemology. That, by dispossessing Korkus of their trees around which their lives and cultures had grown, colonialism also took away their ways of thinking through and knowing the world. This is the point that Indigenous scholars and activists have repeatedly brought forth – that decolonisation is not only about resistance to colonialism but also about finding means to bringing back local ways of knowing things, of epistemological autonomy – a point that I will come back to via Senior's poetry.

While the dialectic between colonial–capitalist modernity and ecological damage is clear in the quoted passage above, the third argument to follow is 'stylistics'. Note that the passage on 'Segun or saga trees are their god . . .' is written in single inverted commas. Given that this follows Dr Apte's conversation with Kapoor who mentions his autobiographical work on the Korkus and their refusal to eat, this passage could be read as an excerpt from his book. Readers well-versed with Devi's writings would have known of the complex weaving of styles in her work (Salgado; Menozzi; Bhattacharya). The discussion, then, may not be so objectively historical here, as Kapoor's somewhat morally superior self-appointed status suggests. This is, however, not the case as there are passages such as the one immediately prior about forests and life systems dying together, which are not reported passages but narratorial interventions suggesting there is truth to Kapoor's findings. Unlike the testimonial episodic style in Bama's *Karukku* pointing to the oppression of Dalits by the Catholic-upper caste coalition in rural India, Devi's piece is less about the tribe (the oppressed) than the way the tribe's welfare is misunderstood and mishandled by state and non-state actors. So, Devi's stories on forests and tribal hinterlands often include researchers and administrators who write 'correct' documents on their lives but do not want to 'know' them (recall Tuhiwai Smith's call against this neocolonising enterprise of the postcolonial state and researcher in the first chapter). In her conversation with Spivak, Devi reflected that Adivasi and mainstream lives have never intersected: 'The tribal and the mainstream have always been parallel. There has never been a meeting point. The mainstream simply does not understand the parallel' ("The Author in Conversation" x). Indeed, in her novella *Operation?—Bashai Tudu*, Devi's narrator is acrimonious in this context: 'Where were the research analysts of the future who would salvage the truth from the mountains of untruths and set the records straight?' (41). In short and long stories like 'Shishu' or 'Pterodactyl, Puran Sahay, and Pirtha', administrative truths (although not incorrect assumptions) abound.

In 'Mahadu' too, much of the discussion is between administrators, nutrition specialists, NGOs and medical researchers. Hence, Devi uses these statements in their objective form as an ironic way of entering the discourses of truth-making on the issue. This ironic narrative style is ingeniously extended in the end of the story when scientists Suvadra Joshi, niece of the local politician, and her husband kidnap Mahadu and take him to their research headquarters in Mumbai to test and dismantle the myth of their not eating. Their hypothesis is that Korkus will eat if they are fed well. So, they cover Mahadu's body with nutrient drips and saline bottles, and the body begins to extract the liquid food making the researchers initially feel that they will receive international fame from their research. But as they discuss the ramifications of this 'miracle', Mahadu suddenly grows very large until his body smashes out of the research building. He then stands up and with a thunderous voice blurts out, 'I'm hungry. Give me food' ("Mahadu" 299). The narrator then tells us that he lifts his hands and starts eating everything around him, from large complexes to hotels, the Gateway of India to the Chhatrapati Shivaji railway terminal – at which he specifically roars in cosmic anger, 'my segun forests'. The narration ends with these utopian statements:

> No Mahadu, no Korku will ever be a myth again.
>
> This is how real Korku life will be written. Mahadu will write on the canvass of the sky. He will tear apart the stars to draw his alphabets. Mahadu stands on one leg in the depths of the western Arabian Sea and extends the other towards the east. His eyeballs reflect the lively segun trees, their beautiful leaves and flowers. (298)

These resisting sentiments remind us of the ending in Raihan's film *Stop Genocide,* which called for a utopian future of egalitarianism and solidarity. But whereas the innovative composition in Raihan's film is geared towards a relatively straightforward political agenda of solidarity and freedom at the 'second' birth of a nation, Devi's story points to a more complex form of life and livelihood for a postcolonial marginalised population. For our eco-materialist reading, this ending is particularly important. The story acknowledges through narrative reporting that the Korkus are dying: this is the 'narrative truth', as mentioned through reports above. But throughout the narration, Devi shows that the Korkus have struggled to live in a (post)colonial–capitalist world where their livelihoods now depend on government-sponsored small businesses such as making thread out of grass; that they are starved and suffer from malnutrition and often die in youth. The other 'narrative truth', as it appears in the earlier critical reading, is that the government is not feeding them properly. Devi has long questioned the fleeting and unreliable methods of welfare engagement from government channels. India's contemporary hunger situation is critical in the rural and tribal districts. This is not temporary hunger, but a chronic case of starvation and malnutrition (Drèze and Sen; Mander). 'Myth', in this administrative/rational sense, is appropriate in conveying the narrative sarcasm and irony as the term exposes our urban, objective and un-empathetic interpretation of the tragic incidents of people dying in marginal areas due to governmental and civic neglect.

Unlike Bama's *Karukku* which is about the challenges of growing up Dalit in a rural society controlled by upper castes, this is a story about trying to understand the Korku situation by an author who is an outsider-insider. Devi, thus, can offer multiple and often contradictory viewpoints in an attempt to understand the situation. This can be read, following Lazarus in the first chapter, as Devi's narratorial and critical consciousness, her positionality. Labelling the situation as a myth from the outside grows out of colonial and postcolonial governments' misgivings about tribal life and customs and their inability to feed or make a cause out of them (the 'parallel' that never meets, according to Devi). While the Joshi's burst the 'myth' of the Korkus's long fast, the result is another 'narrative truth' that cannot be contained within a realistic, objective description. If myth (an archetypal, non-realistic narrative act) has been normalised through bureaucratic and mainstream discourses, we will need a radically new event that can dismantle these discourses and break open the boundaries of the realistic, the probable. Mahadu's 'miraculous' growth and endless destruction of modernity is, thus, Devi's anticolonial counter-myth: the fairy tale. This is the eco-materialist force of the work, which uses the historical conditions of neglect, misreading and abject romanticisation of the tribal and turns them on their head in service of the story's ironic, satirical message. Consider, for instance, the temporal disjunction in the concluding passage above. While the entire story is written in the chiasmic twinning of indefinite and immediate pasts, the ending is a 'changing' present aimed at an anticolonial and properly decolonised future which has dismantled colonialism's material and symbolic presence (I will engage more thoroughly with this feature of postcolonial future-building in the next chapter on 'Futures'). Mahadu's eating of the apartments and colonial buildings is in the present continuous tense ('tearing apart stars', 'setting up alphabets', et cetera.), while his remaking of the cosmic narrative of a socio-ecological life is located in the indefinite future. This is where the objective, governmental myth (used as a cover up for its failures) is displaced by a utopian and equitable fairy tale future.

Fairy tales are about a long-distant past and about monsters which are often killed by good humans with the help of nonhuman animals or cosmic/divine figures, and they are widely told or written to transmit social messages (Zipes). What Devi does is use this style – a cultural form appropriate for the current contradictory socio-economic conditions – and acts upon the fairy tale element in the end with Mahadu's abnormal growth and transformation into a monster. It is not the Mahadu chapter that is the fairy tale; the whole story can be read as one (consider its title). What it means is that the current reality and its 'mythical' rendering are not very different from each other. In a gesture that is remarkably similar to the exiled, spectral and decolonising representations of humans and emotions in Darwish's poems in the previous chapter, Devi suggests that if our current reality can demonise a population, marginalise it and let it die, it is a sinister, dark reality where governments and machines are the monsters. Here, bureaucrats and researchers are the monster's structures and mediators, and together they have made their discourse into 'reality' by the long and repeated telling of this myth or tale. To battle it out, to 'salvage the truth from the mountain of untruths', to rewrite and make this reality self-reflexive, we need another set of protagonists and a new, anti-Anthropocenic, anticolonial and indigenous *kind* of thinking. The complex framing of the story is Devi's nuanced reading of the current situation – a reading that enriches our method of reading literary and cultural works as a way of striving towards that equitable and decolonised future.

EPIDEMICS, POSTCOLONIAL XENOPHOBIA AND THE COMMUNITY OF HEALING IN PHASWANE MPE'S *WELCOME TO OUR HILLBROW*

If European colonisation plays a major role in enabling the 'slow' and everyday conditions of hunger and starvation in the postcolonial world, as in Devi, epidemics and disease – 'spectacular' disasters according to Rob Nixon's theorisation above – also bear a strong link to this world historical event. Disasters are popularly read through socially and culturally damaging discourses of purity, segregation and xenophobia in which postcolonial, environmental and medical or health issues converge. I will argue in this section that the current situation is a legacy of colonialism and imperialism, to battle which a community of healing is imperative. Alfred Crosby in his monumental *Ecological Imperialism* noted that the great migrations of Europeans in the wake of the Great Famine and the Black Death epidemics in the fourteenth century to world-scale colonisation from the sixteenth century onwards had been the prime reason for the spread of epidemics and diseases across the world (37–42). Most colonised territories had seen a rapid rise in diseases and epidemics post colonisation, enabling imperialist practices of 'disciplining' the colonised. The development of Western medicine in nineteenth century India, in the wake of various famines, epidemics and plagues, David Arnold points out, was to manage the post-1857, 'unruly' Indian population and expedite support for the hegemonic imperial administration in the subcontinent (8).

In the case of South Africa, to which we shift our critical register now, colonial and apartheid histories were shaped by the catastrophic consequences of five lethal epidemics, from the smallpox epidemic in 1713 to the HIV epidemic in 1982 (Phillips). Historian of medicine Randall Packard, for instance, reads tuberculosis via the rise of industrial, mine-based capitalism in South Africa (xvi). The Act of Segregation (1910), which Cecil Rhodes and his British government implemented, was based on the rise of industrial capitalism in cities like Johannesburg (where Phaswane Mpe's novel is based) with the arrival of millions of black and African migrant workers to work in the mines. The recommendations made by the Act put restrictions on black and minority people's everyday movement, their ability to own land and property and access to communal spaces, Nancy Clark and William Worger point out. The 1948 Apartheid Act consolidated many of these recommendations; so much so that, 'By the 1980s, many Africans in South Africa would no longer legally be considered citizens of that country but would be categorised as foreigners' (Clark and Worger 37).

It is hardly a coincidence that Mpe's *Welcome to Our Hillbrow* (2001; henceforth, *Hillbrow*) makes 'foreignness' a key issue in understanding the 'medical disaster' of AIDS. *Hillbrow* is a novel about young Refenšte who comes from his rural Tiragalong to Hillbrow, Johannesburg, to work at the University of Witwatersrand, and about his amorous relationships. Like in Darwish, spectrality is a key marker here as the novel is narrated by Refenšte's dead voice (he has died by suicide). This experimental novel on love, community and relationships betrays moments of poignancy at the city's or his rural hometown Tiragalong's deep xenophobia against postcolonial migrants, offering a counter to Adichie's or Hamid's perspectives on the topic earlier. Throughout the book, which is a combination of voices and narratives from Refenšte and his lovers, there is a continuous critical interrogation of rural or suburban values and practices which consign urbanity and urban lives to moral turpitude and sinful living but fail to evaluate their own negative issues. As Refenšte says in relation to his friends' and neighbours' derogatory and culturally offensive remarks on AIDS: 'Who said that the people of Tiragalong were cleaner than everyone else? Were there no stories of Tiragalong people who died of sexually transmitted diseases . . . At least AIDS came by accident, unlike such malicious acts as sending lightning to strike Tshepo' (Mpe 2011, 54–55).

Much like Devi's critical narrator who questions postcolonial forms of welfare and social relation and considers a tribe's slow death as sociopolitically manufactured, there is an increasing realisation in Mpe's novel that a disaster like AIDS is not specific to a certain geography. People in Tiragalong believe that this epidemic is exclusively created and borne by black African foreigners, known as the Makwerekwere. They read it as a result of practising witchcraft on people which thus needs to be eliminated through further bloody, local ritualistic means. Unsurprisingly, this is a belief that Refilwe, Refenšte's beloved from his hometown, also harbours until she herself is diagnosed with the disease, not in South Africa but in Oxford during higher studies. As Refenšte's dead voice makes clear in a passionate monologue, there is no point in finding out where the disease came from in an increasingly globalised world:

> Many of the *Makwerekwere* you accuse of this and that are no different to us . . . They are lecturers and students . . . ; professionals taking up posts that locals are hardly qualified to fill. . . . You would want to add that some *Makwerekwere* were fleeing their war-torn countries to seek sanctuary here in our country, in the same way that many South Africans were forced into exile in Zambia, Zaïre, Nigeria and other African and non-African countries during the Apartheid era. (19–21)

Here is a novel about post-apartheid South Africa slowly coming to terms with the recovery of black and oppressed agency. But all it does in the recovery is find another group of labourers as culprits for the nation's medical debacle – the same colonial logic of blaming and fault-finding with the marginalised that we see in the administrators and citizens in 'Mahadu', hence re-establishing Fanon's proposition that decolonisation must be a long-term process of recovery. The above passage clearly points at the uneven character of a postcolonial city and the meaning it holds for AIDS as a slow disaster in the novel.

In a reading of another Hillbrow-based work, *The Restless Supermarket* by Ivan Vladislavić, Pablo Mukherjee argues that the various contemporary literary and cultural examples of black magic and 'alien-labour' in a global city like Johannesburg 'point to the historical tendencies through which [these practices] operate under conditions of uneven development' ("Ivan Vladislavić" 476). Another critic Rashmi Varma terms the urban postcolonial space as 'conjunctural', which 'produces a critical combination of historical events, material bodies, structural forces, and representational economies that propel new constellations of domination and resistance, centres and peripheries, and the formation of the new political subjects' (1). These sentiments, which I have read elsewhere for postcolonial Indian contexts (Bhattacharya 162, 169), are raised by Mpe too in suggesting that postcolonial cities are historically marked by a conjuncture of migrant labour, uneven development and a coeval culture in which different forms of cultural and social expressions coexist. Not only do migrants 'belong' to a city they live in, but by offering their crucial labour to do things that many long-term residents would be reluctant to do, they also become an integral part of the city. This offers the other side of Adichie's representation of African Americans and the working-class salon in *Americanah*: If Ifemelu has the privilege of not wanting to assimilate here and returning to Nigeria, hard-working migrants working small jobs intending to settle in the host land often have no choice but to assimilate and encounter severe xenophobia. It does not matter if the country is majority white or black. Xenophobia, which comes from making an alien out of a settler as we noticed in the chapter on 'Traumas' through Mamdani, is characteristically postcolonial. Refugees and asylum seekers, as well as racialised migrants, are routinely blamed for every small social disruption, which Mpe ironically suggests here, are not very different from the helpless South Africans who sought sanctuary in other African countries because of their country's ruthless apartheid laws and history. Nothing is sudden and disruptive in the scheme of postcolonial things but deeply social and colonialist.

In this uneven and culturally diverse postcolonial city, epidemics such as AIDS can never be a sudden disaster. While AIDS 'came by accident', as the narrator mentions, the disaster was not 'sudden' as the disease travelled with migrant labourers slowly unfolding its horrible consequences. Howard Phillips has argued that what distinguishes AIDS from previous epidemics is its slow onset, which has allowed not only the possibility of large-scale vaccine production to lessen fatalities but also promote more widespread awareness programmes about the epidemic and fighting the stigma associated with it ("HIV/AIDS in the context of South Africa's Epidemic History" 35–37). As Nixon wrote in *Slow Violence and Environmentalism of the Poor*, slow or attritional disasters are those 'that overspill clear boundaries in time and space (and) are marked above all by displacement – temporal, geographical, rhetorical and above all technological displacement' (2). In order to accommodate the nature of suffering over time and space, literary narratives of attritional catastrophes undergo a significant stretching of their generic and stylistic codes and remodel the literary form.

There is much to talk about AIDS and Mpe's experimental literary form in this novel. AIDS however conflates the two types. It is an event that can be temporally located, which causes a rupture in health and society, but it is also slow and attritional in the way that it affects a wider population and geography through infection and stigma, turning into a pandemic. Speaking about epidemic temporality, medical anthropologist Emmanuelle Roth notes,

> (E)pidemics are acute disease 'events' which problematize time, causing people and institutions to envision and act upon multiple epidemic antecedents and aftermaths. These temporalities may take the form of official tropes enshrined in the outbreak narrative: historical series, "real-time" surveillance and eradication utopias. But beneath the tropes lie the continuities and ruptures which subvert the linear chronology: backward yet emergent diseases and visions of a post-pandemic collapse. The textured experience of outbreaks relies entirely on these overlapping epidemic temporalities. (16)

Looking at the way Mpe brings in the 'overlapping temporalities' of AIDS as a structural and slow form of violence marked by post-Apartheid contexts of racism and xenophobia, witchcraft and rural belief, the narrative itself becomes a gateway to understand the nature of the disease and its impact. Phillips has written that the South African chapter of the AIDS epidemic cannot be read in isolation vis á vis other epidemics, most of which were encountered during the colonial period. Where AIDS differs is the biomedical and socio-cultural response to it because of stigma and government denial of widespread implementation of policy. This cycle was enabled by the sociocultural representation of AIDS. Although widely present from the 1980s, stigma narratives prevented AIDS from being either biomedically or socially established in South

Africa until early 2000. Cultural productions – especially graffiti, photography and literature – as evidenced in Sue Williams's 'From the Inside 2000–2002', pushed AIDS to be more widely discussed in everyday life (Grünkemeier).

Hillbrow, it seems to me, then, is a breakthrough novel that not only falls within this period of early-South African writings on the social stigma of AIDS but also rationalises the situation showing how rural discourses of witchcraft and healing as well as state-sponsored discourses of race and xenophobia have impacted the issue. Nowhere does Mpe dismiss the importance of these contemporary topics, and thus rural faith and customs play a significant role in the novel. Indeed, Refilwe was convinced that AIDS was brought into being by prostitutes, homosexuals and the Makwerekwere women in cities, until her own diagnosis. This dynamic aspect of social and biomedical discourses makes AIDS both a significant discursive factor and a deeply spatialised and temporalised epidemic. As medical and cultural studies scholar Paola Treichler writes, 'We cannot effectively analyze AIDS or develop intelligent social policy if we dismiss such conceptions as irrational myths and homophobic fantasies which deliberately ignore the "real scientific facts". Rather they are part of the necessary work people do in attempting to understand – however imperfectly – the complex, puzzling and quite terrifying phenomenon of AIDS' (265). The critical consciousness in Devi regarding the consigning of myth to an urgent condition of reality finds resonance in Mpe's representations here.

In an essay on decolonised disaster studies, Anthony Carrigan argues that decolonisation in these contexts must rest upon recovering alternative epistemologies or modes of narration which can register the link between long-term colonisation's destructive impact on people and the environment (earthquake and cyclone for the Caribbean world) and a healing-driven and dialect-oriented community voice (Braithwaite's magical realist work for him; Carrigan 126–27). Like Devi's use of a complex narration of voices and the fairy tale trope for the slow disaster, Mpe's narrative also attends to the observation above through a peculiar conjuration of community and healing in the novel. Pallavi Rastogi helpfully discusses this conjuration as the pedagogical function of the novel, in which Mpe engages us in a medical dialogue to cognise AIDS *as* AIDS rather than some form of social aberration that came from ethnic and sexual minorities (122–23). The novel uses the metafiction technique to broaden this message. Refenšte's story-within-a-story of a woman working her way through the city and diagnosed with AIDS, for instance, turns out to be Refilwe's life story. This is a point Mpe repeatedly makes in the narrative, albeit ironically, through the use of plural pronouns – that AIDS needs to be seen as a disease for which the patient needs care, rather than being denied or repulsed by the community. A community that is suffering from the postcolonial materialisation of racial and spatial segregations as well as rural and urban divides cannot choose to further make its people feel more vulnerable and exposed to the world's ugliness. It needs redress and healing. Consider the narratorial sentiments expressed through Refilwe here:

> You have come to understand that you too are a Hillbrowan. An Alexandran. A Johannesburger. An Oxfordian. A *Lekwerekwere*, just like those you once held in such contempt. The semen and blood of *Makwerekwere* flows in your Tiragalong and Hillbrow veins. Now you are the talk of the town and the village, and there is no Refenšte to add his voice to the few voices of reason who say that disease is just disease. That choice is choice, and no one in particular can be blamed for the spread of AIDS. That Tiragalong should know well enough that its children are no better than others. (*Hillbrow* 122–23)

In these observations, the AIDS epidemic does not achieve a temporal or spatialised specificity and yet is markedly South African. The point that Mpe makes is that to fight a disease as globally contagious and socially enabled and layered as AIDS, we need to understand its impact and reach globally – how the world has witnessed many 'contaminated communities' and fought the double pressures of health disaster and social stigma. As Emily Davies writes on the novel,

> If cosmopolitanism has historically – and problematically – assumed as its foundation an individual citizen who chooses to associate himself with a larger community by thinking

of himself as a citizen of the world, Mpe offers a different narrative. In the era of global migration, spurred on by the circulations of global capital, contagion offers a more realistic model for understanding global interconnection. (102–03)

The emphasis placed on the plural pronoun in the end of the novel, 'we' from 'I', is thus a reminder that societies and nations – the plural subjectivities – have an obligation to their vulnerable cohabitants and fellows, the lack of which allows ableist, sexist and racist discourses to grow among us. As another critic of the novel, Carrol Clarkson, writes, 'these pronouns obliquely, but inevitably, call up expectations of a community – but then again, this community, in an ideal, or even in a positively viable sense, never seems to have taken place' (455). This coming community will be, however, an open community as the novel moves from 'Welcome to Hillbrow' to 'Welcome to Our Heaven', which, to echo Ifowodo from the previous chapter, is 'a symbolic return to the past for reconciliation with ancestral origins' (115).

Let me conclude this section on medical disaster, community and healing with a concept of community through storytelling and talking that Mpe spoke of in the final years before his premature death. This appears to me as recognising a disease in its sociocultural context, echoing Ifowodo's and Fanon's calls for a decolonised psychoanalysis of healing:

> I'm not very knowledgeable about this traditional healing, I never really followed it very closely. But of course I know many traditional healers. Beyond using herbs, they are also interested in stories. Because when people come to you and say, "I've got a problem", you don't just say, "Well is it a headache? Here is medicine for your headache", you also want to know how they are doing in their social relationships, because perhaps the headache might come from elsewhere, from a source other than a germ or virus. So you really have to be interested in stories, and I see a connection there. And of course if you hear stories and you see you have experiences of meeting people, then inevitably you'll also tell stories, whether that will translate into writing or not is something else. ("Healing with Words" 146–47)

'ISLAND ECOLOGIES', ANTICOLONIALISM AND PLANT CARE IN OLIVE SENIOR'S *GARDENING IN THE TROPICS*

A community's own means of recovery and healing is crucial to fight the medical emergency of AIDS in Mpe, as it is crucial for Devi to activate a critical agenda through tribal oral narration to fight hunger and species extinction. The question of ecological and cultural reclamation and planetary care is also at the heart of Caribbean writing, which I explored through Dionne Brand's work in the chapter on minorities. The Caribbean archipelago has witnessed five centuries of colonial dispossession and an oppressed humanity's faith in establishing cultural roots and meaning for displaced lives. In the Jamaican Olive Senior's poetry, which I will read below, the historical search for a common humanity appears through the life-affirming values of agricultural work and anticolonial resistance. Elizabeth DeLoughrey writes that in Senior and Jamaica Kincaid, among other Caribbean writers, there is a tremendous emphasis on the historical role of colonisation on the migration and settlement of peoples as well as of plants. She draws upon Glissant's critical insight that 'landscape is its own monument' for the Caribbean people's entangled culture of forced agricultural labour. Richard Grove's concept of the tropical island as Edenic helps build DeLoughrey's key notion of 'island ecologies'. Such ecologies have been historically derived from the colonial construction of islands as remote, paradisical and exotic, the Garden of Eden in contradistinction with the 'modernity' of commodity capitalism, rationalist philosophy and 'civilisational' discourses (299–300).

This deep sense of cultural dispossession is prevalent in Senior's poetry, for whom, much like Devi, the colonial exploitation of land and culture has continued through the neocolonial tourism industry in the Caribbean islands.[5] Senior acknowledges in an interview that European imperialism has now been replaced by American economic and cultural imperialism. She knows that an alternative economic system that prioritises local and Indigenous epistemological and socio-ecological practices needs to be carved out through cultural works, that is, storytelling, orality and poetry:

I don't think there is that much difference in my poems and my stories–apart from the length and complexity, of course. I am in both forms telling stories, exploring consciousness. I can't always decide on what form what I want to say will take. I have started out to write stories that have ended up as poems and had ideas for poems that have ended up as stories. If there is a difference it is that in my poems I am more explicitly political than in my stories. ("An Interview" 482)

Stories and storytelling are the crux of her anticolonial poetic creativity. It is through stories that she reminds both Jamaicans and the world of their histories of colonial displacement and their cultural heritage and togetherness. She writes because she wants 'to reaffirm those parts of our heritage that have been misplaced, misappropriated, subsumed, submerged, never acknowledged fully as the source of our strength'. She adds, 'I want people to know that "literature" can be created out of the fabric of our everyday lives, that our stories are as worth telling as those of Shakespeare or the creators of Dallas' (484). This is classic postcolonial 'writing back' to restore lives and cultures misappropriated and dispossessed by colonialism. For Senior, her poetry is her storytelling. The collapse of genres, from an anticolonial eco-materialist point view, is important here: poetry and storytelling are both tied to oral cultures, and thus it is her responsibility to preserve the heroism and struggle of cultures through poetry. I will show in the discussions below how her instincts towards the reclamation and preservation of land and cultures – her island ecological consciousness – appear through constant references to resource extraction, anticolonial resistance and planting ethics. My brief discussion here will rely on three poems from the collection *Gardening in the Tropics* (1994): 'Meditations on Yellow', 'Anatto and Guinep' and 'Gardening on the Run'.

'Meditations on Yellow' is one of the long poems in the collection that reads the five-centuries of exploitation of Indigenous people in South American and Caribbean islands that occur in search of commodities such as gold and silver. They are followed by further exploitation through the global neocolonial tourism industry. This is how the poem starts:

> At three in the afternoon
> you landed here at El Dorado
> ....
> so in exchange for a string of islands
> and two continents
>
> you gave us a string of beads
> and some hawk's bells (*Gardening in the Tropics* 11)

The poem conjures in the first two lines what DeLoughrey suggests through 'island ecologies' – migrant settlement on tropical islands and their paradisical exoticisation (see also Deckard). El Dorado is a mythic city of gold in the northern parts of the South American continent which attracted several European expeditions and consequently gave rise to unending adventure narratives in the Victorian period. The narrator's ironic tone is clear in the message of greeting in the final lines of the first stanza where she proposes brewing lemongrass tea, a delicacy that she savours throughout the poem. But she would add arsenic to it this time, poisoning the visitors who came to do business and usurped and appropriated two continents full of islands in exchange for a few beads and hawk's bells (jewellery for falconry and animal trade in medieval Europe).

The poem thus yields an underlying historical consciousness which is sharpened by an anguished tone and appeal, reminiscent of Brand in the chapter on 'Minorities'. The poet-narrator wishes that the colonisers/visitors would wake up to the fact that these islands were neither 'the Indies/nor Cathay' (12) and then goes on to say,

> though after you came
> plenty of bananas
> oranges
> sugar cane
> You gave us these for our
> maize
> pineapples
> guavas (12)

Echoing Devi's critique of colonialist deforestation in 'Mahadu', Senior references the commodity industry that these islands were used for by European plantation economies.[6] Bananas, oranges and sugarcane are not native to these islands. They were imported in order to be cultivated to feed an increasingly hungry Europe the civilisational delicacies of pie, scone, marmalade and cake, supplanting local foods such as maize, pineapple and guavas. Jason W. Moore, following Marx and Engels, has shown how these global commodities destroyed soil capacities and, by giving birth to cash crop production, accelerated global hunger in the eighteenth and nineteenth centuries (606–07). This second part of the poem shows a historical continuation of the commodity industry through tourism:

> a new set of people
>
> arrive
>
> to lie bare-assed in the sun
>
> wanting gold on their bodies
>
> cane-rows in their hair
>
> with beads - even bells (*Gardening in the Tropics* 14–15)

Jamaica Kincaid has written caustically about the destruction of community and landscape through the tourism industry in the Caribbean islands in *A Small Place* (1988). Senior shares her anguished anticolonial sentiments in the images of 'bare-assed in the sun' or 'wanting gold on their bodies' (tanning in the sun).

Consider, however, the use of the words 'arrival' or 'gold'. A set of people arriving echoes the 'foreign' arrival five centuries ago detailed in the first part of the poem, and probably most arrestingly captured in Eduardo Galeano's compelling *Open Veins of Latin America* (1971). They wanted gold. Now another set of people want gold, symbolically, on their bodies. While the early colonisers carried gold on ships to decorate the bodies of European men and women or their churches and buildings (the poet talks of the various religious purposes behind extracting silver and gold), contemporary tourists from Euro-America (the postcolonial metropolitan population) come to embody gold again through body tanning. However, as

DeLoughrey notes, 'Like the plantation system, the tourist industry does little to sustain the local economy while fattening the wallets of industrialised Northern states and multinational corporations. . . . To pursue this logic, tropical islands, far from representing the remote and archaic past, embody the earliest structures of capitalist modernity as well as its contemporary global inequities' (308). Gold also brings back the dominant metaphor of yellow that occurs throughout the poem. If it was the yellow of the gold and the banana or oranges or sugar cane that once mesmerised the European coloniser, it is now the yellow of the sun and the tan that brings thousands of foreigners to the islands. Despite these colonialist continuities, the poet asserts that the ex-slaves and the Indigenous populations will not submit to the exploitative, subsumptive vigour of (neo)colonial exploration; and like the yellow macca that finds a way to rise through the soil despite the monoculture of food commodities, like the wailing of Bob Marley, their songs cannot be torn from their throats, 'you cannot erase the memory/of my story' (*Gardening in the Tropics* 17) This is powerful counter-imagery about historical modes of resource extraction that reduced the islands to what Macarena Gómez-Barris in a 'decolonial' perspective calls 'the extractive zone', to restore which one needs to address the social ecologies of network and care and the force of epistemological autonomy and embodied knowledge (xv).

In the resistances through body, language and epistemology above, there is a clear indication of moving beyond the extractive zone, which finds an unusually novel treatment in the poem 'Anatto and Guinep'. This is a poem about fruits which have now become undervalued in the commodity industry. The narrator speaks of how 'No one today regards anatto and guinep/as anything special'. They are no longer used on stamps or for festivals. These fruits are no longer used by 'country people' to colour their food and can hardly be found in the market. Guinep seems to hold an even more precarious place as 'Big people/scorn it' even as they use it for food sometimes. It is only children who 'confess they love it' (76). These poems on fruits and plants are from the section, 'Nature Studies'. Senior here speaks about them in a language and tone comparable to the imagination of a child enthralled by them, recalling Bama's descriptions of the joy of planting seeds and agriculture in her Dalit community in *Karukku*. And like Bama's retrospective and historical narrative, she also brings in notions and images that belie her mature and historical consciousness (note the simplicity and restraint in her interview statements referenced previously). Thus, the use of 'No one' in the poem is important, especially when read against the global market in the third stanza.

Since the marketisation of fruits, for which the Caribbean islands have been used by colonists, pre-colonial fruits which have had long-term symbolic meaning for the Arawaks or for historically-older generations are of no 'use value' any longer. As Jordan Stouck writes, 'Anatto and guinep signify multivalently, recalling a lost indigenous past that valued the plants, as well as a present in which the non-commercial crop is denigrated as backward and (literally) distasteful. This devaluation of native crops, and consequently native knowledge and history, is a contentious issue in global culture' (12). Along with the marginalisation and wiping out of Indigenous peoples, upon which colonialism rested, their valued foodstuffs are gone too (like segun trees for the Korku tribe in Devi's work). Anatto paste or guinep stain, the poet continues, was used to decorate bodies for various occasions, to mark festivals, war or even for medicinal purposes. To restore the heroic significance of these plants associated with people who were heroic, tolerant and simple, Senior elevates them to an anticolonial cosmic importance, redolent of 'Mahadu' above, as she asks in hyperbole in these final lines:

> How do you think Moon got stained
> black like that?
>
> What do you think Sun used to redden
> its face? (*Gardening in the Tropics* 77)

Life in pre-colonial times was deeply connected with the cosmic. Indeed, the prefatory pattern poem of the collection, 'Gourd', mentions how this plant and food are associated with the genealogies of birth and genesis for the African people (7). Senior revitalises the plant in the current poem. Because of the colonial–capitalist system, the undervaluing of the fruits has rendered them useless and thus excessive (garbage). Following Michael A. Bucknor's reading of waste and rejected weeds in Senior, it can be argued that through revaluing these fruits, Senior 'salvag(es)' black or Caribbean subjectivity from the sediments of imperial constructions and rehabilitating our conceptual horizons of community and humanity' (Bucknor 34). As Senior reminds us through the anticolonial and organic metaphor of the cosmos, these fruits shaped the cosmic imagination of the world as stars did for human imagination of the beyond in Indigenous philosophies.

This creative and restorative element in plants and food sets us up for our final thoughts on 'Gardening on the Run' which also brings back the question of epistemological autonomy for the enslaved and the colonised, echoed above. This poem appears in the section, 'Gardening in the Tropics' which starts all poems with the section title to expose readers to the challenges, joys and multiple facets of gardening in the tropics. Critics have pointed out that gardening here refers both to the critique of the Edenic gardens that we mentioned in the beginning, and to the culturally integral task of planting, agriculture and horticulture in African and Indigenous societies. Jamaica Kincaid, in a vein similar to Pratt earlier, has written about plants and taxonomy in *My Garden (Book)*:

> (C)ountries in Europe shared the same botany, more or less, but each place called the same thing by a different name; and these people who make up Europe were (are) so contentious anyway, they would not have agreed to one system for all the plants they had in common, but these new plants from far away, like the people far away, had no history, no names, and so they could be given names. And who was there to dispute Linnaeus, even if there was someone who would listen? (122)

To stand guard to this meaning and to restore gardening's restorative, intersubjective and anticolonial meaning, Senior introduces, much like Brand earlier, a mixture of Jamaican Patois and Standard English suggesting, through the author's hybrid language, a counter-exotic meditation on landscape. 'In these collections', Myriam Moïse comments, 'the Caribbean flora is personified through her multiple pigments, her capacity to resist, to reproduce and cross-fertilize under all circumstances' (46).

We note in the series of poems that gardening in the tropics can lead one to the shocking excavation of human or animal bones ('the disappeared ones'), to precious and holy stones, to a never-ending growth of weed and dense jungle, banana plantations, differently-coloured birds, old love, deforestation and finally to stories. This poem is the story of slaves:

> Gardening in the Tropics for us
>
> meant a plot hatched quickly,
>
> hidden deep in forest or jungle,
>
> run to ground behind palisade or
>
> *palenque,* found in cockpit, in
>
> *quilombo* or *cumbe.* (*Gardening in the Tropics* 107; emphasis in the original)

The metaphor 'hatching a plot', it seems to me, has a double meaning here: carving a plot for agriculture and for writing a narrative of escape suggesting that agriculture and storytelling are intrinsically related. Sylvia Wynter in her essay 'Novel and History, Plot and Plantation' writes that European colonisation of the Caribbean islands and the resultant plantation systems were resisted agriculturally by plots (and the plotting system) given to African slaves and creoles to grow their food, surrounding which their cultures of fractured unity with the African continent grew. 'This culture', she continues, 'recreated traditional values — use values. This folk culture became a source of cultural guerrilla resistance to the plantation system' (100). The historic references above to plot and Palenque are indicative of this 'organic' resistance here. Palenque was a Mayan city in the Chiapas state of today's Mexico known for its wonderfully carved and plastered buildings and temples. But in conjunction with Quilombo it receives the liberatory meaning of anticolonial, anti-slavery resistance and self-determination. Quilombo is a nickname/epithet for hinterland settlements of marooned or escaped slaves in sixteenth and seventeenth century Brazil. In Spanish-speaking Latin America, they were called palenque. Quilombos or palenques were known to have been the bases from which active slave resistance movements began across Latin America and the Caribbean, which then led to more widespread resistance movements in the eighteenth and nineteenth centuries (Davis 110–12). Clearly then, much like Dionne Brand's reference to Phyllis Coard or Mama Prater in *No Language is Neutral*, the reference to plot is as much about claiming one's liberated land, territory and food as about weaving narratives that have been marginalised and/or misplaced – the method of knowing the world and living in it, the epistemology of inhabiting the planet, is interconnected. We witness in these lines a poet-narrator, a 'historic' slave, who might have been brought to these islands in the early-sixteenth century tied in chains, who then escaped, was caught and escaped again, until he was killed. These slaves only witnessed death, starvation and mutilation – the worst kept were the native Indians who were wiped out and who 'were born to know nothing but warfare and gardening on the run'. 'Run' then signifies both the nomadic hunter-gatherers' social world which the slave labour-based, capitalist plantation system had not yet invaded, for whom sowing and agriculture were seasonal and cyclical. It also stands for the constant escape and marooning of slaves, children, tribes and societies from the bloody hands of colonialists and plantation owners.

As the narrator then reminds us, despite the brutalities of colonialism which led to the extinction of species and peoples, there were important historic resistances to exploitation which are worth quoting here:

> from Jamaica, Nanny of the
> Windward Maroons, Cudjoe and
> Accompong who forced the English
> to sign treaties; in Mexico,
> Yanga and the town of San Lorenzo
> de los Negroes; all the *palenques*
> of Cuba; in Hispaniola, le Maniel;
> the Bush Negroes of Suriname;
> the many *quilombos* of Brazil (*Gardening in the Tropics* 109; emphasis in the original)

These world-changing examples of slave resistance build the fabric of an internationalist 'Black Republic' which is both historical and contemporary, indicating the continuity of colonialism and its resistance for centuries. The poem ends with the assertion that these people, the 'we' (recall Bama's or Mpe's 'we' in the end for resonance), cannot be written out of these histories as they had always existed in the pages of diaries, letters and notebooks of expeditions, military triumphs and plantations by colonialists. Now that time has finally come for the decolonised who,

> spent so many years in disquiet,
>
> . . . .
>
> am amazed to discover, Colonist,
>
> it was *you* who feared *me*. (110)

The colonists who tamed and suppressed 'savages', or brought over the tools of law, order and civilisation to discipline them, did it out of the fear that freedom for the Indigenous would render the colonisers meaningless, forgotten and side-tracked in history. The poem thus offers not only a psychological understanding of the master fearing the slave, which resonates with Homi Bhabha's understanding of the complex role of mimicry and power, but also gives us a restorative, anticolonial reading of epistemological autonomy through gardening – that peace and relaxation will finally return to the peoples and tribes lost to world ecological extraction and species slaughter. As Senior states in her interview, these stories will be written out and these plots of resistance will be hatched again – the extraordinary stories of the Jamaican and the Caribbean people will be written back. In that sense, especially in the anticolonial, internationalist sense mentioned above, the garden, as Stouck following Glissant writes, is 'an open potential, an unceasing process of transformation'. It is 'a figure for regional affirmations of identity, as well as for fertile and often painful cross-cultural exchanges' (2).

The anticolonial restorative consciousness accessed through gardening, plants, fruits, vegetation and agriculture points to the issue of care at a planetary level. While the question of care has been suggested in my eco-materialist reading of Devi's and Mpe's call for social justice and communities of healing, Senior's work helps us frame the topic amidst emerging conversations on 'critical plant studies'. As Randy Laist observes, the Aristotelian rendering of the plant at the bottom of the taxonomic order and in between the categories of living and non-living has hardly allowed plants any agency in literature and art (12). While he acknowledges that the 'western modernity'-enabled ecological crisis as being chiefly responsible for the relegation of plants from human imagination (15), neither a vague term such as Western modernity nor the Euro-America-oriented essays in his collection help us imagine a plant studies that is critical of the way plants and animals – their ecosystems, to recall Huggan and Tiffin – were uprooted and commodified on a planetary scale. In my eco-materialist reading, Senior offers a far more compelling rendering of such plant studies in these poems, engaging with plants and their cultural, historical and anticolonial meanings and their restorative and healing powers for non-European or Indigenous cultures and minds. Further, Senior's poems in the collection and elsewhere indicate the importance of agriculture – the production process through which grains and plants become food. Agriculture is a cultivation of the soil which is deeply related to the songs and poetry of the soil. This is what, it seems to me, Senior's poetry wants us to remember: that the conversations of sustenance and resilience in postcolonial studies must consider the methods through which food becomes food – processes which have become reified in the neocolonial capitalist system. As we argued in the first chapter, the fight for food and land in decolonisation is not separate from the fight for culture and reading. Senior suggests here, through her readings of tribal agricultural and slave rebellions, that the point is to build a 'vegetal consciousness' through narratives in which 'plants are no longer the passive object of contemplation but are increasingly resembling "subjects," "stakeholders," and "performers"' (Brits and Gibson 13). As Sumana Roy, author of the critically acclaimed, *How I Became A Tree*, writes on the emerging field of plant humanities,

> Calculate backwards — from the plate to the soil, all the joints in the process, every bend, from production through distribution through the kitchen and the people cooking it

to our plates. The linguistic history, the layers of travel and argument in it, the farmer's history, the distributor's history, the history of the marketplace. I call it "The History of Your Breakfast assignment". Maybe we could begin from there?'
(*The Hindu*)

Senior's poetry makes an embodied offering of this backward-forward process turning into a symbol of planetary care – that is, via DeLoughrey and Handley, care for the planet in the way it comes to us and what we can give back to the ecosystem. Senior's poetry, like the works of Devi and Mpe, urges us to consider futures of care and multidimensional solidarity in envisioning breaking through colonial and neocolonial systems of oppression in the Anthropocene; writing about resistance to the species-destructive methods of extraction in the postcolonial world; and offering a resilient view of community and hope in a connected ecosystem. In the final chapter of this book, I will offer a focussed reading of form and genre to understand how futures of care are imagined and implemented in postcolonial speculative works.

NOTES

1. See the works of Guha and Arnold; Griffith and Robin; MacLeod; Chakrabarty; DeLoughrey and Handley; Iheka; Manjapra; and DeLoughrey, among others.
2. These were codes or laws which were instituted during the colonial period to define what would constitute a famine and how to arrange state relief according to these definitions.
3. All quotes from this story have been translated by me, unless otherwise mentioned.
4. This has been a thorny issue in Indian politics as the Supreme Court has ruled for the eviction of about 40 million forest dwellers in favour of the conservation of forests, while high courts have begun to listen to court cases against eviction. See Chandran; for a historical view, see Saravanan.
5. Indeed, it will not be entirely wrong to say that much of Caribbean poetry shares this critical 'double consciousness' with neocolonial modernity. Recall, for instance, the first stanzas on fisherman and

tourism in Derek Walcott's *Omeros*, 1990.
6. See the work of Sharae Deckard (2017) and Mike Niblett (2020) on this topic.

REFERENCES

Aguiar, Marian. *Tracking Modernity: India's Railways and the Culture of Mobility*. U of Minnesota P, 2011.

Anderson, Mark. *Disaster Writing: The Cultural Politics of Catastrophe in Latin America*. U of Virginia P, 2011.

Arnold, David, and Ramachandra Guha, editors. *Nature, Culture, and Imperialism: Essays on the Environmental History of South Asia*. Oxford UP, 1996.

Arnold, David. *Colonizing the Body: State Medicine and Epidemic Diseases*. U of California P, 1993.

Beinart, William, and Lotte Hughes. *Environment and Empire*. Oxford UP, 2007.

Bhattacharya, Sourit. *Postcolonial Modernity and the Indian Novel: On Catastrophic Realism*. Palgrave Macmillan, 2020.

Brits, Baylee and Prudence Gibson. "Introduction: Covert Plants". *Vegetal Consciousness and Agency in an Anthropocentric World*, edited by Prudence Gibson and Baylee Brits, Brainstorm Books, 2018, pp. 11–25.

Bucknor, Michael A. "Conceptual Residues of Imperialist Ruination: Waste, Weeds and the Poetics of Rubbish in Edward Baugh's *Black Sand* and Olive Senior's *Gardening in the Tropics*". *Journal of West Indian Literature*, vol. 28, no. 1, 2020, pp. 33–45.

Buell, Lawrence. *The Environmental Imagination: Thoreau, Nature Writing and the Formation of American Culture*. Harvard UP, 1995.

Carrigan, Anthony. "Towards A Postcolonial Disaster Studies". *Global Ecologies and the Environmental Humanities: Postcolonial Approaches*, edited by Elizabeth DeLoughrey, Jill Didur and Anthony Carrigan, Routledge, 2015, pp. 117–39.

Chakrabarty, Dipesh. "The Climate of History: Four Theses". *Critical Inquiry*, vol. 35, no. 2, 2009, pp. 197–222.

Chandran, Rina. "India's top court to rule on eviction of millions from forests". *Reuters*, 23 July 2019, https://www.reuters.com/article/idUSKCN1UI1VD/. Accessed 19 June 2021.

Clark, Nancy L., and William H. Worger. *South Africa: The Rise and fall of Apartheid*. Routledge, 2013.

Clarkson, Carrol. "Locating Identity in Phaswane Mpe's *Welcome to Our Hillbrow*". *Third World Quarterly*, vol. 26, no. 3, 2005, pp. 451–59.

Crosby, Alfred. *Ecological Imperialism: The Biological Expansion of Europe, 900–1900*. 1986. Cambridge UP, 2004.

Currie, Bob. *The Politics of Hunger in India: A Study of Democracy, Governance and Kalahandi's Poverty*. Palgrave Macmillan, 2000.

Das, Pallavi V. *Colonialism, Development, and the Environment Railways and Deforestation in British India, 1860–1884*. Palgrave Macmillan, 2015.

Davis, Darién J., editor. *Beyond Slavery: The Multilayered Legacy of Africans in Latin America and the Caribbean*. Rowman & Littlefield, 2007.

Davis, Emily S. "Contagion, Cosmopolitanism, and Human Rights in Phaswane Mpe's *Welcome to Our Hillbrow*". *College Literature*, vol. 40, no. 3, 2013, pp. 99–112.

Deckard, Sharae. *Paradise Discourse, Imperialism, and Globalization: Exploiting Eden*. Routledge, 2010.

---. "Cacao and Cascadura: Energetic Consumption and Production in World-ecological Literature". *Journal of Postcolonial Writing*, vol. 53, no. 3, 2017, pp. 342–54.

DeLoughrey, Elizabeth. "Island Ecologies and Caribbean Literatures". *Tijdschrift voor Economische en Sociale Geografie*, vol. 95, no. 3, 2004, pp. 298–310.

---, and George B. Handley, editors. *Postcolonial Ecologies: Literature and the Environment*. Oxford UP, 2011.

DeLoughrey, Elizabeth. *Allegories of the Anthropocene*. Duke UP, 2019.

Devi, Mahasweta. "Mahadu: Ekti Rupkatha". *Mahasweta Devi: Srestha Galpo*. Dey's Publishing, 2004, pp. 292–99.

---. *Operation?—Bashai Tudu*. Translated by Samik Bandyopadhyay, Thema, 1990.

---. "The Author in Conversation". *Imaginary Maps: Three Stories by Mahasweta Devi*, translated by Gayatri Chakraborty Spivak, Routledge, 1995, pp. ix–xxii.

Dhanagare, D.N. *Peasants Movements in India, 1920–1950*. Oxford UP, 1983.

Drèze, Jean, and Amartya Sen, editors. *The Political Economy of Hunger: Endemic Hunger Vol 3*, Oxford UP, 1991.

"Ecology". *Oxford English Dictionary*, https://www.oed.com/dictionary/ecology_n?tab=meaning_and_use#5964959. Accessed 12 Jan 2022.

Fanon, Frantz. *The Wretched of the Earth*. Translated by Constance Farrington, Grove Press, 1963.

Gadgil, Madhav, and Ramachandra Guha. *This Fissured Land: An Ecological History of India*. U of California P, 1992.

Garrard, Greg. *Ecocriticism*. Routledge, 2012.

Galeano, Eduardo. *Open Veins of Latin America. Five Centuries of the Pillage of a Continent*. 1971. Monthly Review P, 1997.

Glotfelty, Cheryll, and Harold Fromm, editors. *The Ecocriticism Reader: Landmarks in Literary Ecology*. U of Georgia P, 1996.

Gómez-Barris, Macarena. *The Extractive Zone: Social Ecologies and Decolonial Perspectives*. Duke UP, 2017.

Griffiths, Tom, and Libby Robin. *Ecology and Empire: Environmental History of Settler Societies*. U of Washington P, 1997.

Grove, Richard. *Green Imperialism: Colonial Expansion, Tropical Islands Edens and the origin of environmentalism, 1600–1800*. Cambridge UP, 1995.

Grünkemeier, Ellen. *Breaking the Silence: South African Representations of HIV/AIDS*. James Currey, 2013.

Guha, Ramachandra. "Radical American Environmentalism: A Third World Critique". *Environmental Ethics*, no. 11, 1989, pp. 71–83.

---. *The Unquiet Woods: Ecological Change and Peasant Resistance in the Himalaya*. U of California P, 1990.

Huggan, Graham, and Helen Tiffin. *Postcolonial Ecocriticism: Literature, Animals, Environment*. Routledge, 2010.

Ifowodo, Ogaga. *History, Trauma and Healing in Postcolonial Narratives: Reconstructing Identities*. Palgrave Macmillan, 2013.

Iheka, Cajetan. *Naturalizing Africa: Ecological Violence, Agency, and Postcolonial Resistance in African Literature*. Cambridge UP, 2018.

Kincaid, Jamaica. *A Small Place*. 1988. Daunt, 2008

---. *My Garden (Book)*. Farrar, Straus and Giroux, 1999.

Laist, Randy. "Introduction". *Plants and Literature: Critical Essays on Future Plant Studies*, edited by Randy Laist, Brill, 2013, pp. 9–18.

Maathai, Wangari. *The Green Belt Movement: Sharing the Approach and the Experience*. 1985. Lantern Books, 2003.

MacLeod, Roy M. *Nature and Empire: Science and the Colonial Enterprise*. U of Chicago P, 2000.

Malm, Andreas. *Fossil Capital: The Rise of Steam Power and the Roots of Global Warming*. Verso, 2016.

Mander, Harsh. *Ash in the Belly: India's Unfinished Battle against Hunger*. Penguin, 2012.

Manjapra, Kris. *Colonialism in Global Perspectives*. Cambridge UP, 2020.

Martínez-Alier, Joan. *Environmentalism of the Poor: A Study of Ecological Conflicts and Valuation*. Edward Elgar Publishing, 2002.

Menozzi, Filippo. *Postcolonial Custodianship: Cultural and Literary Inheritance*. Routledge, 2014.

Moïse. Myriam. "Jamaica Kincaid and Olive Senior Gardening through History, Cultivating Rhizomic Subjectivities". *Wagadu: A Journal of Transnational Women's and Gender Studies*, no. 19, 2018, pp. 41–51.

Moore, Jason W. 'The Capitalocene, Part I: On the Nature and Origins of Our Ecological Crisis.' *The Journal of Peasant Studies*, vol. 44, no. 3, 2017, pp. 594–630.

Mpe, Phaswane. *Welcome to Our Hillbrow: A Novel of Post-apartheid South Africa*. 2001, Ohio UP, 2011.

---. "Healing with Words: Phaswane Mpe Interviewed by Lizzy Attree". *Journal of Commonwealth Literature*, vol. 40, no. 3, 2005, pp. 139–48.

Mukherjee, Upamanyu Pablo. "Ivan Vladislavić: Traversing the Uneven City". *Journal of Postcolonial Writing*, vol. 48, no. 5, 2012, pp. 472–84.

---. *Natural Disasters and Victorian Empire: Famines, Fevers, and Literary Culture of South Asia*. Palgrave Macmillan, 2013.

---. *Postcolonial Environments: Nature, Culture and the Contemporary Indian Novel in English*. Palgrave Macmillan, 2010.

Niblett, Michael. *World Literature and Ecology: The Aesthetics of Commodity Frontiers, 1890-1950*. Palgrave Macmillan, 2020.

Nixon, Rob. "Environmentalism and Postcolonialism". *Postcolonial Studies and Beyond*, edited by Ania Loomba, et al., Duke UP, 2005, pp. 233–51.

Packard, Randall M. *White Plague, Black Labor. Tuberculosis and the Political Economy of Health and Disease in South Africa*. U of California P, 1989.

Phillips, Howard. "HIV/AIDS in the context of South Africa's Epidemic History". *AIDS and South Africa. The Social Expression of a Pandemic*, edited by Kyle D. Kauffmann and David L. Lindaur, Palgrave Macmillan, 2004, pp. 31–47.

---. *Epidemics: The Story of South Africa's Five Most Lethal Human Diseases*. Ohio UP, 2012.

Pratt, Mary Louise. *Imperial Eyes: Travel Writing and Transculturation*. Routledge, 1992.

Rastogi, Pallavi. *Postcolonial Disaster: Narrating Catastrophe in the Twenty-First Century*. Northwestern UP, 2020.

Roth, Emmanuelle. "Epidemic Temporalities: A Concise Literature Review". *Anthropology Today*, vol. 36, no. 4, 2020, pp. 13–16.

Roy, Sumana. "Plant Humanities: A Discipline Takes Shape". *The Hindu*, 23 July 2021, https://www.thehindubusinessline.com/blink/explore/plant-humanities-a-discipline-takes-shape/article35482656.ece. Accessed 7 June 2022.

Salgado, Minoli. "Tribal Stories, Scribal Worlds: Mahasweta Devi and the Unreliable Translator". *Journal of Commonwealth Literature*, vol. 35, no. 1, 2000, pp. 131–46.

Saravanan, Velayutham. *Colonialism, Development and Tribals in South India, 1792-1947*. Routledge, 2017.

Saro-wiwa, Ken. *Genocide in Nigeria: The Ogoni Tragedy*. Saros, 1992.

Senior, Olive. "An Interview with Olive Senior". Interviewed by Charles H. Rowell, *Callaloo*, no. 36, 1988, pp. 480–90.

---. *Gardening in the Tropics*. 1994. Insomniac Press, 2005.

Shiva, Vandana. *The Violence of the Green Revolution: Third World Agriculture, Ecology and Politics*. Zed Books, 1993.

Stouck, Jordan. "Gardening in the Diaspora: Place and Identity in Olive Senior's Poetry". *Mosaic: A Journal for the Interdisciplinary Study of Literature*, vol. 38, no. 4, 2005, pp. 103–22.

Triechler, Paula. "AIDS, Homophobia and Biomedical Discourse: An Epidemic of Signification". *Cultural Studies*, vol. 1, no. 3, 1987, pp. 265–306.

Varma, Rashmi. *The Postcolonial City and its Subjects: London, Nairobi, Bombay*. Routledge, 2012.

Walcott, Derek. *Omeros*. 1990. Faber and Faber, 2002.

Wenzel, Jennifer. "Forest Fictions and Ecological Crises: Reading the Politics of Survival in Mahasweta Devi's 'Dhowli'". *Postcolonial Ecologies: Literature and the Environment*, edited by Elizabeth DeLoughrey and George B. Handley, Oxford UP, 2011, pp. 136–58.

Wynter, Sylvia. "Novel and History, Plot and Plantation". *Savacou*, no. 5, 1971, pp. 95–102.

Zipes, Jack. *The Irresistible Fairy Tale: The Cultural and Social History of a Genre*. Princeton UP, 2012.

Chapter Six

Futures

UTOPIA, DYSTOPIA AND PLANETARITY IN ROKEYA, PADMANABHAN AND OKORAFOR

We may have noticed by now that postcolonial works are characteristically future-oriented or futuristic. By futuristic, I do not mean the technophilic art movements of futurism or vorticism in early-twentieth century Europe often associated with fascism. Nor do I mean a futurological thrust similar to how think-tanks, policy makers and corporate strategists build designs and scenarios of future (urban) spaces (Paul 131–44). I rather mean that the works we have read reflect critically on the oppressed pasts and presents of their local and national histories, from which they also envision and point us toward futures of social and material transformation. Be it Devi's short story, 'Mahadu: Ekti Rupkatha', Thi Bui's graphic novel, *The Best We Could Do* or Steve McQueen's film, *12 Years A Slave*, the decolonising impulse of postcolonial works (which I started the book with) is a perennially future-directed endeavour to anticipate change for the good; for social, political, economic and cultural emancipation, justice, equity and egalitarianism. This is what my Benjaminian historical materialist method of 'reading for decolonising' has aimed to do: to uncover, through the colonialist crystallisation of 'thoughts' of oppressed pasts and histories, the transformative futures to come.

However, there is another, and perhaps more concrete, way that 'futures' have been imagined in postcolonial works. In these works, primarily known as speculative fiction – I am using the term SF – futures are both the works' imaginative content and their scholarly objects of study. While I have been arguing in the book to read literary and cultural works through their generic and stylistic elements for the not-yet futures to come, in this chapter I will show that postcolonial authors have consistently drawn upon the future-directed, world-building genres of SF. Unlike technophilic, 'energetic' future worlds, these futures, true to their postcolonial ethos, are critical of colonial–capitalist extractivisms or neocolonial–technocratic enterprises of the past and the present. They ask us to collectively imagine futures, not necessarily without technology, but in which technology's terrible extractive logics have been unconcealed or harnessed to greater human use. Or, in which its presentist Eurocentric agenda has been deconstructed to make way for a future of coexistence and collective learning from technology and the environment. To do that, I will first critically introduce genres and 'genre fictions' – a key constituent of SF – for postcolonial studies and then engage with the conceptual rubric of futures through the thematic topics of utopia, dystopia and planetarity. My aim here is to demonstrate the critical richness of postcolonial SF, which has become more academically visible in the last decades, and to interrogate the immense stake that technology and digital use hold for humans and nonhumans in the postcolonial world.

Genre, Postcolonial Studies and SF: Building Anticolonial Future-Worlds

In literary studies, genres can mean many things. As we have noted throughout the book, it can mean a type of work such as novel, poetry or short story; meaning the classification of literary works into specific categories. It can mean literary rules and conventions – or features – through which a piece of work becomes a specific genre. It can be the practice of labelling a piece of work for marketing and distribution. It can also be a way of interpretation – a method of meaning-making out of the world. What unites these definitions is a cognitive practice of stylistic classification through which a piece of work makes meaning out of the social realities and the historical–material events it describes and reproduces. As John Frow notes, genres produce constraints on the production and interpretation of meaning, by which he means the structuring effect which gives form to social realities at work allowing for the heterogeneities of realities to take shape. Genres, for him, are inherently plural and transgressive. Unlike the biological taxonomic practices associated with genres, these genres are open-ended, interfertile and formative (Frow 53).

That genres are plural and interfertile was famously argued by Jacques Derrida in his essay on 'The Law of Genre'. For Derrida, the law postulates that genres are not to be mixed, but the same implies a counter-law that challenges the purity of the same, contaminates it and makes it transgressive. 'What if there were', Derrida posits, 'lodged within the heart of the law itself, a law of impurity or a principle of contamination? And suppose the condition for the possibility of the law were the a priori of a counter-law, an axiom of impossibility that would confound its sense, order, and reason?' ("The Law of Genre" 57). Because of this transgressive nature of genres, critics have called for historicist readings demonstrating how genres have emerged in robust dialogue with historical and social conditions, as well as with existing aesthetic styles and genres. For Tzvetan Todorov, genres are social in content and form and mobilise historical change by giving a 'codification of discursive properties' for shifting hierarchical structures (17–18). The shifting hierarchy of genre systems, Frow writes following Hans Robert Jauss (97), is 'made up of tensions between "higher" and "lower" genres, a constant alternation of the dominant form, and a constant renewal of genres through processes of specialisation or recombination. Genres, it follows, are neither self-identified, nor self-contained' (71).

These scholarly discussions assert that genres are inter-mixing categories and need to be understood, much like decolonisation, in the historical and aesthetic meanings of a 'process'. Peter Hitchcock in "The Genres of Postcoloniality" – one of the earliest readings of genres in postcolonial studies – asks that we focus on the cultural specificities and sociohistorical ruptures producing a counter-discursive use of the novel genre. Hitchcock writes, 'What is required is a mode of analysis that takes genre seriously enough to fathom the conditions under which particular genres may appear and expire (like the romance and the lyric in Western literature) while allowing for a law of genre that is not in itself ahistorical' (311). This line of thought is taken up by later engagements with the topic. Jane Hiddleston comments that in postcolonial studies 'the verbal artifice' of ambiguity, ambivalence or indeterminacy are ignored for content and political meaning of texts. Like Hitchcock, she indicates the need for a more nuanced, committed method of reading along with stylistics (Hiddleston 2). In another volume, Walter Goebel and Saskia Schabio, echoing our concern in the book, argue that postcolonial perspectives have predominantly prioritised the contemporary novel genre without properly historicising it (2). A cogent attempt at narrative decolonisation is found in the edited volume *Minor Genres in Postcolonial Literature* by Delphine Munos and Bénédicte Ledent, who also note the field's continuing aversion to exploring aesthetic matters beyond the novel thereby contributing to 'the containment of postcolonial criticism within a set of prescribed paradigms' (1). Not only are genres plural and malleable as a one-size-fits-all label as these scholars suggest, but there are also several genres through which authors and cultural producers have been expressing their postcolonial concerns and sensibilities. This is something I have tried to capture in this book – that we will have to read across genres to understand how these works have used their aesthetic properties and innovations to construct their specific narrative arguments. I have further argued that at the heart of decolonisation remains an anticolonial, socialist drive to break free from the chains of colonial–capitalist and neocolonial forms of exploitation, and hence these works, their contexts, and genres are also comparable.

These points on the radical political commitment in genre-use have been made most cogently for genre fiction and SF in the postcolonial context. Bodhisattwa Chattopadhyay, Aakriti Mandhwani and Anwesha Maity comment in their 'Introduction' to *Indian Genre Fiction* that since 'genre' practically means to paste an interpretive label on a piece of work, this leads to deeper biases against genre literatures 'as being fundamentally trivial, concerned with cheap thrills, and offering escapist fantasies and gratuitous titillation – a literature consumed by an undiscerning reader belonging to the nameless masses' (2). On the other hand, while pleasure is key to genre fiction, this fiction is deeply critical of the genre forms themselves or politicise the social realities they represent. 'Genre fiction', they write, 'is directly political: it politicises what is taken for granted, bringing the unquestionable such as the sanctity of myth into a space where it can be questioned for relevance and critiqued for social, ethical, and moral values'. They add, 'Genre fiction maintains its political relevance through a healthy use of satire and other comedic devices, challenging authority accorded to figures of power and influence' (7). That genre fiction is deeply political and subversive in nature is famously argued by Rosemary Jackson in *Fantasy: The Literature of Subversion*. She comments that fantasy 'characteristically attempts to compensate for a lack resulting from cultural constraints: it is a literature of desire, which seeks that which is experienced as absence and loss' (3). Following Jackson's aesthetic reading through the genre, Mark Bould and Sherryl Vint note, 'All fantasy is political, even – perhaps especially – when it thinks it is not. From the abstruse literary confection to the sharecropped franchise series, a fantasy text at the very least functions like any cultural text to reproduce dominant ideology' (102).

SF, which includes science fiction, horror, and fantasy, among others genres (together as 'fantastika', as John Clute (2007/2011) termed it), then, is a political project not only because it offers an understanding of a recognisable but different reality, but because it also attempts to subvert or supplement what is marginalised or castrated in the bourgeois representation of reality: an epistemological-aesthetic project per se. This was made clear in the notable use of the genre by black (and postcolonial) authors such as Octavia Butler and Samuel Delaney in the 1980s and 90s who used it to critically comment on the future horrors of race and class-based social segregation in the USA. Nalo Hopkinson and Uppinder Mehan's ground-breaking collection on *Postcolonial Science Fiction and Fantasy*, Dimitra Fimi's scintillating reading of race and culture in Tolkien, and John Rieder's path-breaking arguments that science fiction was used as a method to imagine and materialise imperialist projects made important breakthroughs in the field demanding more robust academic studies of postcolonial SF. As Upamanyu

Pablo Mukherjee's *Final Frontier: Science Fiction and Techno-science in Non-Aligned India* shows, Nehruvian socialist developments in science and technology in a recently decolonised India, and the internationalism of the Third World (the ex-colonised Afro-Asian countries) which had pledged to work together in the historic 1955 Bandung Conference in Indonesia, allowed for the emergence of an internationalist science fiction and fantasy genre in postcolonial India.

This in no way means that postcolonial SF happened only after a colonised country had formally received political independence. As I will show below through a reading of Rokeya's 1922 science fiction short story, SF was used by colonial writers to envision a postcolonial world of social liberty and equality. However, as Padmanabhan's play and Okorafor's novel suggest, the postcolonial world might have a different reality that is set against in the globalisation of the technological world order, a world of dystopia calling for a resistant and decolonising ethics of planetarity. We will note that these works offer incisive political arguments, on gender, capitalism, class and race among others, and demonstrate specifically how women writers have used these genres and topics to imagine an anticolonial, anti-capitalist, and anti-patriarchal world of multispecies inclusivity.

UTOPIA: EMPIRE, TECHNOLOGY AND ANTICOLONIAL FEMINISM IN ROKEYA SAKHAWAT HOSSAIN'S *SULTANA'S DREAM*

This section will engage with colonial utopia as SF. Utopia is a Greek word derived from Thomas More's sixteenth century tract, *Utopia*, which means, paradoxically, a place that does not exist now but will arrive soon. Barnita Bagchi writes that in modern use, it has come to be understood as 'social dreaming' for hope and a better future from the capitalist and colonialist exploitation of humans, animals, vegetation and the environment (qtd. in Paul 327–28; see also, Bloch; Levitas). In *Archaeologies of the Future*, Fredric Jameson observes, 'Utopian form is itself a representational meditation on radical difference, radical otherness, and on the systemic nature of the social totality, to the point where one cannot imagine any fundamental change in our social existence which has not at first thrown off Utopian visions like so many sparks from a comet' (xii). Jameson distinguishes between the utopian programme and the utopian impulse and favours the latter as the moment of initiating the anticipated fundamental change in the future for social transformation and political emancipation. The utopian impulse, as we have argued above, is crucial for postcolonial works too. Bill Ashcroft has suggested that rather than foreseeing a particular utopia, 'the function of postcolonial utopianism is to open up a space for political action that is buoyed up by the possibility—indeed, the probability—of social change. The prominent feature of postcolonial utopianism, then, is critique' (44). This element of social critique for utopian transformation has widely appeared in postcolonial genre fiction. For instance, critic Greg Forter has demonstrated that the role of 'postcolonial historical fiction to totalized understanding is dialectically related to the utopian project of negating what *is* in the name of what could be' (6; emphasis in original). In another work, Andrew Baldwin has usefully interrogated the inadequacy of postcolonial methodologies that excavate the past for understanding the 'colonial' present, but cannot confidently set up meaning for a 'future-conditional form of difference found in the figure of the yet-to-come . . . the climate change migrant' (295). 'Speculating' about a socially transformed future to come through the epistemological–aesthetic agenda of fiction, albeit with its problems, is fundamental to the utopian element of SF.

Utopia's anticolonial socialist impulse in the colonial Indian context was first noted in the revival of the SF genre in Bengal and Calcutta – colonial India's capital until 1911 – during the high tide of British imperialism in the 1870s and 80s. Debjani Sengupta finds that the inculcation of rationality and scientific temperament was encouraged among the educated elite mainly by two competing schools of thought in contemporary Bengal: the Derozian Young Bengal Movement and the Brahmo Samaj. 'This was because of a rapid mechanization of English businesses by the 1880s that led to a growing desire among the colonized Bengalis to master the alien technologies and sciences, largely perceived as a remedy against superstitions and ignorance. It was a way in which colonial modernity could be mastered and understood' (D. Sengupta 116). In the next two decades, amidst the political turmoil of the anticolonialist, nationalist Swadeshi movement, SF had already achieved an underlying political agenda. Consider these words from Rabindranath Tagore's 'Introduction' to Dakshinaranjan Mitra Majumder's *Thakurmar Jhuli*:

> Is there anything more quintessentially indigenous than *Grandmother's Bag of Tales*? Alas, even this golden bag had been manufactured and sent over to us from Manchester's factories until now. English fairy tales became the main source of education and entertainment for our children. Our indigenous grandmother's company was made completely bankrupt. Searching in their school bags, you might spot Martin's *Ethics* or Burke's notebook on the French Revolution – but not the princes and fairies of our beliefs. Where have these princes and the speaking birds of Bengama and Bengami gone? Where have the treasures of the seven kings from the seven seas and the thirteen rivers disappeared? (9–10; my translation)

Apart from his satiric anti-imperialism, Tagore uses the words 'swadeshi' and 'indigenous' several times. 1905 was witness to Lord Curzon's proposal to divide Bengal into two parts to administer it more efficiently. This was mainly meant to effectively suppress anticolonial insurgencies as well as divide the region's spirit of integration and assimilation through a religious identity-based partition which finally materialised in 1947. While the Partition of Bengal led to long-term nationwide protests, its immediate impact was the rise of the Swadeshi movement. Tagore was one of the architects of the cultural and political side of the movement – writing songs and supporting indigenous commercial and social projects. Fantasy and fairy tales, science and horror fiction – or, together as SF – saw a spectacular revival during this period as a political project to mobilise human consciousness around cultural traditions and to satirise discriminatory conditions of life and living under colonialism. From Sukumar Ray to Premendra Mitra to Leela Majumder to postcolonial fantasy and SF, the speculative could hardly ignore the political nature of self and collective mobilisation towards a utopic new political future of anticolonial imagination and self-determination, making it imperative to go back to the past to understand its directions in the now.

Rokeya Sakhawat Hossain's (henceforth Rokeya's) short story, 'Sultana's Dream' was published in the *Indian Lady's Magazine* (1905) during this period of sociopolitical turmoil in India. Rokeya, born in Rangpur district in colonial Bengal and representing Bangladeshi literature and political life now, was a lifelong activist, a major figure for women's education in South Asia, and a robust critic of the orthodoxy of patriarchy and religion in Hindu and Muslim worlds (Ray 434–46). This short story, which has been compared in Anglophone academic circles to the works of Charlotte Perkins Gillman and Virginia Woolf (Quayum xiii), was originally written in English. Narrated by Rokeya's protagonist Sultana, the story begins one evening as Sultana broods over 'the condition of Indian womanhood' and falls asleep. She dreams of a place, Ladyland, where men have been outwitted and relegated to a secluded domestic space called 'mardana' or manliness (where they laze around, eat and sleep), as opposed to 'zenana' or womanliness, the women's secluded space in a Muslim household in her times. Like in her novella, *Padmarag* (*The Ruby*; 1924), women govern this place. They are strong, intelligent, kind and drawn to learning and science. Rationality and affection coexist in this society. Sultana is bemused at the reversal of roles in her dream, to which her guide, Sister Sara, suggests that her puzzlement comes from her unquestioned absorption of patriarchal and colonial discourses of science and religion. As SF scholars Chloe Campbell (2007) and Helen Young (2016) have argued for their individual critical contexts, Sultana's philosophical tendencies seem to be directly related to contemporaneous discussions in the space of colonial–imperial science and eugenics which had equated science with masculinity and racial purity. This story not only criticises the purdah or zenana system which Rokeya has written widely about in her non-fiction work but proposes the reversal, that is, relegating men to seclusion and yet not imprisoning them against their wish (Mookerjea-Leonard 149–50). This aspect of ruling a world with consent and yet radically changing it, overthrowing established traditions in a society which is not entirely different from the real world, was radical enough for her time and remains so even today;

a point which Rokeya scholars have long written about. I will focus here on the example of renewable energy in the narrative, which should be able to suggest the kind of feminist, anti-capitalist, anticolonial utopic imagining that SF as a genre or a political project enables.

During her conversation with Sister Sara Sultana discovers that the queen of Ladyland, a connoisseur of science and technology, declared one day that all women in Ladyland need to be educated and were not to get married before the age of twenty-one. She established several all girls' schools and colleges and two universities. These universities began to invent environmentally sustainable technologies for rainwater harvesting, solar-heat trapping and electric cars which were rubbished by the rival kingdoms of men, rulers and administrators as 'a sentimental nightmare'. When a war broke out and the military and administrative skills of men looked to be in danger of falling apart, the enemy was defeated by the technological innovation of solar heat invented by the women of Ladyland. This heat also powered household activities, commercial and transport systems. To give some examples from the text:

> 'Will you care to see our kitchen?' she asked me.
>
> 'With pleasure,' said I, and we went to see it. Of course the men had been asked to clear off when I was going there. The kitchen was situated in a beautiful vegetable garden. Every creeper, every tomato plant was itself an ornament. I found no smoke, nor any chimney either in the kitchen — it was clean and bright; the windows were decorated with flower gardens. There was no sign of coal or fire.
>
> 'How do you cook?' I asked.
>
> 'With solar heat,' she said, at the same time showing me the pipe, through which passed the concentrated sunlight and heat. And she cooked something then and there to show me the process. (Hossain 29)

And

> 'Our fields are tilled by means of electricity, which supplies motive power for other hard work as well, and we employ it for our aerial conveyances too. We have no rail road nor any paved streets here.'

'Therefore neither street nor railway accidents occur here,' said I. 'Do not you ever suffer from want of rainwater?' I asked.

'Never since the "water balloon" has been set up. You see the big balloon and pipes attached thereto. By their aid we can draw as much rainwater as we require. Nor do we ever suffer from flood or thunderstorms. We are all very busy making nature yield as much as she can. (36)

Apart from the story's remarkably advanced thinking in terms of sustainable technologies, two aspects stand out for my interest in this chapter: conveyance and nature. There are no streets, roads and railways in this world: conveyance is aerial and the ground is a giant green garden, on in which I will focus soon. Masquerading in these visions is a strong case for anticolonial critique. As we noticed through Devi's short story, 'Mahadu: Ekti Rupkatha' in the previous chapter on 'Ecologies', roads and railways are the prime markers of colonial–capitalist modernity of the Anthropocene. Railways are often mentioned as the gift from the British Empire which led India's rise to modernity (Tharoor). What is not mentioned in this kind of imperial apologia is the relative ease with which resource extraction and commodity production could be mobilised across the nation through this technology. In this story, the narrator reminds us that they did not want roads or railways because these meant greater environmental pollution. While the language of climate crisis that we are familiar with today may not be available to Rokeya, but by the late nineteenth century filth and pollution had already become a key debate (Stephen Mosley's *The Chimney of the World* comes to mind). Natalka Freeland tells us that the utopian science fiction of the Victorian period by H.G. Wells and others repeatedly focused on the overt presence of urban poor and filth in Victorian London and Paris, appearing at times as instructive manuals for waste management (225). Hence, city planning in the late-nineteenth and early-twentieth centuries made green spaces and hygiene a key policy topic (Datta). This is why botany, green space and gardening are fundamental to this reimagining of the city for Rokeya. Indeed, Sister Sara tells Sultana, 'Our noble Queen is exceedingly fond of botany; it is her ambition to convert the whole country into one grand garden' (Hossain 36).

However, botany in the eighteenth and nineteenth centuries was understood as feminine and thus a lesser science. As Ann B. Shteir comments, 'During the later eighteenth century women had more culturally sanctioned access to botany than to any other science: they collected plants, drew them, studied them, and named them, taught their children about plants, and wrote popularizing books on botany. Botany came to be widely associated with women and was widely gender coded as feminine' (29). It is not surprising then that the queen of Ladyland's interest in botany or in the scientific–religious notion of the kingdom as a giant garden was ridiculed by men as 'a sentimental nightmare'. Apropos of the current ecofeminist scholarship such as Henrietta Nickels Shirk's project of retrieving eighteenth-century female botanists' work as contributing to a feminine green tradition, and the postcolonial botanical discourses that we noticed through Kincaid and Senior in the previous chapter, Rokeya's story not only draws from the colonial realities of pollution, hygiene and green city-planning but also challenges what Deepika Bahri calls colonial–masculinist biopolitical thinking.

But Rokeya does not stop with roads and railways – markers of a polluting modernity. Unlike the anticolonial nationalist leader Mahatma Gandhi's aversion to modern technology, Rokeya – as an activist for women's emancipation – knew that technology was needed for social reform and could be beneficial if harnessed thoughtfully. So, if we recall the quote – 'We are all very busy making nature yield as much as she can', a suggestion may arise in favour of exploiting ('yield') nature through speed and extraction. But Sister Sara tells Sultana that the women in Ladyland do not work for more than two hours a day because the nine-to-five workday is a regimentation that capitalism has chained us with where men mostly while away time by chatting with colleagues or smoking cigarettes. Two hours are adequate for pursuing scientific and administrative work. What is suggested here is a paradigm for the management and organisation of resources for a utopic social life. Maitreyee Chaudhuri comments on the use of utopia in the story noting that 'Organization is the utopianist device to manage issues of supply (of satisfactions) with those of demand (of human desires). Efficient management of natural resources (solar heat and water balloons) and time (for unlike men they do not dawdle away time smoking) is what makes this utopia possible' (109). Interesting is also the word 'yield' here which has a religious–agricultural meaning, that is, produce, pay or repay. The *Oxford English Dictionary* informs us that 'yield' develops its current meaning from crops, return, worship and sacrifice. This religious understanding of crops and food is still prevalent in agricultural societies, especially in India. Later, Sister Sara tells Sultana that the women of Ladyland dislike the ownership of land and possession of wealth and do not trade with men who are habitual liars and exploiters. To quote her again,

> Men, we find, are rather of lower morals and so we do not like dealing with them. We do not covet other people's land, we do not fight for a piece of diamond though it may be a thousand-fold brighter than the Koh-i-Noor, nor do we grudge a ruler his peacock throne. We dive deep into the ocean of knowledge and try to find out the precious gems, which Nature has kept in store for us. We enjoy Nature's gifts as much as we can.
> (Hossain 39)

As we may notice from the pictorial description of nature here, it is a deep reservoir of precious knowledge which is offered to humanity as a gift. A gift, as Jacques Derrida reminded us, is as much about giving as about radically withdrawing from the positionality of giving. Giving is a form of hospitality that recognises the giver or the receiver but does not bind them into a legitimate demand of return. What it asks for in its anonymity of exchange is a recognition of the gift in itself (Derrida, *The Gift of Death* 47–53). Nature is the gift here which the receiver must recognise. It is through collaboration between the human and the nonhuman, between labour and the environment that nature as a gift is formed (recollecting Pablo Mukherjee's eco-materialist framework discussed in the previous chapter). As Suchitra Mathur perceptively notes that in 'Sultana's Dream',

> (T)he technological innovations are designed to work in collaboration with nature instead of competing with it. ... The optimization of natural resources rather than material wealth is the driving force behind technological developments

in Ladyland. Hossain thus redefines scientific progress by measuring it in terms of collective harmony, of how far a 'we' (not an 'I') can benefit from 'Nature's gifts' (not extracted wealth). It is this recognition of Nature as a subject, as a living collaborator rather than an inert object to be manipulated, which most clearly represents Hossain's feminizing of science as an activity. (Mathur 123)

To achieve such an anticolonial, inclusive and utopic vision, Mathur continues, Rokeya's aesthetic method is dreaming, which blurs the material and the non-material and is disallowed in current discourses of Western colonial science. Dreaming, as Parna Sengupta notes, is also important for its religious meaning. Islam, especially the Sufi tradition, uses dreams as a way of not only revealing some fundamental knowledge of immediate social and individual crises but also to foster a community-driven tradition of cure and therapy ("Writing, Dreaming and Freedom"). The Bangladeshi literary tradition has a few noted literary examples of this, including perhaps the most famous one by Akhteruzzaman Elias's novel, *Khoabnama* (1996; *Dreambook*) in which dreaming is shown to be a fundamental practice in the social life of the Muslim fishing community, bringing about a collective therapy for the socially marginalised community. To recall Bagchi, anticolonial critique through the means of political allegory was pervasive in Rokeya's essays indicating how 'British colonialism perpetuated itself by using lies that it disguised as moral welfarism' ("Ladylands and Sacrificial Holes" 172). If the nightmarish social reality is morphed through lies into acceptable truth, Rokeya then counters such a reality and uncovers the potential for a more sustainable reality through dreams. Like the fairytale genre for Devi's 'Mahadu: Ekti Rupkatha' in the previous chapter, dreaming offers an important formal aspect to the story: it allows a journey towards a more community-oriented and equitable world to take place making sure that this world can be seen as just another aspect of everyday reality where technological and social revolution is just a matter of time. But unlike Devi's complex use of the narrative voice and tropes, the narrative arc for this anticolonial story is simpler. The speed and straightforward agenda with which the story moves from reality to dream in the beginning, and then returns from dream to current reality in the end, suggests that the speculative is hardly an unrecognisable extra-real world. The radical imagining of uprooting the current order in the story is thus given a realist utopic potential through dreaming. Considering women's ongoing struggle to make use of technology and the internet for social-political and economic emancipation in contemporary South Asia, Rokeya's 1905 short story reminds us, apropos Fanon, that political decolonisation and social equality are a long-term process, for which the utopic fight needs to continue.

DYSTOPIA: AI, BIOCOLONIALISM AND FEMINIST RESISTANCE IN THE POSTCOLONY IN MANJULA PADMANABHAN'S *HARVEST*

If Rokeya's tale imagines a utopian feminist counter-narrative through technology, the dystopic possibility of a nightmarish postcolonial reality governed by Artificial Intelligence (or AI) is not too far from this utopia. Jameson observes in *Archaeologies of the Future*, 'The term dystopia has traditionally been used (as it is here) to designate representations of the future best characterized as "new maps of hell" (Kingsley Amis), and such predictions have loosely been grasped as anti-Utopias' (154). Dystopia meaning 'dys' or 'bad' utopia ('An imaginary place or condition in which everything is as bad as possible', according to the *OED*), is what authoritarianism, violence and the corruption of 'ideal types' have reduced everyday 'normal' reality to. Noting the inherent relation between utopia and dystopia, Bagchi writes, 'Utopian and dystopian writing and practice thus offer a complex interplay between the actual and the possible, dream and reality, spaces and temporalities, and competing versions of the ideal and the monstrous communities' (5). This point could be best captured by a counter-argument to the introductory section of this chapter: if postcolonial works were future directed and written for a world of emancipation and equality, their current reality was, properly speaking, dystopian. It is no surprise that scholars have widely written on the dystopic elements in 'realist' postcolonial works (Nnodim; Varughese). But the etymological meaning of what a bad utopia, or anti-utopia, could be is best gathered through postcolonial science fiction. We will see how AI technology could lead to the 'extraction' of the human body and life in the postcolony through Indian playwright Manjula Padmanabhan's *Harvest* (2015). Written in 1995 for the Alexander S. Onassis Public Benefit Foundation International Cultural Competition where it won the first prize, and published in 2003, the three-act play, can easily be categorised as a domestic play – a kitchen-sink drama – engaged in exposing the harsh and abusive realities of the everyday life of postcolonial India's urban poor. What is fresh about the story is the rarely-used medium of science fiction theatre. Set in a future Bombay of 2010, the story is about a migrant family of four, settled in a single-room accommodation in a tenement building. The eldest son, Om, has recently lost his job as a clerk; his younger brother, Jeetu is a scandalous male prostitute involved in a romantic relationship with his sister-in-law, Jaya, who is constantly verbally abused by her mother-in-law, Ma, for being 'barren'. Ma uncritically glorifies Om and abhors Jeetu for his profession and relationship with Jaya. All these fall neatly, albeit complexly, into an everyday social drama until Om gets an offer of a job at InterPlanta Services which excels in organ transplantation, a fully institutionalised service in the India of the play. The description of this company sets up the scientistic discourse of the narrative: 'The water is hot, scented. Then cold. Then hot air. Then again, the water. . . . It stings a little, this second water. Smells like some medicine. Then air again. Then we pass through another place' (12). In Om's abrupt and failed attempts to make sense of what happened in the 'job interview', Padmanabhan foreshadows how the 'normal' domesticity of the play is disrupted by the monstrous encroachment of the machine (cf. Devi), now transformed from the colonial machinery of the railways to the postcolonial biopolitics of body monitoring. This part of the chapter will engage with organ transplant, or AI-induced means of biocolonialism, and Jaya's utopic feminist resistance.

Transplanting organs from black and poor bodies to white and rich ones is not new. Writing about the curious case of a heart transplant from a black donor to a white recipient in the racially-charged America of 1968, Maya Overby Koretzky observes that cornea and kidney transplants from black to white bodies had become commonplace in the US by the 1950s. Anthropologist Nancy Scheper-Hughes informs us that it is the Third World which has now become the hub for the trafficking of human organs into the First World. This is especially true for India (Scheper-Hughes 197), a country which needs 200,000 kidneys per year, of which only up to ten percent is supplied legally, leading to 'transplant tourism' in the country and abroad (Masoodi). This demand for healthier organs from poorer peoples who would need the money to pay off debt or avail basic necessities began with the rise in AI-led biotechnological and genomic research in richer countries, encouraging notions of reproductive longevity and transplantation of body parts – in short, the rise of what critics call 'biocolonialism'. Laurie Ann Whitt writes, 'If colonialism encompasses the interlocking array of policies and practices (economic, social, political and legal) that a dominant culture can draw on to maintain and extend its control over other peoples and lands, then biocolonialism emphasizes the role of science policy' (33). Debra Harry, the executive director of the Indigenous Peoples Council on Biocolonialism (an NGO which resists biocolonialism) states, 'Biocolonialism extends the reach of the colonial process into the biomes and knowledge systems of Indigenous peoples in the search for marketable genetic resources and traditional knowledge' (702).

If scholar-activists like Harry or Vandana Shiva (who spoke about 'biopiracy' in 1997) have long critiqued biotechnological research into human bodies and knowledge systems of deprived nations, another compelling source of critique has often come from science fiction. Brittany Anne Chozinski argues that, while the term 'organ donation' previously carried within it a sense of gift or giving, the success rate of the transplantation of organs since the 1960s has meant that bodies are mappable and thus re-organisable, leading to their fearful presence in science fiction writing. She advises, 'Just as organ transplantation was starting to gain a foothold as medically possible, we see the simultaneous emergence of a fear of colonialism in science fiction literature' (61). Chozinski gives examples from American works such as Larry Niven's *The Gift from Earth* (1968) to Margo Piercy's *Woman on the Edge of Time* (1976) in which debates about organ harvesting and the colonial domination of bodies for a dystopian future are ripe, to those about the current world of AI robots, clones and the posthumanist normalisation of transplantation in the twenty-first century as in Kazuo Ishiguro's *Never Let Me Go* (2014).

Padmanabhan's *Harvest* falls into this category of dystopian science fiction on AI-controlled biocolonialism. What is notable in the invasion of the machine into the domestic is the biopolitical production of the body among poor donors. Consider this passage in which Ginni, who is later identified as a 'computer generated wet dream', that is, a sexy female AI voice-over of Virgil, an American male buyer, informs us how the donor needs to be happy at all times for their organs to be healthy:

> Ginni: It's a scientific fact that people who smile longer live longer...
>
> Jaya: I'm smiling!
>
> Ginni: But not enough, Zhaya. . . . if you're not smiling, it means you're not happy. And if you're not happy, you might affect your brother's mood...?
>
> Ginni: The Most Important Thing is to keep Auwm smiling. Coz if Auwm's smiling, it means his body's smiling and if his body's smiling, it means his organs are smiling. And that's the kind of organs that will survive a transplant best – smiling organs. (Padmanabhan 38)

If this passage anticipates the everyday role of smart technology globally (our smartphones, computers, AI and robotics), it also strikingly conveys that health and happiness are not a result of the simple joys of life any longer but must be methodically cultivated for longer life. Happiness is calculable here. Like transplantation, following Chozinski above, which allowed bodies to be mappable and re-organisable, happiness, mood, sorrow – matters of emotion and affect – are now seen as a flexible assortment of body parts which can be bettered and made more durable if they are kept at an optimum level (echoing the increasing use of smart technology and the rise of chatbots such as ChatGPT for optimum regenerative learning techniques as industry best practices).

Eric P. James and Rebecca Gill argue, via a Foucauldian biopolitical approach, that this fascination with keeping the body and mind at an optimum fitness level, is a neoliberal reorganisation of the body which is 'a particular organizational commodity that is not only incorporated into organizational branding, but which may also become a crucial element of one's own self or personal brand' (708–09). Organisations encourage their employees to be fit as a 'democratic choice' – to reclaim something lost, be self-made and exceptional – which means the communicative labour (mechanisms/methods) to manage and produce bodies for the 'normalisation of these types' (722). Neoliberalism's win, to follow Suchitra Mathur's comparative essay in the previous section, is not to produce and export this dogma globally thanks to multinational capitalism, but to continue to extract raw materials from cheap, ex-colonised sources such as Om's family. However, despite the glitter and freedom of fitness, (rich) society has lost emotional value and connection with people. Ginni (Virgil) is jealous of the 'special bond' between Om's family members and laments, 'people in my country, at my age, they just don't have any worthwhile friends, you know? Nothing to hold onto – nothing precious. Nothing like… this'. But then he reminds us that if Western society has forgotten the emotions of love and relationship, they can all be 'harvested' and synthetically produced because what he can do is buy life: 'I get to give you things you'd never get in your lifetime and you get to give me…well…maybe my life' (41). I will come to the question of life soon, but clearly in these conversations Rokeya's dream of equality and exceptionalism through access to technology is shattered as the First World can literally buy the body of a Third World citizen. It is not surprising that with the recent world-changing rise of AI and robotics, postcolonial digital humanities critics have urged for community and affect-based learning and placed a premium on the important issues of access and equity to prevent a technology-driven neocolonial unequal world (Risam; Mohamed, Png, and Isaac) – issues that we argued in the first chapter are at the heart of decolonisation.

The biocolonial extraction of bodies and body parts in order to fuel a neoliberal dream of access to the richer world reaches a climax as Ginni exposes herself as Virgil, who now has the body parts of Jeetu, wrongly identified as Om. Om who wanted to be with Ginni and experience her clean, lush and beautiful world goes out to lodge a police complaint of treason against the Company, and Ma buys herself a self-contained Video Couch (a TV-cum-cabin) which she does not need to get out of. As Virgil then woos an abandoned Jaya, we are told that he always wanted Jeetu's body parts because the ultimate plan was to impregnate Jaya to have perfect children:

> Virgil: We lost the art of having children... We began to live longer and longer.... soon there was competition between one generation and the next – old against young, parent against child. We older ones had the advantage of experience. We prevailed.... So we designed this programme. We support the poorer sections of the world, while gaining fresh bodies for ourselves. (Padmanabhan 86)

This passage is both poignant and frightening, talking about the imminent future of neoliberalism's dystopian dreams (and hence the burning question of ethics for AI in postcolonial studies). As we noted in James and Gill previously, the competition in sports and professional industries to regiment bodies and cultivate 'exceptionalism' is a clear pathway towards this competition of who has a better, healthier life. The Darwinian competition that has seen the end of nature in society needs to now artificially fill it with 'nature' and more importantly with 'life' (for which both fresh body parts and wombs are necessary). Reproductive longevity will need to come from cheaper and poorer sections of the world which may not have money and capital (which will be given to them) but enjoy a healthy, communal life (which will be taken away from them) – a case of racialised gendered debt between the First World and the Third World in Jodi Kim's insightful reading of the play. There is a strong resonance of the current condition in two contemporary dystopic examples: Ann Patchett's novel, *State of Wonder* (2011), where a Kurtz-like scientist, Dr Annick Swenson, works with the Indigenous Lakashi tribe to mine knowledge on reproductive longevity; and Jordan Peele's widely acclaimed film, *Get Out* (2017) which shows a wealthy white family in the American Deep South trading in black bodies through romantic relationships and the neurosurgical transplantation of organs to old, wealthy white figures. Indeed, Peele's work harks back to the historical biocolonialist extraction of labour through chattel slavery that we noticed earlier in McQueen's neo-slavery film, *12 Years A Slave*. Virgil seems to come directly from this latter example. The similarity of Peele's film with *Harvest* is so compelling it would not be wrong to say that the play – which was made into a New York production called *Wanted: Organ Donors* (2006) – anticipated the film.

Like the final sequence of *Get Out*, in which the black protagonist's friend finds and restores him after he has killed the white scientist's family, we notice Jaya resisting Virgil's all out technological assault. In Jaya, Padmanabhan builds a pragmatic and independent character who, despite her poverty and dependence on Om's family, never gives up on what she thinks is right and fair. She is not scared to assert her sexual relationship with Jeetu. She matches Ma's vitriolic abuse with acerbic wit and indomitable strength and keeps Om on his toes with her relentless comical jibes. Indeed, Jaya is the only person suspecting and resisting the organ transplantation programme throughout. While Jeetu once declared he enjoyed the freedom of being a male prostitute as his body could be bought but not owned, he also gives away his 'real' eyes in return for an artificial world of riches through 3D spectacles. Jaya retorts, 'What happened to your ideals, your freedoms? Your pride? All gone, so easily gone' (Padmanabhan 74). She struggles to resist the god-like figure of Virgil persuading her to have a sexual relationship with him because he is Jeetu incarnate in 'a red-blooded all-American man'. This is then followed by another extraordinary assault on her to remind her of her maternal wants, 'You've longed for a child. Your arms cry out for that sweet burden' (86), and scientifically breaking Jaya's astrologically-obtained and domestically-accepted belief that she was reproductively infertile. Just when Jaya seems persuaded by Jeetu's body and love, Virgil reminds her that the process of lovemaking is stripped off all human contact as Jaya's womb will be impregnated with seeds from a device, making the procedure painless. This is where Jaya's humane-ness again breaks open as she demands pain and warmth in lovemaking and asks him to come in person and make love with her (which Virgil cannot do because Jaya's residence is too polluted for him). Jaya thus wins by claiming both her victimised, subaltern position and reclaiming her body. These final lines are deeply suggestive:

> Jaya: Stupid or not, if I lose my life, I win this game.
> ...
> But I'll die knowing that you, who live only to win, will have lost to a poor, a weak and helpless woman. And will get more pleasure out of the first moment of death that I've had in my entire life so far! (91)

Padmanabhan ends the play with Jaya feeling relaxed and happy after a long time, watching TV and eating her fill, suggesting that she has earned her anticolonial freedom and independence by defeating a neocolonial Virgil through addressing the very basic feature of human life: the warmth of togetherness. Sujatha Moni offers a fine reading of this sense of humanist pride: 'Jaya's contradictory move, of on the one hand privileging physical contact and desire over the virtual and technological and, on the other hand, risking her own physical existence in order to seize control over the liminal space of her apartment, represents a counter-hegemonic move on the part of the subaltern to fiercely assert agency' (326). In another compelling reading, Shital Pravinchandra observes that Jaya's agency can be seen as resistance to the post-racial, molecularised, ahistorical and postmodern notion of 'basic commonality' that borders on species vulnerability, and yet disregards the vast socio-economic, racial and gendered differences in her milieu leading to what she calls 'a regenerative ethic', of survival and longevity in the current 'western' life system (40–44). Drawing from them, it can be argued that Jaya wins life by owning death. While the necropolitical aspect of neoliberal body regulation through 'death' is indicated in Jaya's family, Jaya thralls this posthumanist politics by taking pride in owning her death. Like Bama's and Jackie Kay's protagonists who earn life-affirming consciousness in the end, or Mama Nadi in Nottage who stands up to a postcolonial- and species-destructive military–technological power, Jaya's resilience and strength marks a humanistic politics of anticolonial resistance by her choice of taking full control of her body and living it back again – a fully decolonising and rehumanising practice.

This transformation is also convincing because of the genre of theatre's aesthetic efficacy in creating social change, as we noted in Nottage's *Ruined*. While science fiction theatre is not very common, the key aspect is what theatre critic Theodore Shank calls its 'actuality' on stage: the sheer tangibility of the physical presence of characters, gadgets, props and dialogues that other genres simply cannot import (9). The theatrical scene allows the audience to witness first-hand the biological–affective impact of extractive colonialism on the body of the recipient and on their family – anxiety, greed, rage and sheer tragedy in the lives of the postcolonial poor. Like in advanced capitalism, where people shop sanitised, preserved body parts of animals (chicken, beef) without witnessing the torment animals go through and thus do not need to be grateful for or pained by their sacrifice (which is almost always reversed for poorer, local communities in the Third World), here too they see human body parts up for sale; sanitised, reified and commodified. This tangible biological aspect of 'live theatre' is heightened by the use of advanced communications technology, AI gadgets like Virgil's voice-over Gini, and various stage props, which, according to Jenni G. Halpin, offers its audience 'a shocking occasion for thinking through the relationship among self, body, and scientific advancement' (222). While one keen example of this shocking occasion can be the installation of Ma's Video Couch, the use of lighting is particularly compelling in the play. The final scene, for instance, starts with the Contact Module emanating a fluorescent light, bathing Jaya's face in an 'unearthly radiance' symbolising her forced sexualisation before the act itself (89). As an angry Jaya breaks the Module, a cracking sound follows a blue and purple light showing a darkened globe of the Module; or, a triumphant Jaya in the end is synoptically joined by 'rich, joyous music filling the room' as the lights fade out. The strategic use of light, music and noise allows for the stage to create both the aura of posthumanist technological and digital domination of human life (without using expensive technology on stage) and the time-tested literary/symbolic examples of pathetic fallacy signifying human resistance. Dialogues, another fundamental cog in the wheel of theatre, further extend this sense of lively resistance.

As can be obtained from the dialogues in the quoted passages above, the play lacks sentimentality, which is replaced by burlesque and comical satire. This satire is most significantly brought out through the sharp-witted dialogues given to Jaya to counter the ruling discourses of patriarchy which are weaponised by Om's mother. Like Mama Nadi's resistance to military power and sexual violence in Nottage's play, Jaya is never seen as succumbing to the pressures of family or the technological reorganisation of life. In doing so, she reminds us of the strong female characters in Mahesh Dattani's plays, especially *Bravely Fought the Queen* (1991), who never shy away from acknowledging their sexual identities and freedom. If technology is used to extract 'life' out of the urban poor in the Third World, Jaya's theatrical presence (in both senses of the term) makes her into an appropriate rival from this world: desperate, vulnerable, anxious and yet self-confident, demanding, and passionate.

PLANETARITY: POST-APOCALYPTIC EMPIRE, RACE AND MULTISPECIES INCLUSIVITY IN NNEDI OKORAFOR'S *BINTI*

Ayesha Ramachandran reads Jaya's feminist resistance in *Harvest* as Padmanabhan's 'utopian gestures' (172), recalling our suggestions throughout the book that utopian resistance is inherent in postcolonial 'dystopic' reality. Feminist resistance and a utopic reimagining of the world are also at the centre of the Nigerian-American Nnedi Okorafor's speculative series, *Binti* (2015). Okorafor's work is among the most notable in the rising field of African/African-American SF. Sometimes known as 'Afrofuturist' – a term coined by Mark Dery in his essay 'Black to the Future' (180) – these fictional works, most notably by Octavia Butler, stand guard against the technology-driven, white, masculine world and imagine a socially-transformed reality for black people in outer space through the means of futuristic technology and the recovery of oppressed and lost cultural traditions. The term broadly incorporates the interlinked SF genres of science fiction, fantasy, folklore and magical realism in which Samuel R. Delany, in a critique of the term, reminds us that black people and their creative fusion cultures have to be at the centre of thought and not as marginal subsidiaries (Dery 191). Following Delany's critique, Okorafor thinks Afrofuturism does not always centre African cultures and traditions but rather African-American cultures in an Americanised conceptualisation of science fiction. She uses the term 'Africanfuturism', 'a sub-category of science fiction' that is 'similar to "Afrofuturism"' but more deeply rooted in African culture, history, mythology and point-of-view as it then branches into the Black diaspora, and it does not privilege or center the West' (qtd. in Wabuke). Afrofuturism or Africanfuturism has come to mean black liberation in the face of contemporary social realities of hostility, racism, and neocolonialism in the twenty-first century (Hamilton). But liberation through futuristic technology has also been critiqued. In a revealing essay on African SF, Matthew Eatough shows how the rise of speculative fiction in contemporary Africa and the African diaspora is related to the nationalisation of the Structural Adjustment Plans and Poverty Reduction Schemes of the World Bank and IMF in African metropolises. Eatough argues that scenario planning, a method through which archaeological think-tanks (essentially neoliberal) imagine an elongated temporality to tackle poverty through the gentrification of space and long-term capitalistic solution to social ills, has grown in the recent decades with active collusion from science fiction writers (239–48).

While criticisms of Afrofuturism/Africanfuturism and the neoliberal tendencies within African science fiction are suggestive, there is little doubt that this genre offers a solid platform for understanding colonialism's link with science fiction and a postcolonial reimagining of human–nonhuman relationships through the reconstruction of identities and values on a planetary scale. Planetary or planetarity has a particular meaning for this genre of SF. In *Death of a Discipline* (2003), Gayatri Chakravorty Spivak writes that comparativists and literary studies scholars need to renounce the concept of the globe in favour of the planet:

> The globe is in our computers. No one lives there. It allows us to think that we can aim to control it. The planet is in the species of alterity, belonging to another system; and yet we inhabit it, on loan. It is not really amenable to a neat contrast with the globe. I cannot say "the planet, on the other hand."

When I invoke the planet, I think of the effort required to figure the (im)possibility of this underived intuition. (72)

Conceptualised as a form of close reading that demands patient commitment to linguistic and ethical othering in the trainer, planetarity, for Spivak, is based on a Derridean notion of friendship which derives its meaning from acknowledging difference in forming 'collectivities'. To think of living on this planet as a form of loan dismantles anthropocentric desires of owning and controlling its life and resources. Loan also means borrowing and sharing to form collectivities with unknown peoples, animals and forms of living and non-living entities. Spivak, thus, asks comparativists to practise a close reading of 'peripheral' literatures in order to imagine a more humane world in which reading takes on the character of collective responsibility of building an environmentally sustainable world. As Hayley Toth argues through an attentive reading of these concepts, 'A focus on literariness does not mean depoliticizing reading and literature or turning toward the text and away from the world. It is instead intrinsically worldly and political to the extent that its obligation to the text is returned to the world in potentially critical and revisory ways' (463).

While these posthumanist-guided conversations can echo our anticolonial method of reading for decolonising in the book, the environmentalist lesson in reading through differences beyond identity politics and anthropocentric emphasis may be best understood through Okorafor's *Binti* series (I focus mainly on the eponymous first novella, *Binti*) in which humans, non-humans and planets engage with each other to recover black African epistemological and cultural traditions of planetary collectivity and multispecies inclusivity through decolonising Eurocentric epistemologies. Echoing Ytasha Womack's definition that Afrofuturism is about people of 'non-Euro descent', *Binti* offers the story of an eponymous sixteen-year-old maths genius of the Himba tribe of planet Earth who has been given full scholarship to study at the prestigious Oomza University. Binti's tribe, which Okorafor builds upon the Himba tribe of Namibia, excels in mathematics and is 'obsessed with innovation and technology' (*Binti* 21). They make astrolabes for the Khoush people, who are known as cultural and politico-economic elites on planet Earth. The narrative is about Binti's escape from her people to study at the university – an act of blasphemy for her tribe. Like Bama's *Karukku* is about a Dalit woman growing up and gathering a resilient consciousness in an upper caste-dominated world, in this postcolonial *bildungsroman* narrative Binti wrestles with identity loss and her social, ethnic and spatial alienation from family and culture. After an attack on the transport ship for the Uni (university) by an alien, scorpion-like race, Meduse, Binti is kidnapped and offers to mediate between the Meduse and Oomza University, which has taken away a sacred stinger from the Meduse for research. Binti, the master harmoniser, recovers the sacred stinger for them and restores solidarity between the warring groups.

I would like to engage with three specific aspects in the novella to offer a study of planetarity here: identity, technology, and narrative perspective. Identity is a key topic in this post-apocalyptic ('post-climate change') African novel. There are no white-Caucasian characters here, although colonial and imperialist power relations and racialised cultural traditions remain suggestively strong (reminding us of the reading of decolonisation as a process). As Binti leaves, she takes some *otjize* with her – a red powder like substance applied to the hair and skin by her tribe – and her *edan*, an object of faith that keeps one safe. As a panicked Binti reflects in the beginning, 'We Himba don't travel. We stay put. Our ancestral land is life; move away from it and you diminish. We even cover our bodies with it. *Otjize* is red land. Here in the launch port, most were Khoush and a few other non-Himba. Here, I was an outsider; I was outside' (13). The concept of carrying one's land through one's body is fundamental to many Indigenous cultures which makes Binti feel like an outsider in a modernised Khoush-majority port town where people consider such customs rustic and polluting (recall here Olive Senior's poem 'Anatto and Guinep'). As Binti is kidnapped, she is asked to throw away her astrolabe and edan and become like the Meduse so that the latter can trust her. Once stung by the Meduse, Binti realises the Meduse are 'not what we humans think. They are truth. They are clarity. They are decisive. There are sharp lines and edges. They understand honor and dishonor' (66). In a marked difference from Bama's work here, as Binti's blood is mediated by the currents of Meduse life her anxieties of becoming an outsider materialise. In the end, Binti realises her locks now glowed 'a strong deep blue . . . like Okwu and so many of the other Meduse' (80). Okwu is a Meduse friend of Binti's who would be studying at Oomza with her, and in the second book travels to her homeland with her. Sandra Lindow has argued that Okorafor's YA (Young Adult) novels are a *bildungsroman* of a girl's moral development. Identity is forged through the adventure form: separation from family for a social reason; rites of passage; finding superpowers through reclaiming hybrid cultural traditions; and harnessing the emotions of anxiety, fear, rage and depression that constitute YA fiction (50–55). Binti's continuous struggle with her own self and her simultaneous recognition of truth and beauty in the Meduse life is a reminder from Okorafor that identities can never be pure or kept in isolation. Like in Spivak, there is always a radical sense of connecting, evolving, mutating and resisting homogenisation for a planetary collectivity, which Bettina Burger (via Donna Haraway) effectively calls Binti's 'multispecies muddle'; to which I will come back shortly.

It is worth noting that Okorafor not only builds the question of identity through Binti's characterial development but also through the loss of Binti's collective racial identity. This loss is engendered by the suggestion of the colonial plundering of sacred objects from Indigenous cultures as well as their subsequent restitution. Okwe the Meduse, tells Binti that they do not like humans or Oomza people because both looted their sacred objects and culturally valuable artworks: 'In your university, in one of its museums, placed on display like a piece of rare meat is the stinger of our chief . . . We will land on Oomza Uni and take it back' (*Binti* 56). As suggested in the first chapter of this book, this is a burning issue in contemporary public conversations about colonial looting and plundering of objects and cultures, their dehumanising usage of Indigenous cultural values in museums and the postcolonial means of repatriation and restitution (Hicks). This is important in the current context because Namibia (where the Himba people in the book are drawn from) was colonised by Germans. Joshua

Yu Burnett notices that in 2011 the German government returned eleven skulls, stolen for 'research' purposes and stored in Berlin's Charité Hospital, after more than a century. He adds, 'The conflict also echoes Saartjie Baartman, whose large buttocks led her to be displayed as a spectacle for the European public for many years; indeed, her genitals and brain, after being pickled, were displayed at Musée de l'Homme in Paris for many years after her death' (Burnett 125). This practice agonisingly resembles the Meduse chief's story but also indicates how violent, dehumanising and dismembering colonialism as a global historical episode has been. In returning the plundered objects, the anticolonial possibility of restitution and a decolonising recognition of respect and humanity as guiding values of life (to recall Fanon or Tuck and Yang again), can be forged. As the head of professors at Oomza University accepts, 'Museum specimens of such prestige are highly prized at our university, however such things must only be acquired with permission from the people to whom they belong. Oomza protocol is based on honor, respect, wisdom, and knowledge. We will return it to you immediately' (*Binti* 78).

This turn of events reminds us of Aboulela's short story 'The Museum' we read in the first chapter where the Sudanese student Shadia feels distraught and disoriented at the culturally reductive representation of her nation and continent in the Scottish museum, and Sumaya Kassim and her team's decolonising work at the Birmingham Museum two decades later. In these last few years, museums, like literary studies, have come under tremendous pressure from academics, activists and the public to acknowledge the provenance of their objects and their collecting and preserving cultures, as well as decolonialising to facilitate the repatriation and restitution of objects and pasts. As Amy Lonetree writes in *Decolonizing Museums*, 'Objects in museums are living entities. They embody layers of meaning, and they are deeply connected to the past, present, and future of Indigenous communities. Every engagement with objects in museum cases or in collection rooms should begin with this core recognition' (xv). In the head of Oomza Uni's speech about honour, dignity and permission, we see how Okorafor forwards the anticolonial notion of restitution and the decolonising values of humanity and respect through seizing back one's land, sacred objects and cultures, and restoring through them Binti's 'postcolonial' identity.

However, this episode is publicised through rumours among the Oomzas: 'It was said that a human tribal female from a distant blue planet saved the university from Meduse terrorists by sacrificing her blood and using her unique gift of mathematical harmony and ancestral magic' (Okorafor 82). The Meduse, in common parlance, are known as terrorists and Binti, a mathematical genius, a tribal woman. As Binti reflects, '"Tribal": that's what they called humans from ethnic groups too remote and "uncivilised" to regularly send students to attend Oomza Uni' (82). There are two important suggestions here. First, Binti recognises what is honourable and truthful in the Meduse by radically 'becoming' one of them through reading and communicating with them, or, in Spivak's terms referenced above, by patiently committing to ethical othering in her training of planetarity. Most of the misconceptions about the Meduse arise from a lack of communication and conversation, as Brand and Senior would also point out in their creative works and interviews. That no one from the Himba study at Oomza because of their cultural inwardness is understood as their being too remote and uncivilised – again a lack of communication which Binti and her bodily transformation point out. Second, through naming the Meduse terrorists and Binti uncivilised by academics, it is also made clear how ruling discourses of race and racism have emerged as much from cultural ignorance between communities and nations as from purpose-driven research which attempts to look at the dismembered body parts of a race as a marker of its defeat and of its subservience to the triumphant race (recall our conversations on race and anatomy for neo-slavery narratives in 'Minorities'). Indeed, Okorafor adds another level of complexity to the question of colonising identity in the Meduse's stinging of Binti. If it is via the *edan* that Binti connected to their world, by forcing her to throw it away and assuming another identity to offer a reliable means of negotiation, the Meduse – to draw from Burnett again – have 'colonized Binti's body and taken away her otjize-covered dreadlocks, the symbol of her Himba culture' (125). In these actions and suggestions, Okorafor offers the most piercing depiction of scientific and discursive colonialisms which continue to this day. She also offers that the possible path forward to overcome this struggle for a 'planetary' postcolonialism must need communication and respect between races, conversations across cultures (Spivak's 'peripheral literatures') and an acknowledgement that identities are always fluid, mobile and violently born and reborn – which Jenna N. Hanchey rightly reads as Okorafor's 'queer/feminist' and radical enunciation (122).

If conversations and dialogues are central to the reconceptualising of historically racialised human relations, they are represented in the novella through technology and species mediation, my second point. In Africanfuturism, as Okorafor mentions, technology is used to retell cultural histories. In the introduction to *Postcolonial Science Fiction*, Nalo Hopkinson writes that science fiction allows for a reinventing of tribal and cultural relations and reclaiming lost stories: 'from the experience of the colonizer, critique it, pervert it, fuck with it, with irony, with anger, with humour' (9). Reclamation, as we noted in the first chapter, is an anticolonial and decolonising task. Much of the reclamation in this narrative happens through the use of mathematics and species inclusivity. Mathematics is not about coding and encoding nature for its human exploitation but is part of how cultures communicate and develop themselves. In an insightful reading of mathematics and magic in the trilogy, Burger notes that 'mathematics may actually be the universe. Binti's mathematics points towards a dismantling of traditionally Western concepts of science in favor of the "speculative powers" of the imagination' as being intimately connected with mathematics and science rather than 'a "theoretical truth" of the world' (Burger 367). Reading the books with Stenger's use of mathematics as a creative force and Dabiri's historical readings of mathematics in Africa, Burger situates the 'rooted' African philosophical tradition of mathematics in the trilogy. This aspect is most clearly visible in two examples: Binti's hair and the notion of science as culture among the Himba people. While Binti's hair-braiding and *otjize* spark concerns among the Khoush, she explains her braiding as representing decoding and communicating in African tribal traditions. While hair is a tremendous source of postcolonial debates on cultural recovery in African fiction, as we noted through Adichie's *Americanah*, recovering traditional methods of wearing hair and dreadlocks assumes a refreshingly new meaning only through an age-old custom of cultural communication through hair (again, a matter of cultural ignorance and hubris that informs the ruling classes when it comes to demonising black communities).

The other example is useful here for its references to science and technology. Consider Binti's anxious thoughts on her hair after her blood mediation with the Meduse: 'There were ten of them [the *okuoko* dark blue dots on her hair] and I could no longer braid them into my family's code pattern as I had done with my own hair. I pinched one and felt the pressure. Would they grow like hair?' (*Binti* 87). What is read as culturally savage, tribal or animist is rather a set of codes and formulas that were mathematically, scientifically mediated. What is further useful is to note how Binti's mediation has made her body coeval and opened her species to 'foreignness'. This, in one way, reminds us of Foucault's prescient analysis in *History of Madness* of how foretelling and oracular power were understood in post-Enlightenment Europe – which was rearranging its ruling values via instrumental rationality – as madness and thus disciplined via regimentation (238–42). In another way, this could be Okorafor's incisive suggestion that human species must learn to go back to pre-colonialist discourses of respect for other species and education from cultural alterity. This, to me, is a politically and ecologically decolonising gesture through which Okorafor, like Rokeya before, suggests the need to understand technology in a broad, cultural and sustainable fashion. In a related reading, Dustin Crowley draws from Cajetan Iheka's notion of 'the critical insight of indigenous cosmologies in Africa', and 'the capacity of nonhumans – water, trees and other inhabitants of the environment – to produce effects on the human.' He argues that Okorafor uses the SF genre to project and 'prepossess a future in which African peoples like the Himba are not shut out of technological agency and its posthuman possibilities' (244). Burger also arrives at a similar conclusion of 'multispecies muddle' through Donna Haraway in her reading of species entanglement and post-human ecologies.

While these readings about multispecies mediation are helpful, I think the first-person narrative perspective adds something striking to the discussion on species inclusivity, my third and final point in the section. Okorafor opined in her essay 'Organic Fantasy' that 'fantasy is the most accurate way of describing reality' (279). In a reading of the trilogy, Gary Wolfe argued that 'Okorafor's genius has been to find the iconic images and traditions of African culture . . . and tweak them just enough to become a seamless part of her vocabulary of fantastika' (qtd. in Lindow 47). It is important, then, to note the question of reality and perspective in her fiction. As we have been arguing above, Okorafor does not necessarily bring in technologies, ideas or objects that are completely new. Indeed, the archetypal novelistic use of first-person perspective allows for a post-apocalyptic, postcolonial 'African' character to emerge whose desperate attempt to mediate between worlds and imagining of utopic harmony between tribes and human and nonhuman groups point at the new age YA climate or education activists such as Malala Yousafzai or Greta Thunberg. Okorafor's radical reconstruction of postcolonial tribal life and politics demands a first-person narrative novel that is intensely brooding and reflective of the protagonist's personal philosophical and cultural troubles throughout.

Indeed, the narration is so deeply personal that we do not get a respite from Binti for a moment, asking from readers a total commitment to Binti's development of character, even if given in fast brushstrokes. There is hardly a third-person, diegetic narration, or free indirect discourse to make Binti's feelings come across as ironic or to allow readers an intervention in the narrative. Readers here are outsiders, and the narration is entirely Binti's. This serves to suggest that Okorafor wants to retain the importance of a decolonised subject's peculiar viewpoints but also keep the possibility open of the viewpoint being widened by coming into contact with other species and their radically different life systems. This does not mean a denial or a forgetting of one's viewpoint but the ability of seeing through multiple viewpoints and mediating between them for the continuous achievement of a democratic and diverse future to come. The utopia then demands a close witnessing of the efforts at reconstruction through a young woman, ridiculed and derided throughout, who stands her ground and builds mediating prowess through the inherited power of her tribe and her faith in its values. This is the project of multispecies inclusivity that I argue Spivak's concept of planetarity and Okorafor's notion of Africanfuturism point at. Following Kristine Kotecki, it can be said with caution that *Binti* does not offer a journey into a nativist archetype or a postcolonial break with colonialism. In the novel's resounding faith in rural and local traditions, in the traditions' scientific and progressive bases and cosmopolitan connectivity across cultures and races, *Binti* offers a notion of a 'critical dystopia' which 'does not find hope in opposition or revolution itself but rather in solidarity with alterity, in the difference and multiplicity . . . organized in a fully democratic alliance politics' (176).

In the end, it could also be argued that Binti's mediating powers between multispecies life forms is a utopian gesture by Okorafor. It is impossible for suppressed traditions and epistemologies to not write anticolonial futures of hope. It is also imperative that these futures of hope are not about replacing one warring 'culture' with another. It is about dismantling anthropocentric desires of controlling the 'globe' and reclaiming lost and submerged lives and cultures, their epistemological differences that were violently suppressed and wiped out, for a planetary (un)making of the world. Marxist scholar Raymond Williams argued that the 'emergent' in culture is not something completely new to the structure/system of culture. Possibilities of the emergent are always submerged in the dominant paradigm/discourse (Williams 123–24). The discourses of colonial rationality have not only suppressed non-colonial, non-rational elements, they have also demonised them by consigning them to reductive tribalism and cultural savagery. Postcolonial writers have widely used different genres and forms – SF in particular – to critique colonialist Eurocentric readings of nationhood, ethnicity, history, identity and storytelling, allowing for the submerged and the emergent to arrive at the forefront of imagination and rebuilding. It is worth remembering Okorafor's prescient idea that fantasy is the most accurate way of describing reality because 'reality' in its current shape, which we often take for granted, is built on a long process of making meaning and standardising genres by suppressing other forms and genres of thinking and interpretation. Like the intermixing and plural nature of genres themselves, postcolonial writing and cultures are about recognising the plurality and multiplicity of life forms and their mediations through decolonising knowledge systems. It is probably in postcolonial SF that such an attempt at decolonising epistemology is at its most concrete and powerful. Rokeya's imagination of the world as a giant garden, Padmanabhan's seizing back of Jaya's everyday life from her family's neocolonial technological death and Okorafor's reclamation of culture and knowledge through species mediation are perhaps some of the most compelling instances of what I have theorised in the book as the 'decolonising impulse' in postcolonial literary and cultural works.

REFERENCES

Ashcroft, Bill. "Unlocking the Future. Utopia and Postcolonial Literatures". *Reframing Postcolonial Studies: Concepts, Methodologies, Scholarly Activisms*, edited by David D. Kim, Palgrave Macmillan, 2021, pp. 43–67.

Bagchi, Barnita. "Ladylands and Sacrificial Holes: Utopias and Dystopias in Rokeya Sakhawat Hossain's Writings". *The Politics of (Im)possible: Utopia and Dystopia Reconsidered*, Sage, 2019, pp. 165–78.

---. "Utopia". *Critical Terms in Future Studies*, edited by Heike Paul, Palgrave Macmillan, 2019, pp. 327–34.

Bahri, Deepika. *Postcolonial Biology: Psyche and Flesh after Empire*. U of Minnesota P, 2017.

Baldwin, Andrew. "Postcolonial Futures: Climate, Race, and the Yet-to-Come". *ISLE: Interdisciplinary Studies in Literature and Environment*, vol. 24, no. 2, 2017, pp. 292–305.

Bloch, Ernst. *The Principle of Hope*. Translated by Neville Plaice, Stephen Plaice and Paul Knight, vol. 3, MIT Press, 1986.

Bould, Mark, and Sherryl Vint. "Political Readings". *The Cambridge Companion to Fantasy Literature*, edited by Edward James and Farah Mendlesohn, Cambridge UP, 2012, pp. 102–12.

Burger, Bettina. "Math and Magic: Nnedi Okorafor's *Binti* Trilogy and its Challenge to the Dominance of Western Science in Science

Fiction". *Critical Studies in Media Communication*, vol. 37, no. 4 2020, pp. 364–77.

Burnett, Joshua Yu. "'Isn't Realist Fiction Enough?': On African Speculative Fiction". *Mosaic: An Interdisciplinary Critical Journal*, vol. 52, no. 3, 2019, pp. 119–35.

Campbell, Chloe. *Race and Science: Eugenics in Colonial Kenya*. Manchester UP, 2007.

Chattopadhyay, Bodhisattwa, Aakriti Mandhwani, and Anwesha Maity. Introduction. *Indian Genre Fiction*, edited by Bodhisattwa Chattopadhyay, Aakriti Mandhwani and Anwesha Maity, Routledge, 2019, pp. 1–14.

Chaudhuri, Maitrayee. "Ecology and Virtue in Rokeya Sakhawat Hussain's 'Sultana's Dream'". *Feminist Moments: Reading Feminist Texts*, edited by Katherine Smits and Susan Bruce, Bloomsbury Academic, 2016, pp. 107–14.

Chozinski, Brittany Anne. "Science Fiction as Critique of Science: Organ Transplantation and the Body". *Bulletin of Science, Technology & Society*, vol. 36, no. 1, 2016, pp. 58–66.

Clute, John. *Pardon the Intrusion: Fantastika in the World Storm*. Beccon Publications, 2011.

Crowley, Dustin. "Binti's R/evolutionary Cosmopolitan Ecologies". *Cambridge Journal of Postcolonial Literary Inquiry*, vol. 6, no. 2, 2019, pp. 237–56.

Datta, Partha. *Planning the City: Urbanization and Reform in Calcutta, 1880–1940*, Tulika Books, 2012.

Derrida, Jacques. "The Law of Genre". *Critical Inquiry*, vol. 7, no. 1, 1980, pp. 55–81.

---. *The Gift of Death*. Translated by David Willis, U of Chicago P, 1995.

Dery, Mark. "Black to the Future: Interviews with Samuel R. Delay, Greg Tate, and Tricia Rose". *Flame Wars: The Discourse of Cyberculture*, Duke UP, 1994, pp. 179–22.

Eatough, Matthew. "African Science Fiction and the Planning Imagination". *The Cambridge Journal of Postcolonial Literary Inquiry*, vol. 4, no. 2, 2017, pp. 237–57.

Elias, Akhteruzzaman. *Khoabnama*. Naba Udyog, 1996.

Fimi, Dimitra. *Tolkien, Race and Cultural History*. Palgrave Macmillan, 2008.

Forter, Greg. *Critique and Utopia in Postcolonial Historical Fiction: Atlantic and Other Worlds*. Oxford UP, 2019.

Foucault, Michel. *History of Madness*. 1972. Translated by Jonathan Mulfy and Jean Khalfa, Routledge, 2006.

Freeland, Natalka. "The Dustbin of History: Waste Management in Late Victorian Utopias". *Filth: Dirt, Disgust and Modern Life*, edited by William Cohen and Ryan Johnson, U of Minnesota P, 2004, pp. 225–49.

Frow, John. *Genre*. Routledge, 2006.

Goebel, Walter and Saskia Schabio, editors. *Locating Postcolonial Narrative Genres*. Routledge, 2013.

Halpin, Jenni G. "Representing Science that Isn't: *Harvest* as Science Fiction Theatre". *Interdisciplinary Science Reviews*, vol. 39, no. 3, 2014, pp. 213–23.

Hamilton, Elizabeth. *Charting the Afrofuturist Imaginary in African American Art: The Black Female Fantastic*, Routledge, 2022.

Hanchey, Jenna N. "Desire and the Politics of Africanfuturism". *Women's Studies in Communication*, vol. 43, no. 2, 2020, pp. 119–24.

Harry, Debra. "Biocolonialism and the Indigenous Knowledge in United Nations Discourse". *Griffith Law Review*, vol. 20, no. 3, 2011, pp. 702–28.

Hicks, Dan. *The Brutish Museum: The Benin Bronzes, Colonial Violence and Cultural Restitution*. Pluto Press, 2020.

Hiddleston, Jane. Introduction. *Postcolonial Poetics: Genre and Form*, edited by Patrick Crowley and Jane Hiddleston, Liverpool UP, 2013, pp. 1–10.

Hitchcock, Peter. "The Genre of Postcoloniality". *New Literary History*, vol. 34, no. 2, 2003, pp. 299–330.

Hopkinson, Nalo, and Uppinder Mehan, editors. *So Long Been Dreaming: Postcolonial Science Fiction and Fantasy*. Arsenal Pulp Press, 2004.

Hossain, Rokeya Sakhawat. *Sultana's Dream: A Feminist Utopia*. Translated and edited by Roushan Jahan, Feminist Press, 1988.

Jackson, Rosemary. *Fantasy: The Literature of Subversion*. Routledge, 1981.

James, Eric P., and Rebecca Gill. "Neoliberalism and the Communicative Labor of CrossFit". *Communication & Sport*, vol. 6, no. 6, 2018, pp. 703–27.

Jameson, Fredric. *Archaeologies of the Future: The Desire Called Utopia and other Science Fictions*. Verso, 2005.

Jauss, Han Robert. "Theory of Genres and Medieval Literature". *Toward an Aesthetic of Reception*. Translated by Timothy Bahti, U of Minnesota P, 1982, pp. 76–109.

Kim, Jodi. "Debt, the Precarious Grammar of Life, and Manjula Padmanabhan's *Harvest*". *Women's Studies Quarterly*, vol. 42, no. 1/2, 2014, pp. 215–32.

Koretzky, Maya Overby. "'A Change of Heart': Racial Politics, Scientific Metaphor and Coverage of 1968 Interracial Heart Transplants in the African American Press". *Social History of Medicine*, vol. 30, no. 2, 2017, pp. 408–28.

Kotecki, Kristine. "Apocalyptic Affect in Nnedi Okorafor's Speculative Futures". *Research in African Literatures*, vol. 51, no. 3, 2020, pp. 164–79.

Levitas, Ruth. *The Concept of Utopia*. Syracuse UP, 1990.

Lindow, Sandra. "Nnedi Okorafor: Exploring the Empire of Girls' Moral Development". *Journal of the Fantastic in the Arts*, vol. 28, no. 1, 2017, pp. 46–69.

Lonetree, Amy. *Decolonizing Museums: Representing Native America in National and Tribal Museums*. U of North Carolina P, 2012.

Masoodi, Ashwaq. "Why Organ Trafficking Thrives in India". *Mint*, 28 May 2015, https://www.livemint.com/Politics/pxj4YasmivrvAhanv6OOCJ/Why-organ-trafficking-thrives-in-India.html. Accessed 13 June 2021.

Mathur, Suchitra. "Caught between the Cyborg and the Goddess: Third-World Women and the Politics of Science in Three Works of Indian Science Fiction". *Journal of Commonwealth Literature*, vol. 39, no. 3, 2004, pp. 119–38.

Mohamed, Shakir, Maria-Therese Png, and William Isaac. "Decolonial AI: Decolonial Theory as Sociotechnical Foresight in Artificial Intelligence". *Philosophy and Technology*, vol. 33, 2020, pp. 659–84.

Moni, Sujatha. "'In Bits and Pieces': Bodies in Movement, Liminality and Subaltern Resistance in Manjula Padmanabhan's *Harvest*". *Journal of Postcolonial Writing*, vol. 50, no. 3, 2014, pp. 316–28.

Mookerjea-Leonard, Debali. "Futuristic Technologies and Purdah in the Feminist Utopia: Rokeya S. Hossains's 'Sultana's Dream'". *Feminist Review*, no. 117, 2017, pp. 144–53.

Mosley, Stephen. *The Chimney of the World: A History of Smoke Pollution in Victorian and Edwardian Manchester*. White Horse P, 2001.

Mukherjee, Upamanyu Pablo. *Final Frontier: Science Fiction and Technoscience in Non-Aligned India*. Liverpool UP, 2020.

Munos, Delphine, and Bénédicte Ledent, editors. *Minor Genres in Postcolonial Literature*. Routledge, 2020.

Nnodim, Rita. "City, Identity and Dystopia: Writing Lagos in Contemporary Nigerian Novels". *Journal of Postcolonial Writing*, vol. 44, no. 4, 2008, pp. 321–32.

Okorafor, Nnedi. "Organic Fantasy". *African Identities*, vol. 7, no. 2, 2009, pp. 275–86.

---. *Binti*. Tom Doherty Associates, 2015.

Padmanabhan, Manjula. *Harvest*. 1998. Aurora Metro Publications, 2015.

Paul, Heike, editor. *Critical Terms in Future Studies*. Palgrave Macmillan, 2019.

Patchett, Ann. *State of Wonder*. Bloomsbury, 2012.

Peele, Jordon, director. *Get Out*. Universal Pictures, 2017.

Pravinchandra, Shital. "One Species Same Difference? Postcolonial Critique and the Concept of Life". *New Literary History*, no. 47, 2016, pp. 27–48.

Quayum, Mohammad A. "Rokeya Sakhawat Hossain: A Biographical Essay". *A Feminist Foremother: Critical Essays on Rokeya Sakhawat Hossain*, edited by Mohammad A. Quayum and Mahmudul Hasan, Orient BlackSwan, 2019.

Ramachandran, Ayesha. "New World, No World: Seeking Utopia in Padmanabhan's *Harvest*". *Theatre Research International*, vol. 30, no. 2, pp. 161–74.

Ray, Bharati. "A Voice of Protest: The Writings of Rokeya Sakhawat Hossain (1880–1932)". *Women of India: Colonial and Post-Colonial Periods*, edited by Bharati Ray, Centre for Studies in Civilizations, 2005, pp. 427–53.

Rieder, John. *Colonialism and the Emergence of Science Fiction*. Wesleyan UP, 2012.

Risam, Rupika. *Postcolonial Digital Humanities in Theory, Praxis, and Pedagogy*. Northwestern UP, 2019.

Scheper-Hughes, Nancy. "The Global Traffic in Human Organs". *Current Anthropology*, vol. 41, no. 2, 2000, pp. 191–224.

Sengupta, Debjani. "Sadhanbabu's Friends: Science Fiction in Bengal from 1882 to 1974". *Science Fiction, Imperialism and the Third World: Essays on Postcolonial Literature and Film*, edited by Ericka Hoagland and Reema Sarwal, McFarland, 2010, pp. 115–26.

Sengupta, Parna. "Writing, Dreaming and Freedom: Rokeya Hossain at the Limit of Freedom in Colonial Bangladesh". *Genre & Histoire*, no. 25, 2020. https://doi.org/10.4000/genrehistoire.5051. Accessed June 6, 2021.

Shank, Theodore. *Beyond the Boundaries. American Alternative Theatre*. 1982. U of Michigan P, 2002.

Shirk, Henrietta Nickels. "Contributions to Botany, the Female Science, by Two Eighteenth-Century Women Technical Communicators". *Technical Communications Quarterly*, vol. 6, no. 3, 1997, pp. 293–312.

Shiva, Vandana. *Biopiracy: The Plunder of Nature and Knowledge*. North Atlantic Books, 2016.

Shteir, Ann B. "Gender and Modern Botany in Victorian England". *Osiris*, no. 12, 1997, pp. 29–38.

Spivak, Gayatri Chakravorty. *Death of a Discipline*. Columbia UP, 2003.

Tagore, Rabindranath. Introduction. *Thakurmar Jhuli: Banglar Rupkatha*, by Dakshinaranjan Mitra Majumder, 1907, Mitra and Ghosh, 1963, pp. 9–12.

Tharoor, Shashi. "But What about the Railways…? The Myth of Britain's Gift to India". *The Guardian*, 8 March 2017, https://www.theguardian.com/world/2017/mar/08/india-britain-empire-railways-myths-gifts#:~:text=In%20their%20very%20conception%20and,%2C%20and%20not%20British%2C%20taxes. Accessed 13 June 2023.

Todorov, Tzvetan. *Genres in Discourse*. Translated by Catherine Porter, Cambridge UP, 1990.

Toth, Hayley. "Spivak's Planetarity and the Ethics of Professional Reading". *Comparative Critical Studies*, vol. 17, no. 3, 2020, pp. 459–78.

Varughese, E. Dawson. "Post-Millennial Indian Dystopian Fiction: A Developing Canon of Precarity, (Im)purity and Ideas of India(nness)". *South Asia: Journal of South Asian Studies*, vol. 44, no. 6, 2021, pp. 1041–55.

Wabuke, Hope. "Afrofuturism, Africanfuturism, and the Language of Black Speculative Fiction". *Los Angeles Review of Books*, 27 August 2020, https://lareviewofbooks.org/article/afrofuturism-africanfuturism-and-the-language-of-black-speculative-literature/. Accessed 14 June 2021.

Whitt, Laurie Ann. "Biocolonialism and the Commodification of Knowledge". *Science as Culture*, vol. 7, no. 1, 1998, pp. 33–67.

Williams, Raymond. "Dominant, Residual, and Emergent". *Marxism and Culture*. Oxford UP, 1977, pp. 121–27.

Womack, Ytasha L. *Afrofuturism: The World of Black Sci-Fi and Fantasy Culture*. Chicago Review Press, 2013.

"Yield". *Oxford English Dictionary*, https://www.oed.com/search/dictionary/?scope=Entries&q=Yield. Accessed 16 June 2021.

Young, Helen. *Race and Popular Fantasy Literature: Habits of Whiteness*. Routledge, 2016.

Conclusion

POSTCOLONIAL STUDIES IN A POST-COVID WORLD

In this book, I have offered a method and a set of examples of reading postcolonial works. I have defined postcolonialism through decolonisation. If colonisation has meant how the world was colonised by 'western' Europe for capitalist and cultural authority since, at least, the fifteenth century, decolonisation stands for the culmination of all of the resistant movements from below to overthrow such authority, most prominently, in the twentieth century. But decolonisation is never fully achieved at the birth of the post-colonial (after-colonial or independent) state as the educated elite's imitative neocolonial and neoliberal practices make the social and political liberation of oppressed communities in the ex-colonised world a long-term process. I have argued that these conditions are not specific to a single post-colonial nation but, rather, are global. At the same time, they are also peculiar to the geographical, linguistic and cultural specificities of a nation. My main contention in the book is that literary and cultural works in the post-colonial period can effectively register the sociopolitical dynamics of these power relations through their complex use of content, style and narration. Through such representation, they enable us to see the peculiar conditions of local oppression but also moments of their global comparability and mutual struggle for continuous decolonisation – their aesthetic and interpretive resonances. Thus, the book offers a new method of reading that it calls 'reading for decolonising'. This method draws from Fanon, Ambedkar, Ngũgĩ, Freire and Anzaldúa, among others, to argue that reading and pedagogy – the symbolic form of decolonisation – cannot be separated from the material form of it, that is, the recovery of land and resources. Reading and decolonising (to be able to recognise dominant structures and resistant methods and working towards sociopolitical and economic egalitarianism) are mutual and constitutive as they are local and global in the post-colonial world. I have read this political–aesthetic strategy for continuous decolonisation as 'postcolonial' here.

The book reads seventeen literary and cinematic works from across the postcolonial world through the relevant analytical concepts of caste, race, gender, sexuality, slavery, hunger, land, poverty, utopia, and so forth. But since these concepts intersect with each other on many occasions, the book reads them together under five conceptual and plural rubrics – Minorities, Migrations, Traumas, Ecologies and Futures. While the rubrics have their own sets of topics, throughout the book I have showed how these topics and literary works have drawn from each other through their aesthetic representation. There are many more topics and works that could not be touched upon here for lack of space. While such omissions are inevitable in a field-specific introductory book, what this book has aimed to do is offer a historical materialist method of reading postcolonial texts and contexts. Here, 'postcolonialism' is an analytical framework through which to recognise the comparative elements between postcolonial works and the universal drive in postcolonial nations for the continuous decolonisation of oppressed groups. Hence, the 'now' in postcolonialism is as much about the way the field and its concerns have developed through literary and cultural works in the last decades, as about taking on a new lens (or method) to organise and read them together, despite their differences. The 'now' also impresses upon us, in conclusion, to reflect on how the field and its concerns may respond to the to the futures of the world-historical event of the COVID-19 pandemic.

The COVID-19 pandemic has posed unique challenges to postcolonial nations which go back, at their heart, to the historical issues of class, gender, race and racism, imperialism and structural inequality. For instance, in the initial days of the pandemic in early 2020, the president of the USA, Donald Trump, called the pathogen the 'Chinese virus' thanks to it possibly originating from a lab in Wuhan, adding fuel to the already fiery situation of racialising and alienating the Chinese and Asian community worldwide for the virus ("Spit on, Yelled at, Attacked"). Later, postcolonial nations such as India or South Africa – which did fairly well in the first wave of the pandemic and contributed widely to the mass manufacturing of COVID-19 vaccines – were allowed lesser quantities of vaccines to inoculate their own populations by patent acts. These countries' vaccines, named differently due to patenting laws, were then declared invalid and prevented their citizens from entering richer Euro-American nations; which was suggested as 'vaccine imperialism' (Liu and Chung). The structural inequalities of the COVID-19 pandemic found its most brutal class and caste articulation in India in the overnight manufacturing of a large precariat community of migrant workers who were employed in urban areas without formal contracts. These workers were abruptly asked by the ruling government to 'walk back' home due to the nationwide lockdown of interstate transport (Biswas). In April 2021, when the Indian government had already assured its population about its swift handling of the pandemic, the second wave of the pandemic proved markedly more fatal. Millions succumbed to the infrastructural lack of oxygen cylinders and medical beds in hospitals (Gentleman, et al.). The world witnessed with horror and pain one of the most harrowing episodes of national tragedy as distraught families in India said goodbye to their loved ones from far and the dead bodies of Covid victims were dumped in rivers (Sharma).

It is only human, as I have been arguing in the book through a global comparability of postcolonial texts and contexts, to seek solace from episodes of shock and pain through observing how others have coped with them. Unsurprisingly, the early months of the pandemic (which birthed the challenging conditions of a peacetime lockdown) social and news media – mostly at a remove from the immediate precarity of the pandemic – were filled with what we could learn from literature to tackle this disaster. Along with many important world literary examples from Daniel Defoe, Albert Camus, Katherine Ann Porter or Ling Ma, the Hindi language memoir of poet Suryakant Tripathi (popularly known in India as 'Nirala'), *Kulli Bhaat* (1939;

translated as *A Life Misspent*), also surfaced. Based on the experiences of the 1919 influenza pandemic in India which vanquished millions including the author's family, Nirala's work achieved wider meaning for an Indian population that had to undergo a similar crisis. Nirala considered suicide until he met Kulli Bhaat, who rescued the depressed memoirist from the burning ghats and brought him to a nearby ashram to start anew. Bhaat, whom the book's Hindi title is based on, is a Dalit activist fighting caste discrimination and the stigma of untouchability. Nirala situates him in his struggles against both a colonialism-enabled casteism (as we noted while discussing Bama's work in 'Minorities') and in the context of pandemic and empire (remember the historical connection between colonialism and epidemics in Phaswane Mpe's representation in 'Ecologies'). There are also resonances of their homosexual relationship. This memoir is extraordinary in the way that it charts colonialism's impact on social life, especially during a human disaster. In its 'Preface', Nirala urges us to read it as a 'comic' work. No doubt that this comedy of human loss is a strategic narrative take masquerading as satire and irony. But the work is also about affection and forming collectivities across caste, class and gender lines in their anticolonial, anti-discriminatory and anti-caste meanings.

The future of collectivity in Nirala's work could be compared with a similar kind of empathetic solidarity expressed in the writings and activism (in the Western world) of the 'Black Lives Matter' and the 'Rhodes Must Fall' debates. Locked down in the tiny quarters of their houses, people took to social media to encourage and support health workers for their tireless and brave work in saving the world from the contingencies of the pandemic; to create communities of trust and inclusivity for minority populations that have faced the pandemic's impact disproportionately; or come out in the public sphere to register their protest against perpetuating discrimination in society. Technology and digital media, as I suggested in the previous chapter, will play an enormous role for postcolonial struggles and their representations. The pandemic has compelled a wider population to depend on technology for survival – a dependence which had already been rising in the twenty-first century with the digital revolution.

As technology creates opportunities for professional improvement and building moments of solidarity for change, it will also be crucial to remain vigilant of technology's hierarchical powers and disproportionate impact in the postcolonial world, especially through the burgeoning impact of AI in a post-Covid world (Stadler, Laursen and Rock; Risam). Through the dominance of social and news media which have exposed us to global struggles, we have also noticed that the last few years have been filled with wars along religious, national and imperialist lines. Consider Russia's ongoing war in Ukraine and its impact on ex-colonial and ex-colonised nations; or the Israel–Palestine conflict with Israel's widespread destruction of Gaza, strategic bombing of aid workers and its forced starvation of Palestinian population, making many call the war as colonialist genocide (which only suggests why Darwish's work, read in the chapter on 'Traumas', continues to be relevant today).[1] Perhaps, apart from the pandemic none of these are new to us. Or, perhaps, epidemics and pandemics have been present in the last two decades as well (through the Ebola, SARS, MARS and Zika outbreaks). As richer economies recover from the pandemic by inflicting even more structural forms of discrimination and dispossession on post-colonial nations, we dreadfully anticipate a longer period of political and social uncertainty; rising austerity and authoritarianism; further decimation of the welfare state and democratic provisions; and a global condition of precarity and social unrest leading to wars. Through the success and 'visibility' of broad-based movements in the postcolonial and global contexts, it can be also argued that there will continue to be coalitional and co-operative struggles to defend territories, land, food, livelihoods, humans, animals, vegetation and, above all, the planet.

There has never been, it seems to me, a more opportune time to do academic postcolonial studies – to witness and experience current social struggles (sometimes from a distance through a critical or narratorial form of consciousness); to read through them and analyse their colonial and anticolonial temporalities; and to explore and interrogate the decolonising impulse in literary and cultural works. This book, through its method of reading for decolonising, explores how postcolonial works have interrogated these issues and called for building a diverse and equitable world of community, affection, inclusivity and solidarity. As students of literature witnessing and experiencing wider cases of discrimination locally or globally during a pandemic and in its aftermath, especially leading to a genocidal war in West Asia, we cannot afford to lose the urgent lens of anticolonialism and postcolonialism. I am tempted to conclude the book with this incidental note: In May 1922, a young anticolonial Indian poet, Kazi Nazrul Islam launched his journal *Dhumketu* (*Comet*), to demand full independence from colonialism – a total reclamation of Indian land and culture from colonial powers (4). A hundred years later, while India and many parts of the ex-colonised world have achieved formal independence from colonialism, the fight to stand against colonialism and neocolonial powers has continued as we saw in the first chapter through Eve Tuck and K. Wayne Yang's work on decolonisation. It will not be over until those in the bottom-most rung of the social order in postcolonial nations do not achieve social and economic equality and dignity. For this, we, as postcolonial readers and activists in our own capacities, need to closely and comparatively attend to literature, culture and imaginative works to point out how populations from across the world in the last decades, at least, have offered examples from their social and material conditions to prepare intellectual horizons for locally-specific yet globally-resonant decolonising movements to come about.

NOTE

1. This book was written in 2022 and published towards the end of 2024. In these two years, the Israel–Palestine conflict has once again showed why settler-colonialism has continued unabated and unabashed in the modern world aided by richer ex-colonising countries, and why, for humanities and postcolonially-minded scholars, anticolonialism and decolonisation will have to be the vital means through which to study postcolonial literatures and practices and advocate for sociopolitical emancipation and economic egalitarianism.

REFERENCES

Biswas, Soutik. "Coronavirus: India's pandemic Lockdown Turns into a Human Tragedy". *BBC*, 30 March 2020, https://www.bbc.com/news/world-asia-india-52086274. Accessed 23 May 2022.

Gentleman, Jeffrey, et al. "The Night the Oxygen Ran Out in an Indian Hospital". *The New York Times*, 28 June 2021, https://www.nytimes.com/2017/08/17/world/asia/the-night-the-oxygen-ran-out-in-an-indian-hospital.html. Accessed 23 May 2022.

Islam, Kazi Nazrul. *Dhumketu*. Nazrul Institute, 2001.

Liu, Joanna, and Ryoa Chung. "Capitalist Philanthropy and Vaccine Imperialism". *The Hastings Centre*, 12 September 2021, https://www.thehastingscenter.org/capitalist-philanthropy-and-vaccine-imperialism/#:~:text=In%20many%20ways%2C%20the%20behavior,patents%20even%20during%20health%20emergencies. Accessed 22 May 2022.

'Nirala', Suryakant Tripathi. *A Life Misspent*. 1939. Translated by Satti Khanna, HarperCollins, 2018.

Risam, Rupika. *Postcolonial Digital Humanities in Theory, Praxis, and Pedagogy*. Northwestern UP, 2019.

Sharma, Sourabh. "Poverty, Stigma behind Bodies Floating in India's Ganges River". *Aljazeera*, 21 June 2021, https://www.aljazeera.com/news/2021/6/2/poverty-stigma-behind-bodies-floating-in-indias-ganges-river. Accessed 23 May 2022.

Stadtler, Florian, Ole Birk Laursen, and Brian Rock, editors. *Networking the Globe: New Technologies and the Postcolonial*. Routledge, 2016.

Tavernise, Sabrina, and Richard A. Oppel Jr. "Spit on, Yelled at, Attacked: Chinese-Americans Fear for their Safety". *The New York Times*, 23 March 2020, https://www.nytimes.com/2020/03/23/us/chinese-coronavirus-racist-attacks.html. Accessed 22 May 2022.

Select Titles from the Series

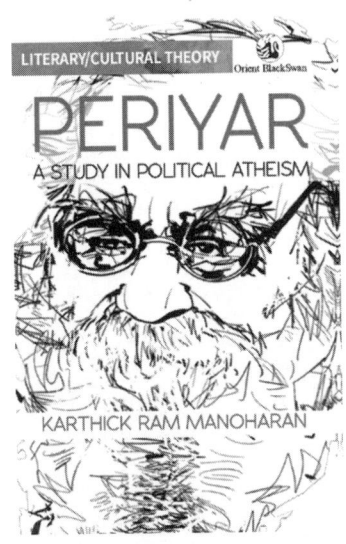
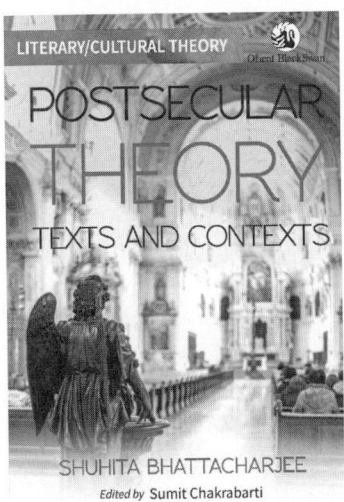

For more information, visit www.orientblackswan.com

Select Titles from the Series

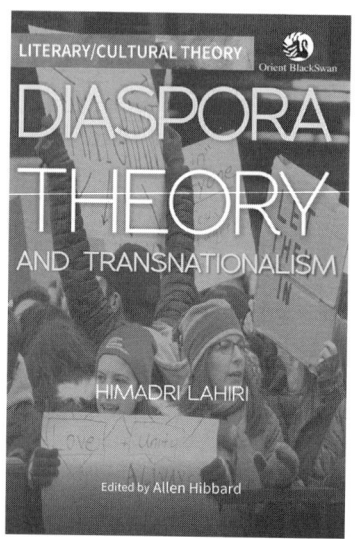
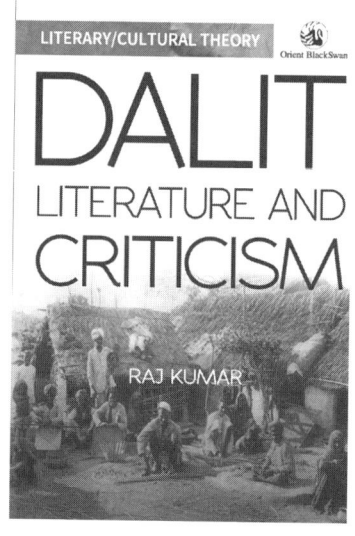

For more information, visit www.orientblackswan.com